IMAGES
of America

RANDOLPH COUNTY

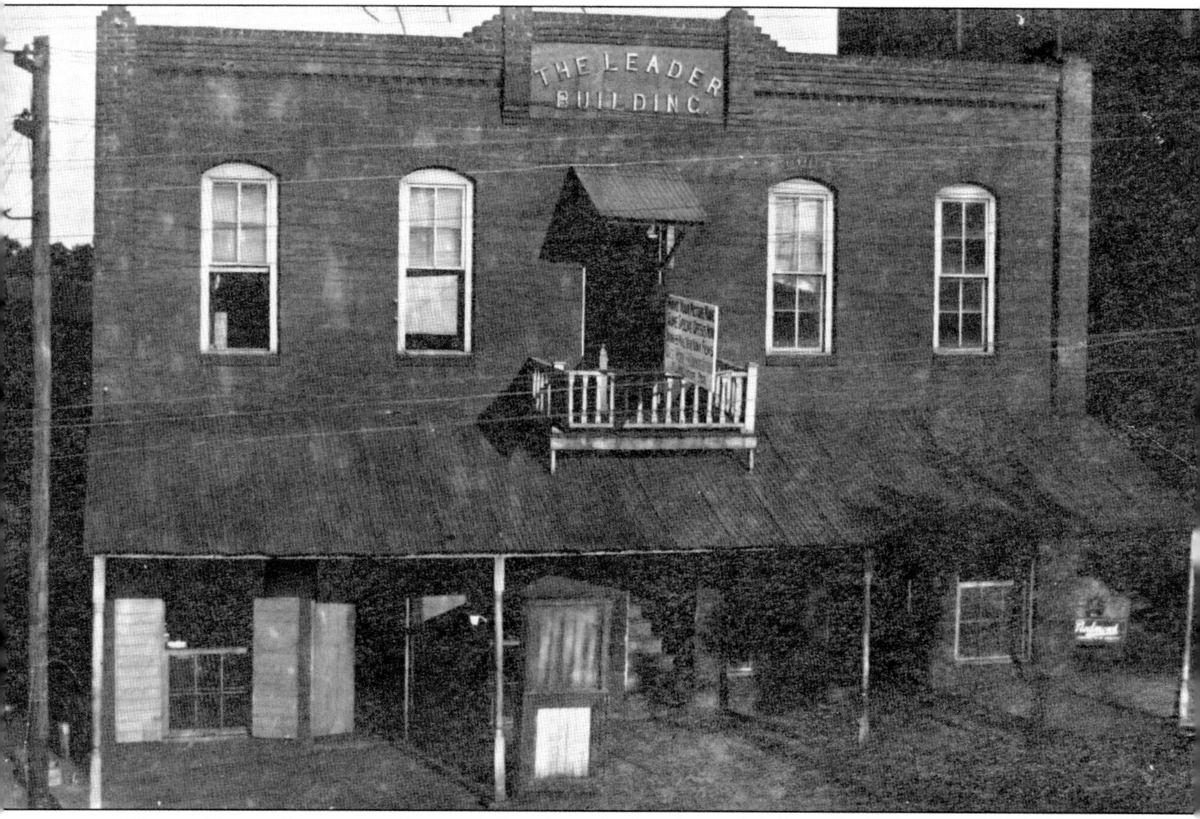

Olin and Leon Stevenson founded the *Roanoke Leader* in 1892, and Olin served as editor until June 1937, when Olin's son John B. Stevenson became editor. After 45 years, John B. passed this position on to his son John W., who is the editor at the present. After several moves, the building pictured on Chestnut Street became the home for the *Leader* in 1910, later burning in 1923. The *Leader* still holds its importance to the county. (Courtesy of John W. Stevenson.)

On the Cover: Alious Elonza Wilson (Mr. Ale) and his youngest son, Linward, sit atop their wagon overflowing with hay while they stop for a moment to speak with his wife, Frances. The hay-filled wagon was a common sight in the early years of Randolph County. (Courtesy of Bernice [Wilson] Burson.)

IMAGES
of America

RANDOLPH COUNTY

Lois Walls George,
Paula Burson Lambert,
and Wyner S. Phillips

ARCADIA
PUBLISHING

ISBN 978-0-7385-4371-0

Published by Arcadia Publishing
Charleston, South Carolina

Printed in the United States of America

Library of Congress Catalog Card Number: 2006932625

For all general information contact Arcadia Publishing at:
Telephone 843-853-2070
Fax 843-853-0044
E-mail sales@arcadiapublishing.com
For customer service and orders:
Toll-Free 1-888-313-2665

Visit us on the Internet at www.arcadiapublishing.com

We dedicate this book to our friends, neighbors, and family members of the past and present: those of the past who led the way and left us a great legacy and those of the present who have helped identify and preserve this legacy.

Contents

ACKNOWLEDGMENTS

There are many people we would like to thank for the help they so graciously gave us and without whom this book would have never been finished. Our families top the list. They encouraged us when we faltered, filled in for us when we missed other obligations, assisted us when asked, and continued to love us when we were unlovable.

The response to our requests for pictures was overwhelming. Not only were we supplied with pictures, those wonderful people who dug through their trunks and scrapbooks to find the pictures also took the time to supply us with information to go with the pictures. To name all those individuals is virtually impossible.

We should also like to thank our editors: Adam Ferrell, who gave us the help and encouragement we needed to get started, and Kendra Allen, for her untiring efforts to help us finish the job.

INTRODUCTION

When Alabama was admitted to the Union on December 14, 1819, most of the eastern section was inhabited by Cherokees and Creeks. There followed a series of Native American treaties, beginning with one entered into by Chief McIntosh, which cost him his life and caused Pres. John Quincy Adams to withdraw the treaty. A final treaty was signed in 1832; the land became part of Alabama and was divided into counties. Randolph was one of those. It was named for John Randolph of Virginia, and the town of Roanoke was named for his home. There were no railroads, no roads, and no post offices. The best road near the area was the McIntosh Trail, and it was hardly a road.

Early historian J. M. K. Guinn wrote a series of articles about Randolph County for the local newspaper, the *Randolph Toiler*, between 1894 and 1896. He referred to the area as "The Red Man's Home—The White Man's Eden." Early settlers left vivid descriptions of the land: virgin forests with lots of wildlife, turkeys, squirrels, rabbits, raccoons, opossums, wild hogs, and others; clear springs, creeks, and rivers filled with a variety of fish; and an abundance of nuts, berries, and grapes. A tea was often made from sassafras roots. Even before the land of Randolph County was ceded, squatters came in by the hundreds and remained. Many of the Native Americans were friendly and very helpful to them. Among other things, Native Americans taught them to use herbs and roots as medicines.

Randolph County is noted for the purest and coldest water in the world, water that has been given credit for the wonderful health of those who live here. The abundance of springs is reflected in the names of different areas: Springhill, Springfield, Big Springs, and Rock Springs. Here the Tallapoosa River joins the Little Tallapoosa. It has been said there is hardly a square 40 acres of land not penetrated by a branch, creek, or river, making Randolph County perfect for small truck farmers, which supported many families in the early years.

Wedowee, the county seat, was named for a Native American chieftain who allowed his wigwam to be used for the first indoor court in Randolph County. The name Wedowee is a corruption of his name.

In 1903, the county had 52 post offices. Today it has four. Many communities flourished and then faded. Louina was such a village. It was named for a wealthy Native American who, along with her two slaves, operated a trading post. For over half a century, it was the largest town and the chief business center, paying over one third of all Randolph County taxes. Today it is difficult to find the site of this once-prosperous community.

The Handley textile mill was located in Roanoke, the largest town in the county. For 70 years, it was the main source of employment in Randolph County. Roanoke is famous for the Ella Smith Indestructible Doll and was again spotlighted when one of its sons, Joe Edwards Jr., was selected by NASA as an astronaut in December 1994.

The town of Wadley was established following the coming of the Atlanta, Baltimore, and Atlantic Railroad (AB&A). Wadley is home to Southern Union State Community College, which began as an institution of the General Convention of Christian Churches in the South and became a state junior college in 1964. A sewing plant and a large outdoor furniture plant have provided employment for people in Wadley and surrounding areas.

In 1982, a dam on the Tallapoosa River created a 10,660-acre lake. Known as Lake Wedowee, it is an attraction to tourists and vacationers and enjoyed by the Randolph County citizens.

One

INDUSTRY

The earliest industries took advantage of the county's natural resources. Alerted to the presence of gold by the Native Americans, a few of the settlers tried gold mining, but this proved unprofitable. Recognizing the high quality of the kaolin, entrepreneurs established potteries in Rock Mills and brickyards in Blake and Dickert that flourished for a time and then died. The forests fostered many industries and have been successful through the years, as the timber was plentiful and the need for lumber and other timber products was great.

Randolph County was primarily agricultural, and many of the successful early industries complemented and/or augmented the agrarian society and, in the process, changed the orientation of the rural areas and the towns. The cotton gins and the gristmills were established early and were successful because they were a necessary adjunct to the farmers' main crops. The syrup mills were another necessary, seasonal industry.

The cotton mills, however, were different. They worked 24 hours a day all year long, requiring hundreds of workers, and eventually causing the demise of this crop as the farmers found it more profitable to work in the mills than to grow the cotton. Roads improved. Members of the rural communities drove busloads of mill workers to town. Fields were abandoned. Some farms were set out in pine trees. Many were sold to lumber and power companies as families found living was better and easier in the towns near the mills. Generations worked in the mills before they closed. The wars brought more changes as the young people took advantage of the G.I. Bill to go back to school and prepare for professions. Due to many extenuating circumstances, the great mills fell silent, and mill hands were forced to move or commute to jobs outside the county.

But one of the county's natural resources, so important in the early years, continues to be one of its most important resources: water. Lake Wedowee, crated by the Harris Dam, has produced a new industry. The lake is filled during the warm months with residents and visitors.

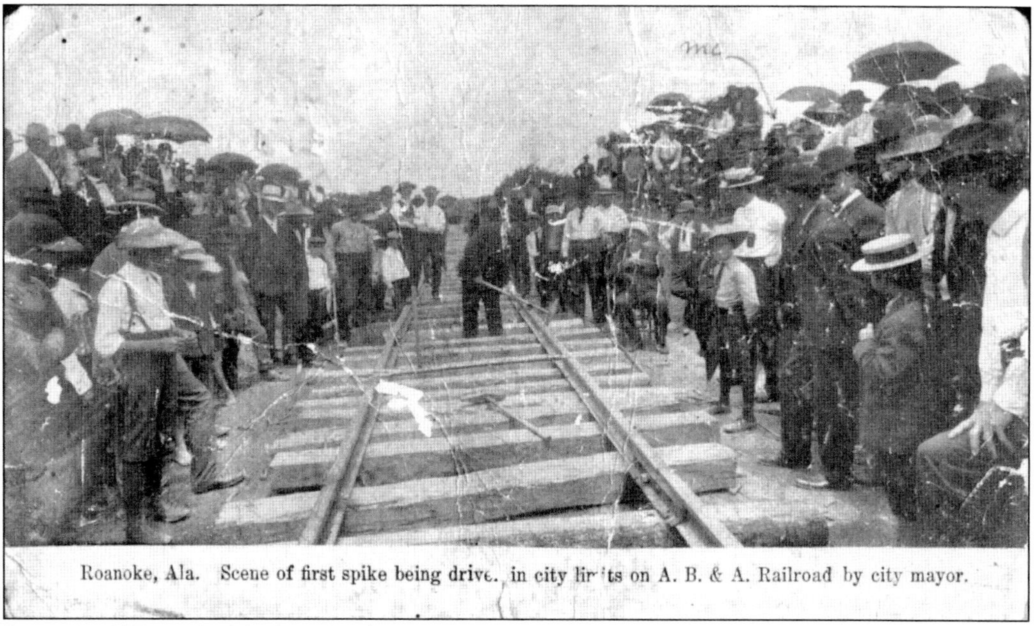

June 14, 1907, at 10 o'clock on Friday morning, Roanoke's mayor, John T. Heflin, drove the first spike inside Roanoke city limits on the Atlanta, Baltimore, and Atlantic (AB&A) Railroad. Photographer Olin Stevenson reported that he took two pictures because, on the first swing, the mayor missed the spike. At this time, Randolph County was primarily an agricultural region, and the railroad was a boon to the farmers. (Courtesy of Ruth Holliday.)

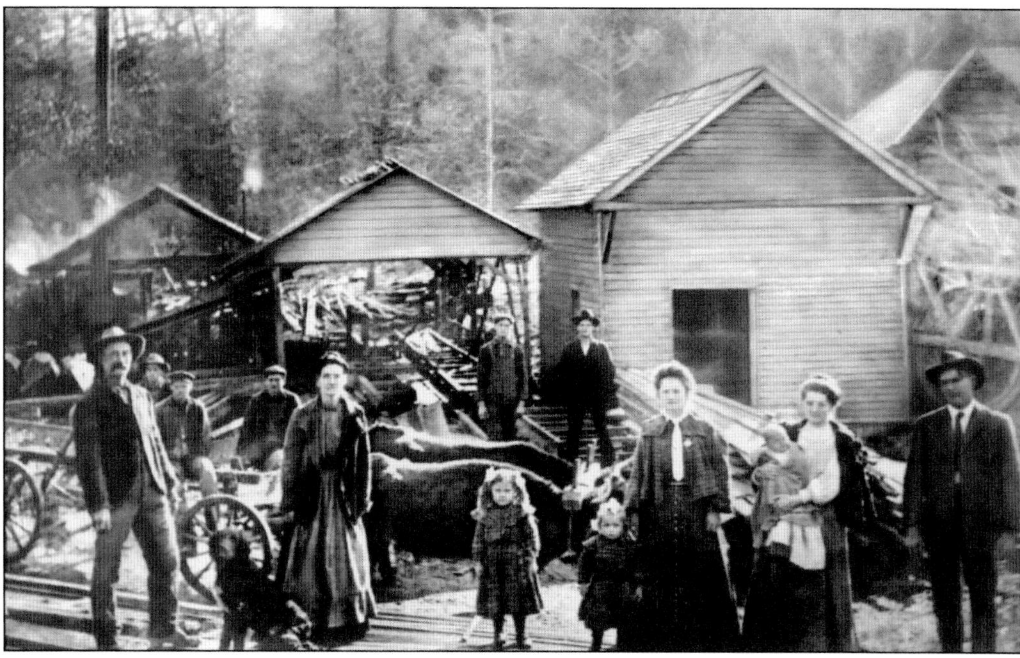

This sawmill, belonging to Pierce Parker in 1907, was located on No Business Creek near what is now County Road 49. The small child in the center of the picture is Bernice Hester Knight. The dog in front is named Slack. Jerome Hester, the grandfather of Bernice Hester, ran the Hester Ferry at Wadley. (Courtesy of Ezra Knight.)

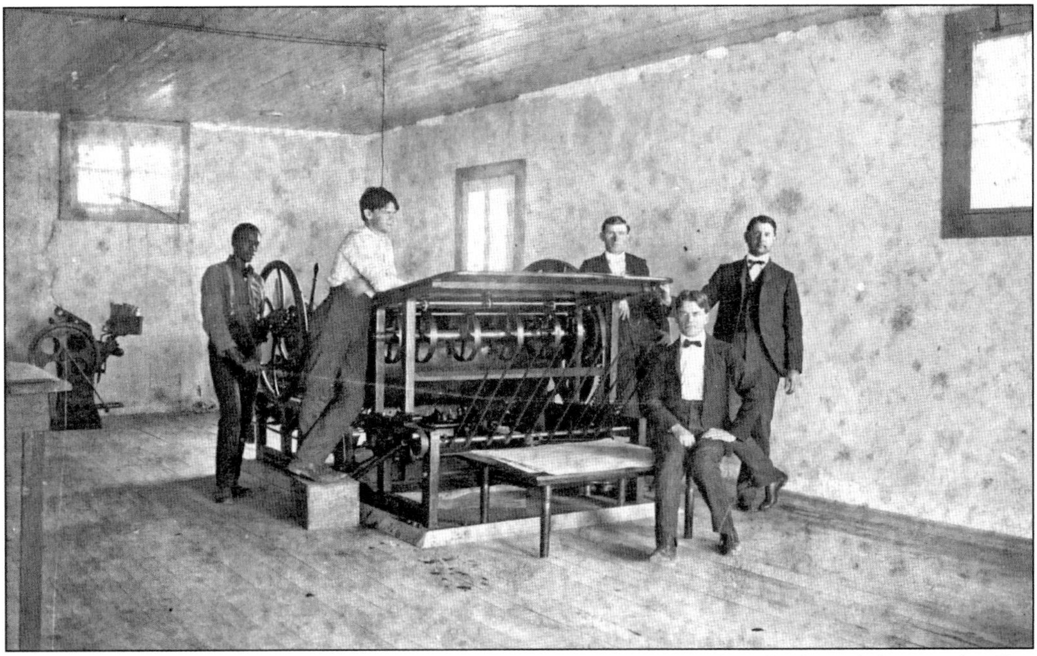

The printing presses of the *Roanoke Leader*, c. 1900, are pictured with, from left to right, Bet Patton turning the wheel, Ike Ballew standing on a box, and Olin Stevenson standing behind the press. The other two are unknown. The press against the rear wall was donated to the Randolph County Museum and is presently on display there. (Courtesy of John W. Stevenson.)

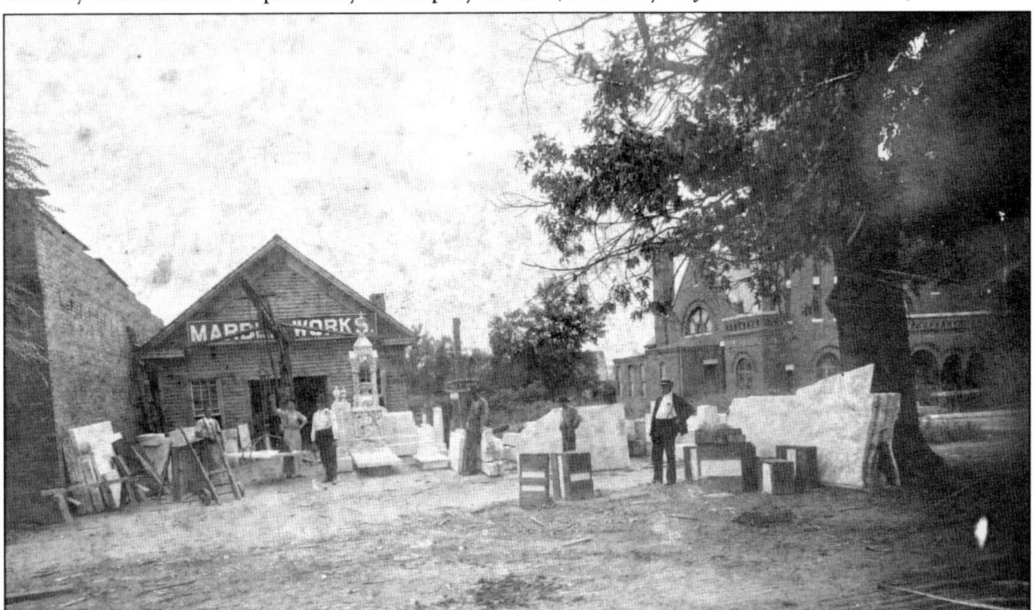

In 1905, the Marble Works was owned and operated by Benjamin James "B. J." Mitchum (pictured in a white shirt) and James Moore Jackson (under the tree). The First Baptist Church is seen to the right of the Marble Works. The front yard is filled with slabs of marble in various sizes, and the ornate monument to the right of Mitchum is in the Roanoke Cedarwood Cemetery, marking the grave of Sue Jessie McDonough. (Courtesy of Jean Windsor.)

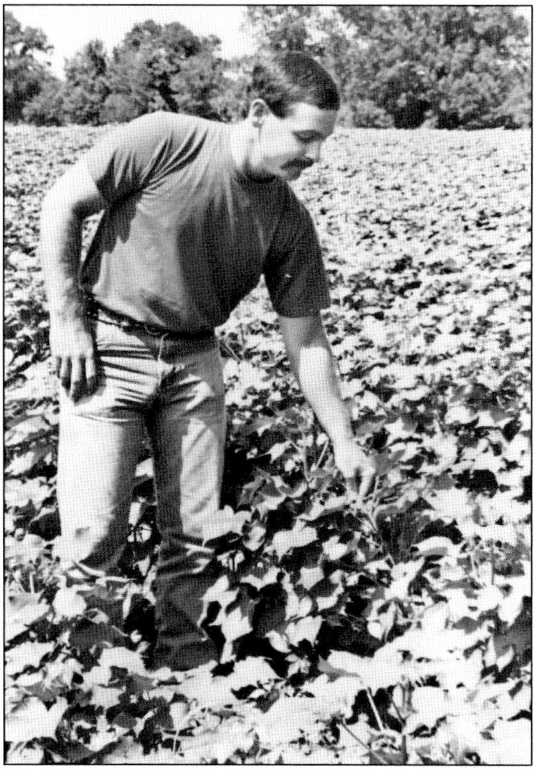

Cotton was the backbone of Randolph County economy for 140 years. In 1935, there were 4,103 farms in Randolph County with 31,277 acres of cotton planted. Roanoke had two cotton warehouses, a textile mill, and several cotton gins. Shown here in 1990 is Drew Phillips in his cotton field, which was the last cotton produced in Randolph County. Since 1990, there has not been a single acre of cotton planted. (Courtesy of Wyner Phillips.)

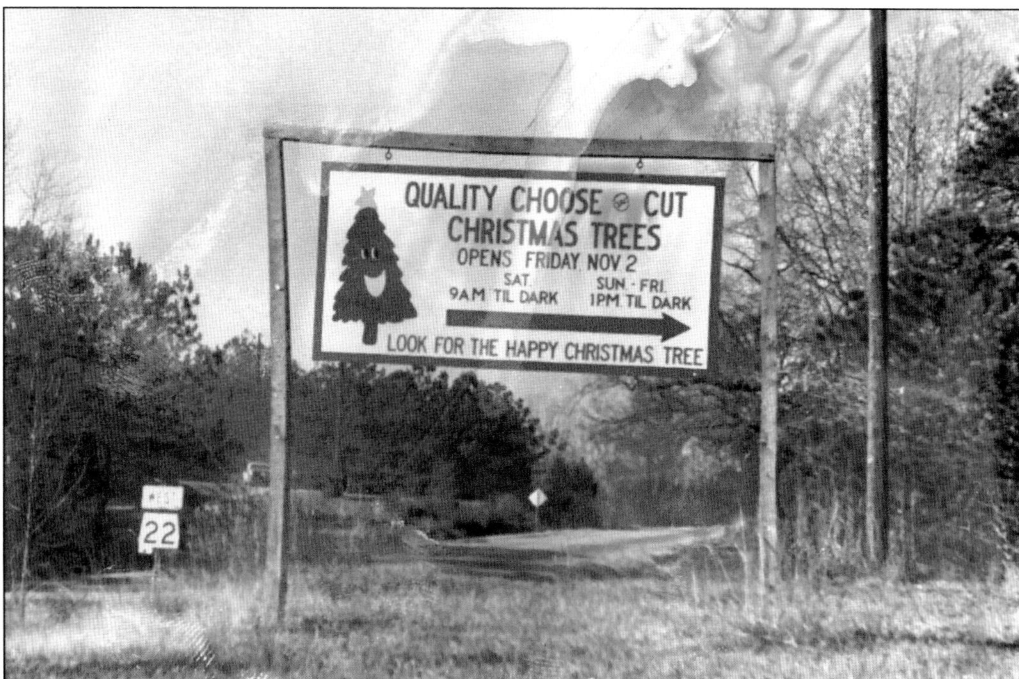

Commonly found in the county are Christmas tree farms. Shown here is Sam Wylie's farm in Dickert. (Courtesy of the *Randolph Leader*.)

Pool Brothers' Bottling Works was established on Louina Street, Roanoke, in March 1907. The name was later changed to Royal Crown Bottling Company and Nehi Bottling Company. The Pool family bottled RC and multiple flavors of Nehi soft drinks for approximately 70 years. This photograph shows the last president, Fred Pool, with the latest product, the Diet-Rite Cola, in 1962. The Piggly Wiggly grocery store is now where the Pool's Royal Crown Bottling Company and Nehi Bottling Company once stood. (Courtesy of Freddie Hill.)

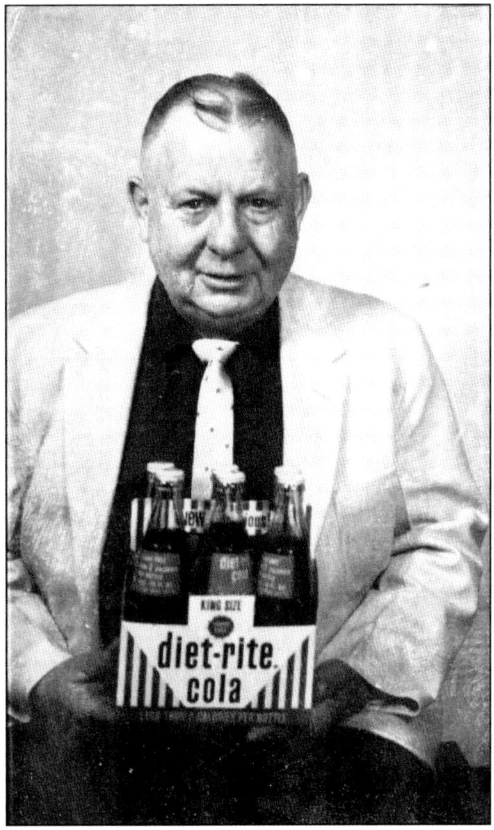

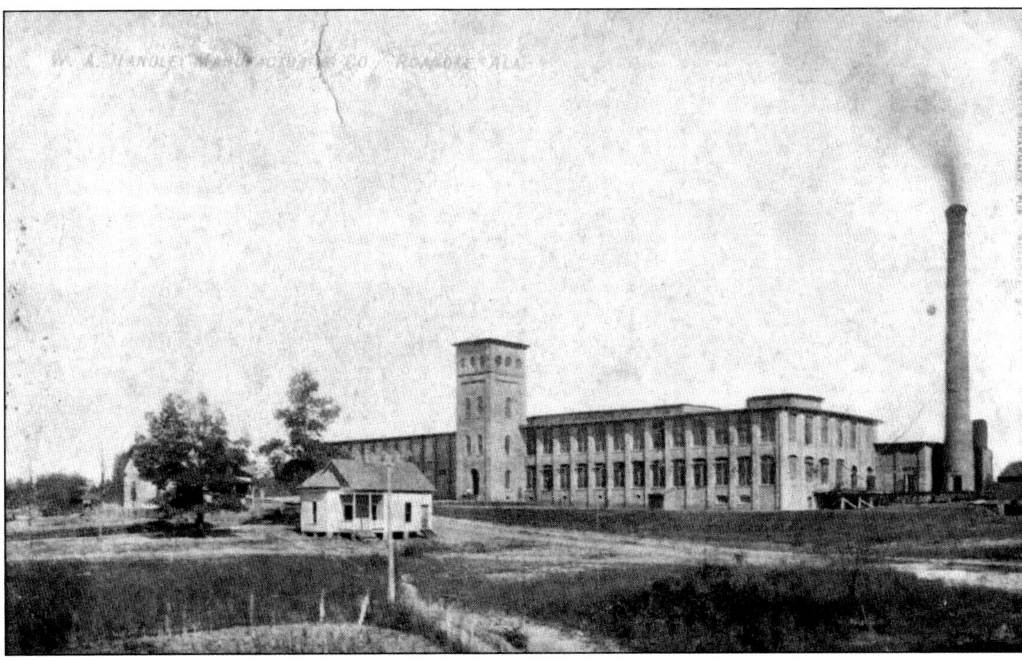

Pictured is the W. A. Handley Manufacturing Company *c.* 1908. The small, white house in the foreground served as the office. (Courtesy of the Randolph County Museum.)

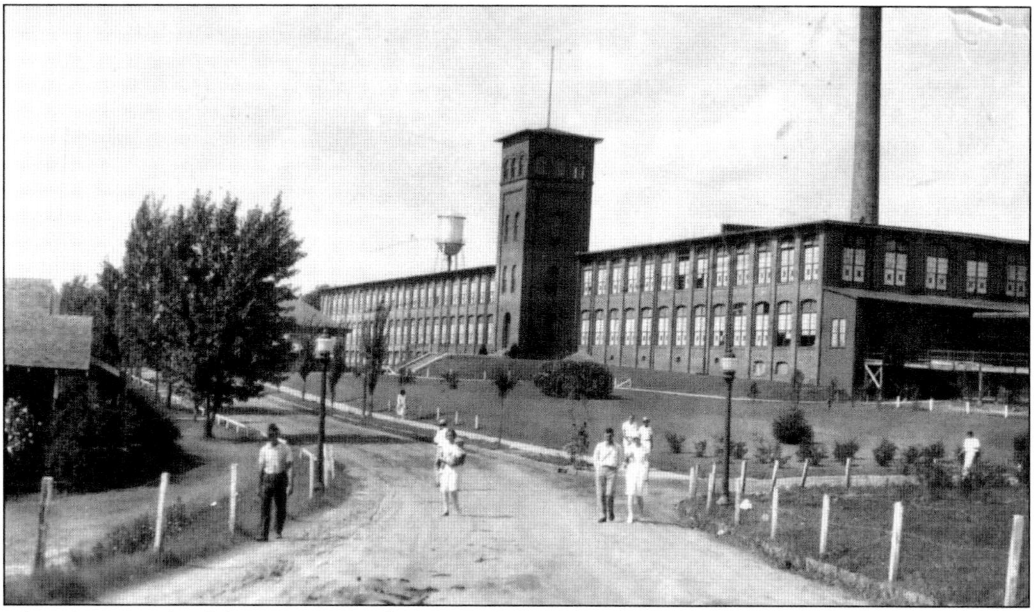

This photograph of the W. A. Handley Manufacturing Company, pictured with well-manicured grounds and unpaved street with no ruts on July 2, 1929, shows the high degree of maintenance carried out by the management and employees. (Courtesy of Gwen Murr.)

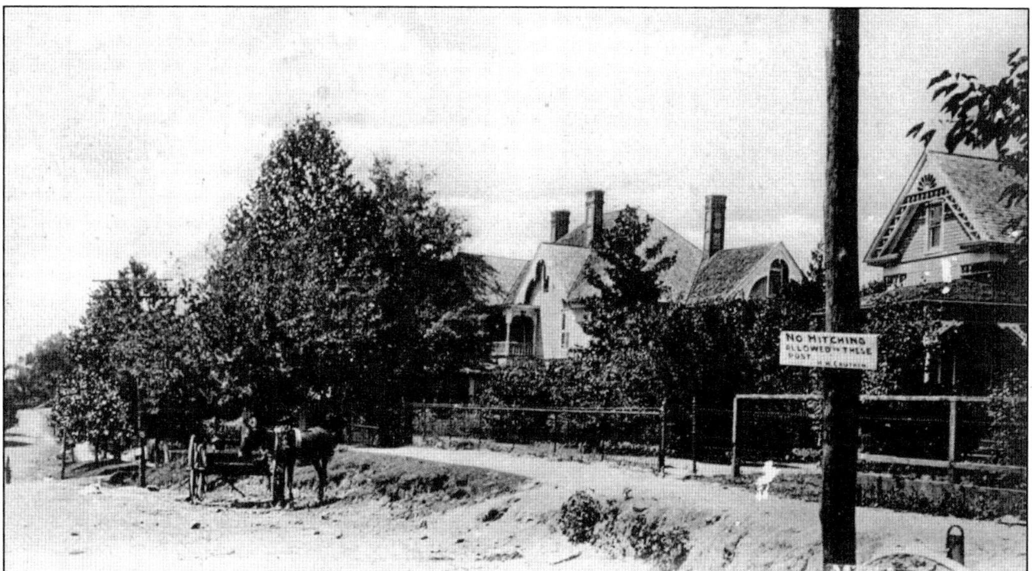

The sign on the utility pole, "No hitching allowed to these post H. H. Cauthen," indicated this was a telephone pole, *c.* 1908. Herbert H. Cauthen purchased the Roanoke Telephone Company in 1902 when it had 17 customers and immediately began installing "first-class, modern phones and raising wires so as to prevent the buzzing which interferes with talking at night, on account of the proximity of the electric wires," according to the local newspaper. After Cauthen's death in 1923, the company was run by his wife, Ethel, with the help of their five sons, serving approximately 800 subscribers. Currently there are more than 5,500. (Courtesy of the Randolph County Museum.)

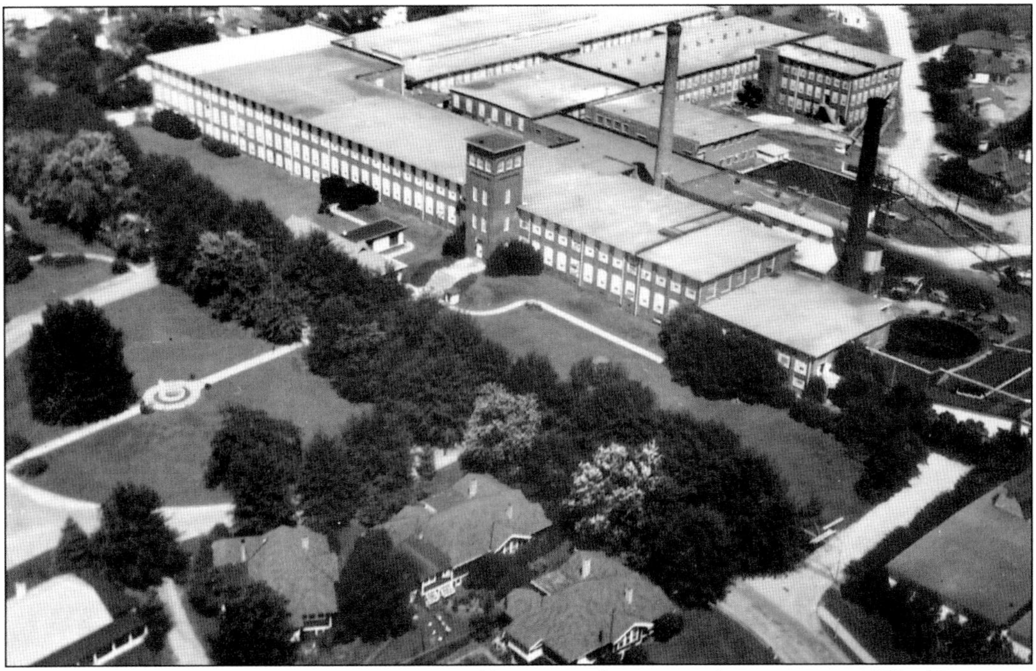

Pictured is the aerial view of W. A. Handley Manufacturing Company c. 1950. (Courtesy of Squat Yarbrough.)

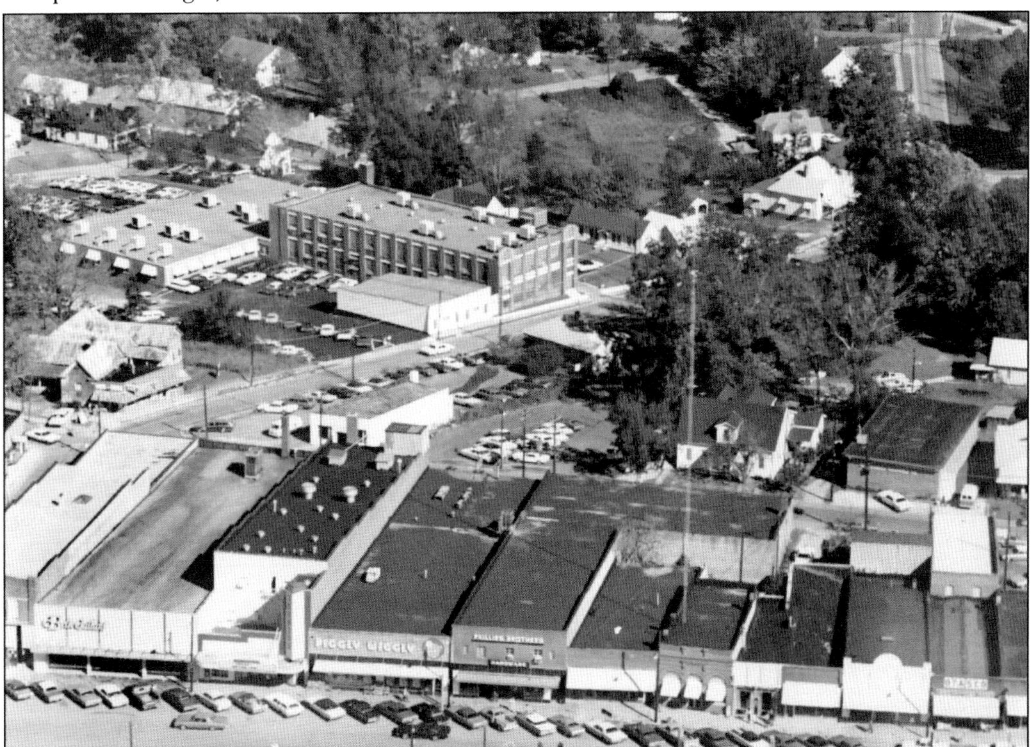

Here is a 1971 aerial view of downtown Roanoke when there were no vacant buildings and the Palm Beach Company was busy making men's suits. (Courtesy of Wyner Phillips.)

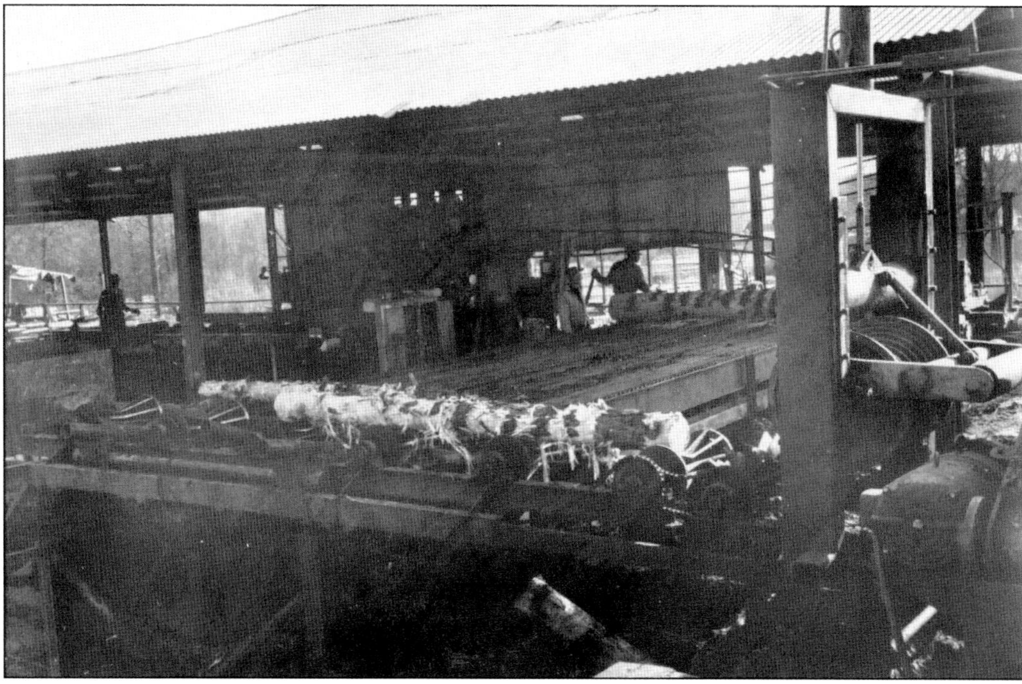

Shown here is Samuel Mark Wylie's sawmill at Dickert. He set up his first sawmill in Wadley in 1929 and moved to Dickert in 1938. The Wiley Lumber Company began with freshly cut logs and ended with finished lumber. (Courtesy of Ellen [Wylie] Sims.)

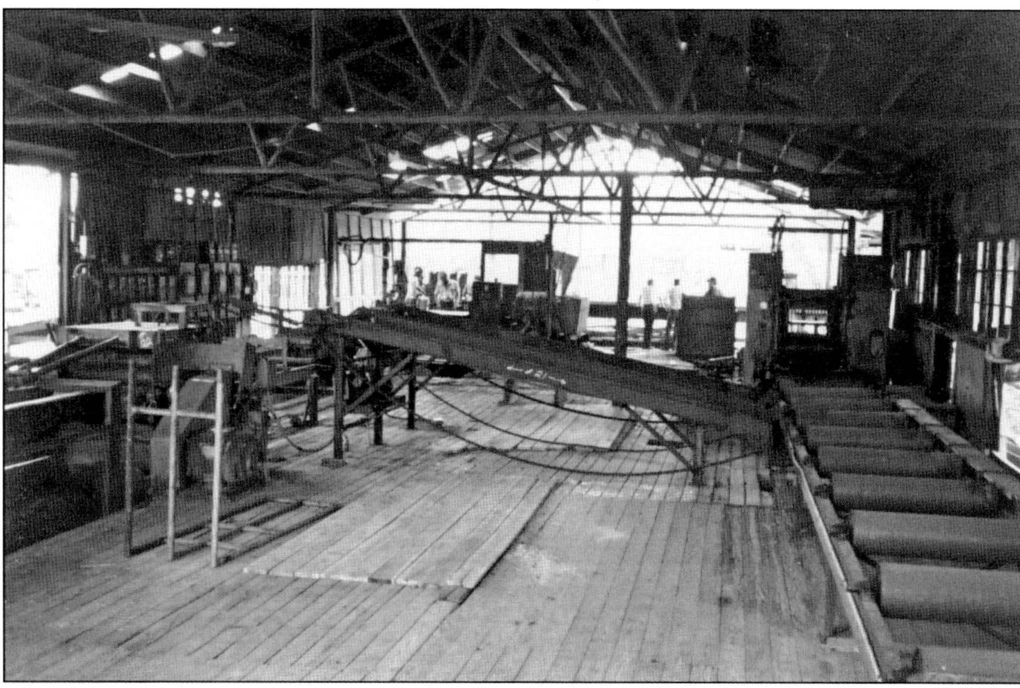

The planer was also moved to Dickert from Roanoke. Having all operations in one location made the process of making freshly cut logs into finished lumber much easier. (Courtesy of Ellen [Wylie] Sims.)

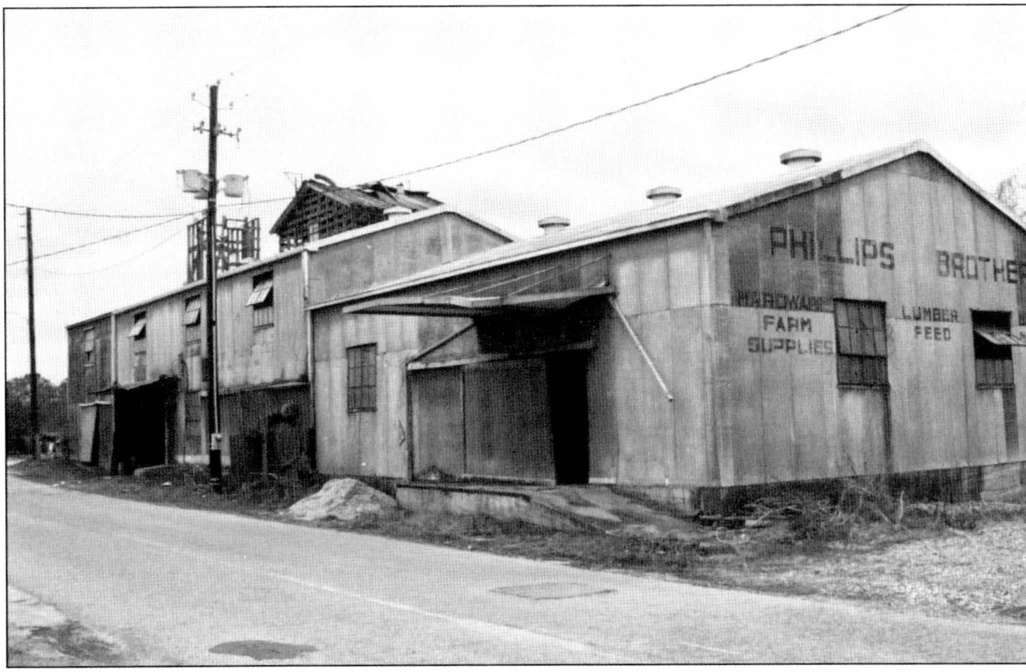

Built in 1945, Phillips Milling Company was a gristmill/feed mill that processed corn and hay and added molasses to produce feed for livestock. Located adjacent to the railroad tracks and next to the Atlantic Coast Line Depot, it operated for 50 years and was razed in 2004. (Courtesy of Wyner Phillips.)

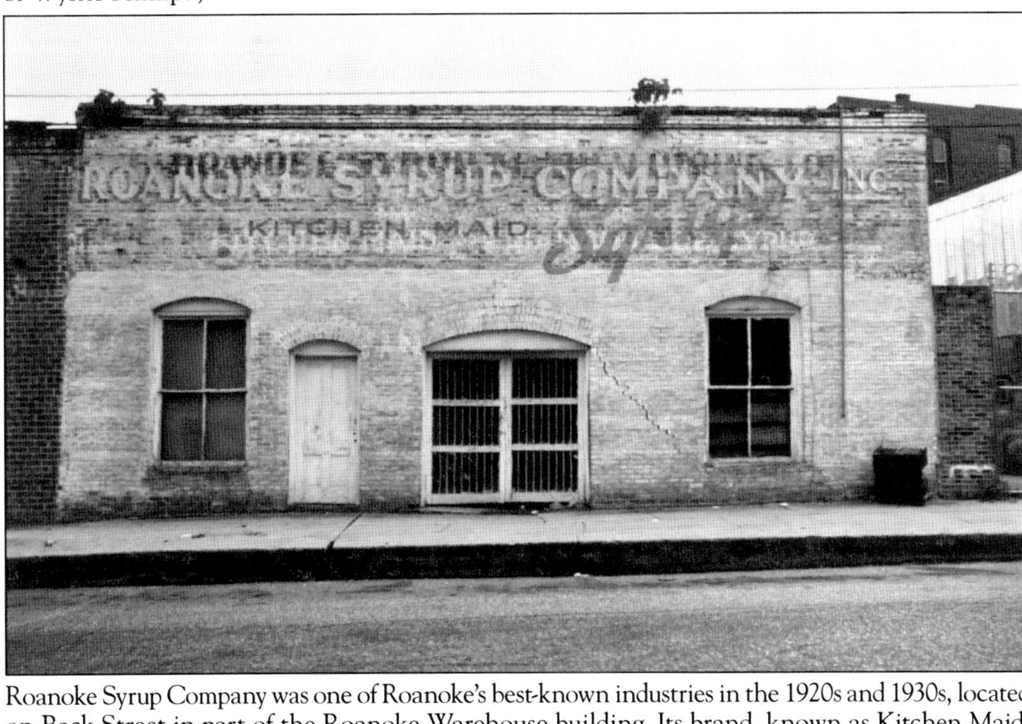

Roanoke Syrup Company was one of Roanoke's best-known industries in the 1920s and 1930s, located on Back Street in part of the Roanoke Warehouse building. Its brand, known as Kitchen Maid, was made and bottled at this location for sales far and wide. (Courtesy of Helen Blankenship.)

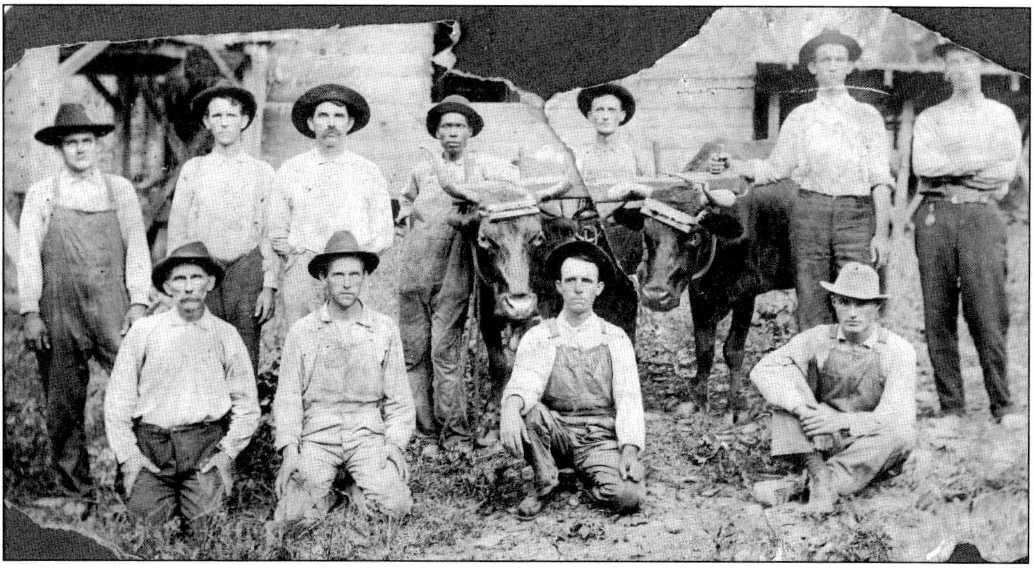

This picture of the Wilson Cotton Gin and Saw Mill workers was made about 1910. From left to right are (first row) Mebane "Mount Budd" Wilson, Alious "Ale" Wilson, David Wilson (owner) and Ollie Teal; (second row) Will Irvin, Walt Wilson, Wesley Shaw, Bud Holliday, Rufus Wilson, Buren Wilson, and Eugene Wilson. (Courtesy of Michael Wilson.)

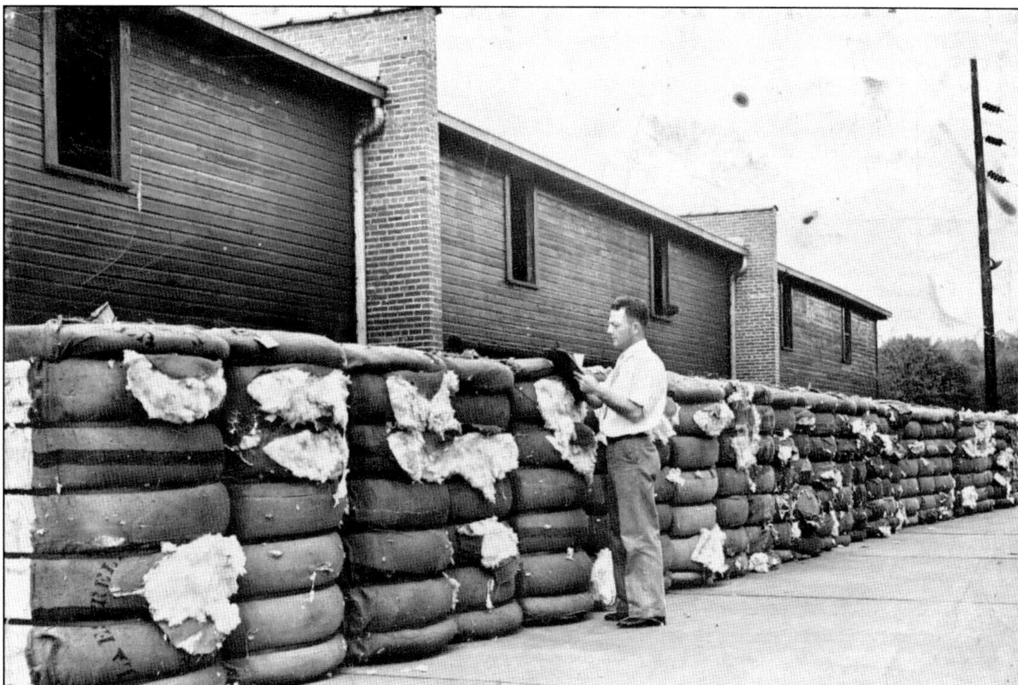

L. Eugene Moore, the cotton buyer, grader, and mixer for W. A. Handley Manufacturing Company, is shown here grading cotton, c. 1948. After the grading, the higher and lower grades were mixed to produce good-quality yarn. (Courtesy of Bonnie Sue Knight.)

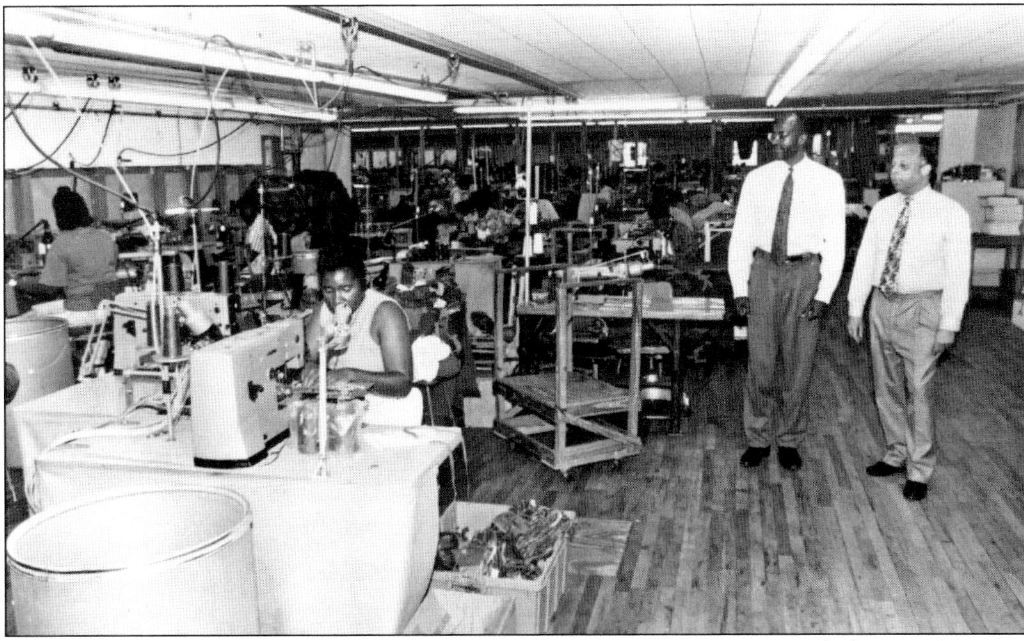

Jesse and Velma Terry founded Terry Manufacturing Company in 1963 with five employees. It ultimately employed 300 and made uniforms for the military, U.S. Forest Service, McDonald's, the National Hockey League, and 1996 Olympics. Their sons, Roy and Rudolph, succeeded Jesse and Velma and operated it until it closed in 2003. Touring the plant with Pres. Roy Terry (left), April 27, 1994, is Edwin Moses (right), winner of an Olympic gold medal. (Courtesy of the *Randolph Leader.*)

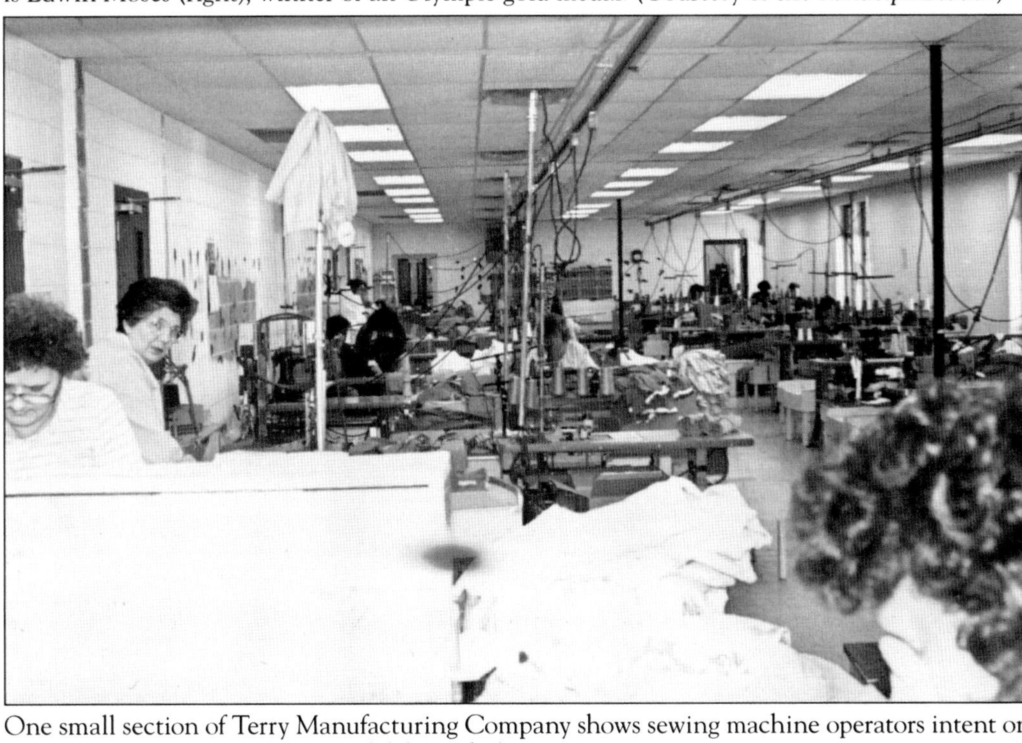

One small section of Terry Manufacturing Company shows sewing machine operators intent on production. (Courtesy of the *Randolph Leader.*)

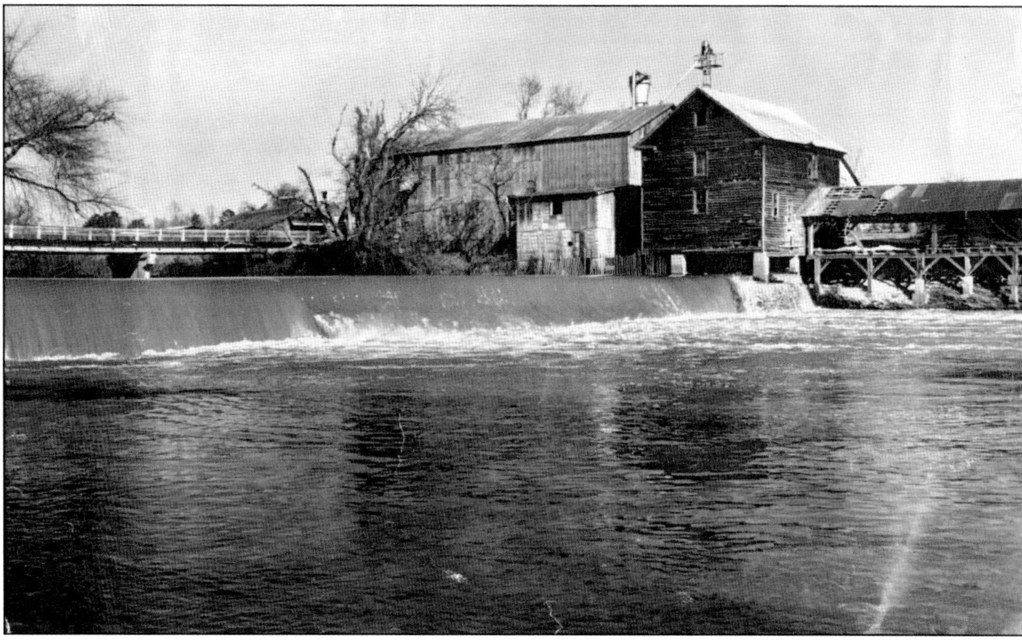

The first mill and dam built by James Saxon was powered with an overshot wheel. In 1881, a new mill house, 30 by 40 feet and 20 feet high, was erected and machinery was installed that would grind wheat and corn. In 1902, the overshot wheel was changed to turbine that would produce 150 horsepower. A gin was added that could gin eight bales of cotton a day. Through the years, improvements were made to the mill, and when it shut down in 1975, 15 bales of cotton were ginned a day. (Courtesy of Bob and Boots Butler.)

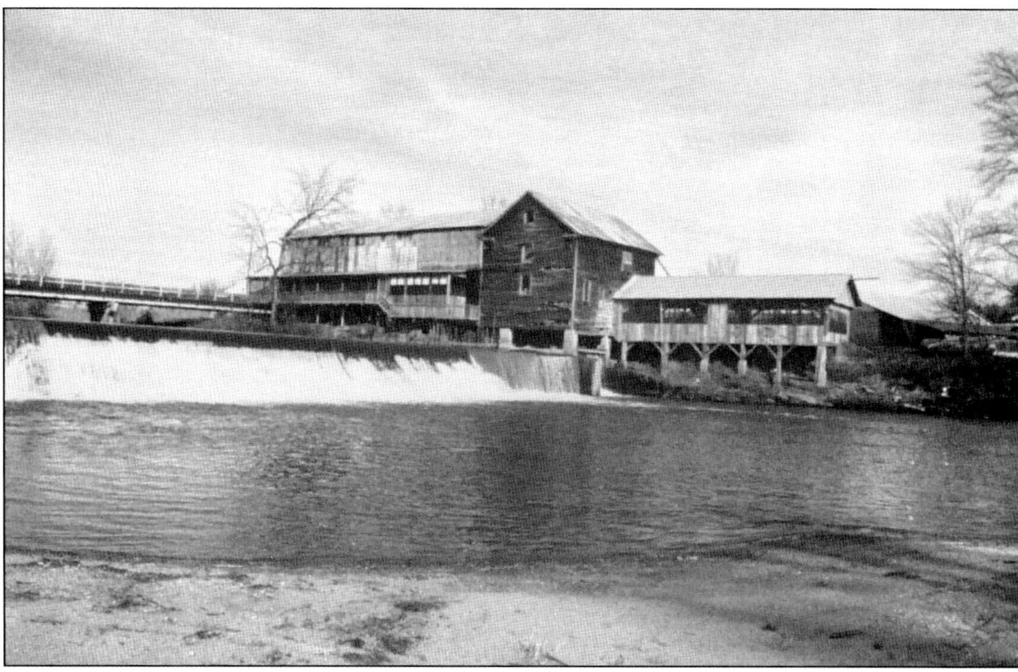

Today the gristmill is still in operation, and the gin house has been converted to a popular restaurant, Butler's Mill. (Courtesy of Bob and Boots Butler.)

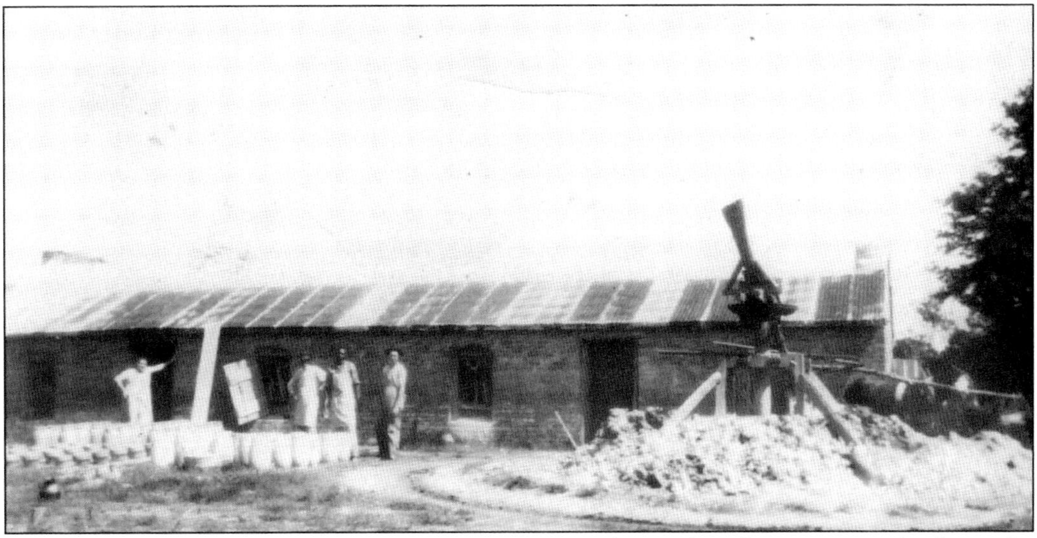

The Rock Mills' Jug Factory business was begun around 1840 by John Leaman, who located a deposit of fine pottery clay, called kaolin, in the vicinity. Three potteries making churns, jugs, vases, and other containers operated in Rock Mills for many years. Here at Pound's Jug Shop are, from left to right, Earl, Will, and Jessie Boggs; ? Scales; and Nell the mule. (Courtesy of Harold Breed and Jeff Towler.)

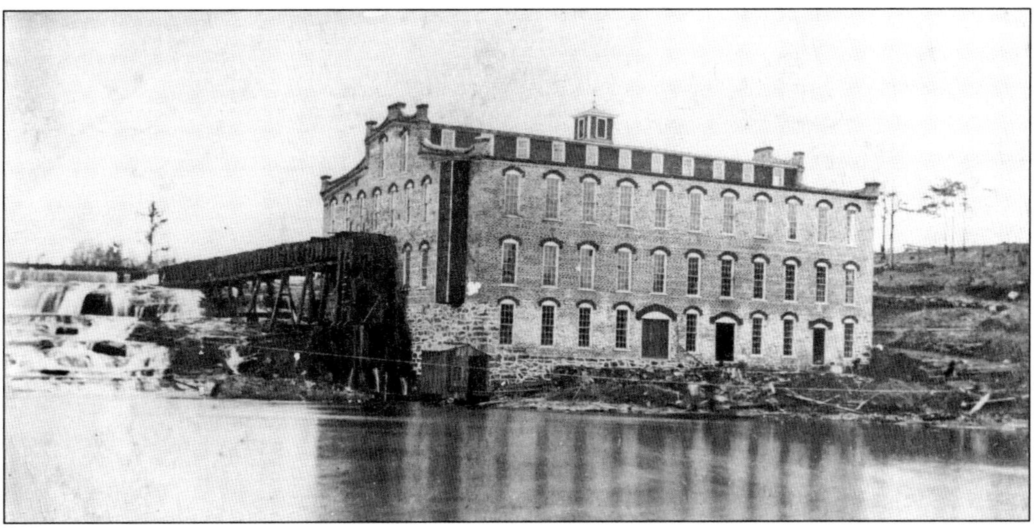

The mill at Rock Mills has always been the center of the community. The first mill on Wehadkee Creek, a small wooden building with little machinery that carded wool for people so they could weave it, was built in 1866. After it burned, it was replaced by a brick building in 1881. A Mr. Barry from Rhode Island installed two big engines that would generate electricity. The first cotton mill was named Rock Mills Cotton Mill. The name later changed to Rosedale Cotton Manufacturing Company, then to Wehadkee Yarn Mill. During World War II, the mill produced cord that was used by soldiers to tie down pup tents. (Courtesy of Harold Breed and Jeff Towler.)

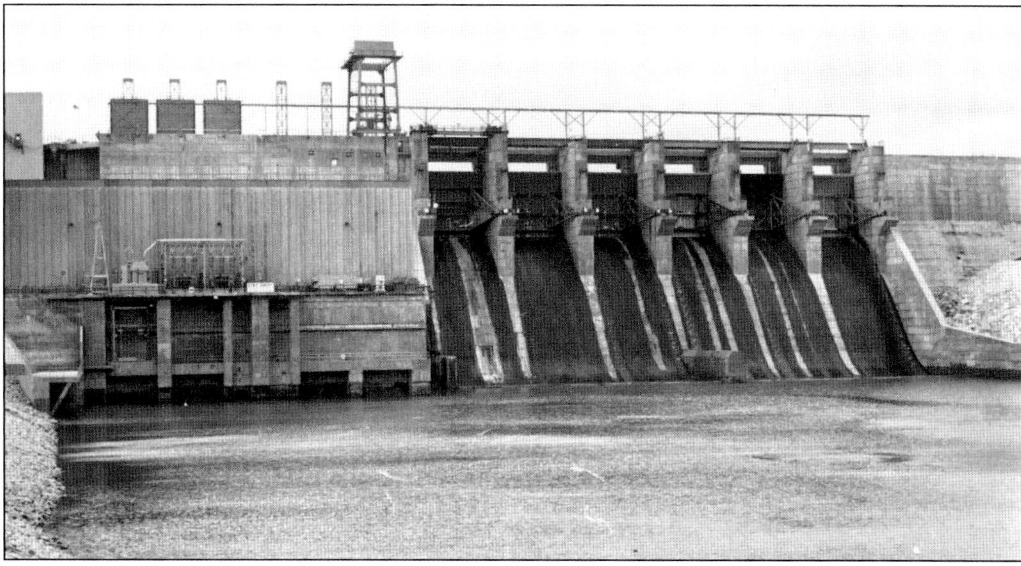

Lake Wedowee and R. L. Harris Reservoir are located approximately 90 miles from Atlanta, Georgia, and Birmingham and Montgomery, Alabama. Lake Wedowee ranks as one of the cleanest lakes and spills its pure, clean water across approximately 11,000 acres. The shoreline stretches some 280 miles, and the lake boasts a maximum depth at the dam of 135 feet. Construction on the dam began November 1, 1974. The dam is 1,142 feet in length and 150 feet high. Two generator units, rating 67,500 kilowatts each, went into service on April 20, 1983. Harris Dam, the newest Alabama Power Company dam, was built at the last major hydro site in Alabama. (Courtesy of the *Randolph Leader*.)

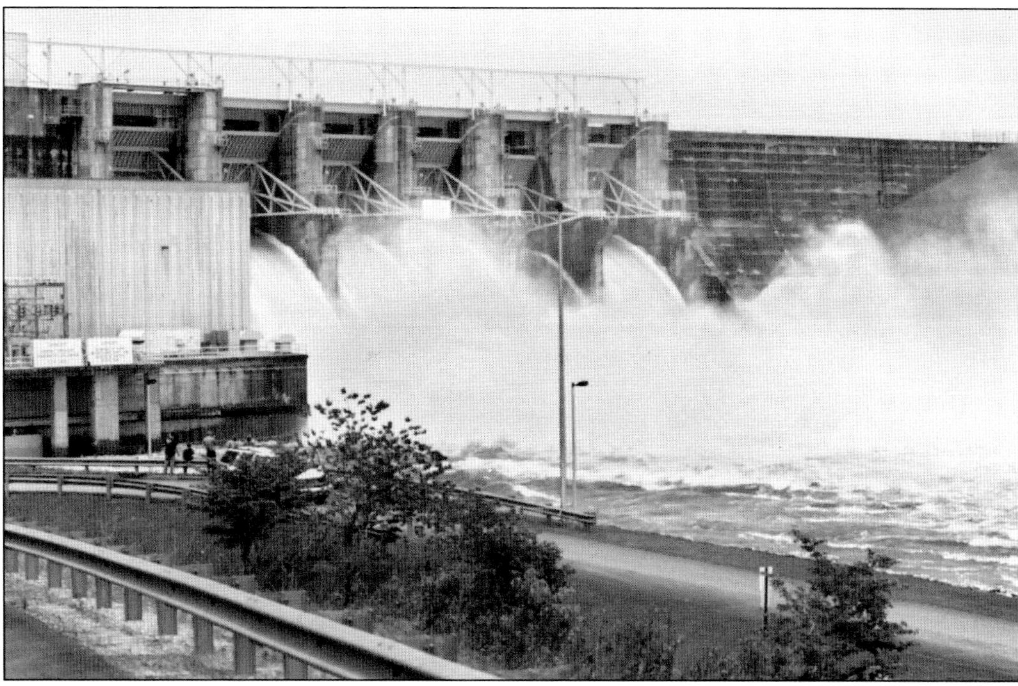

The newest dam was named in honor of Robert L. "Judge" Harris, who retired in 1968 after 45 years of service with Alabama Power Company. (Courtesy of the *Randolph Leader*.)

Two

SCHOOLS AND CLASSES

In the very early years, people were so busy that little thought was given to establishing permanent schools. The families who were financially able sent their children to private schools already established in other areas.

An act of the legislature, which provided for the reserving of the 16th section of each township for school purposes, encouraged the people to build schools and to handle their own school affairs through their own trustees. But no funds were allotted for the schools or anything connected with the schools.

The first schools were organized and built by community members. The men built the schools, usually one room with a huge fireplace in one end and with clapboard windows, the only source of light, which could be opened only when weather permitted. The children walked to school, some for miles. In the beginning, most schools were held only in the summer.

Teachers were hired and paid by the families who sent children to school. The teachers' board was often part of the salary as they lived in the community in the homes of the children they taught. Families often paid a subscription for each child who attended school. In some places, their pay might be in the form of produce from the farms.

In 1834, the legislature set up a state system for schools, and there began to be more regulation, but still no public funds were allotted. In 1899, responsibility for the certification of teachers was transferred to the state department. The State Department of Education began to adopt the textbooks. In 1907, Roanoke became one of the first municipalities in the state to have a city school system when the Roanoke Normal College was donated to the city.

The improvement of roads and transportation and the interest of the state in the education of the young made a big difference in the schools. School buses began transporting the students. Consolidation of the schools began. Laws were passed requiring parents to send their children to school. The state supplied the books. The school year was expanded.

Southern Union, organized in 1927, continued to grow and in 1964 became Southern Union State Community College. Today Randolph County has outstanding public schools and is within commuting distance of several colleges.

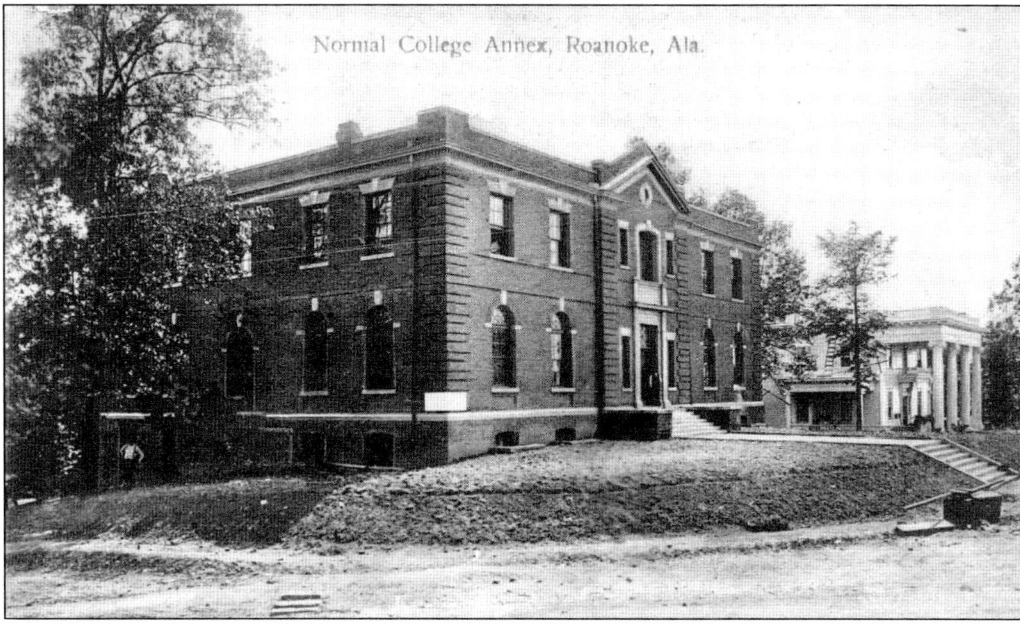

On January 25, 1907, Roanoke Normal College was deeded to the city of Roanoke by the stockholders and at that time became a Roanoke City school. Because of W. A. Handley's generosity, the annex building became Handley High School. In 1963, this building was demolished to make room for a new school building on the site of the Carlisle home, which was sold and moved to Macon, Georgia, where it is still a beautiful home. (Courtesy of the Randolph County Museum.)

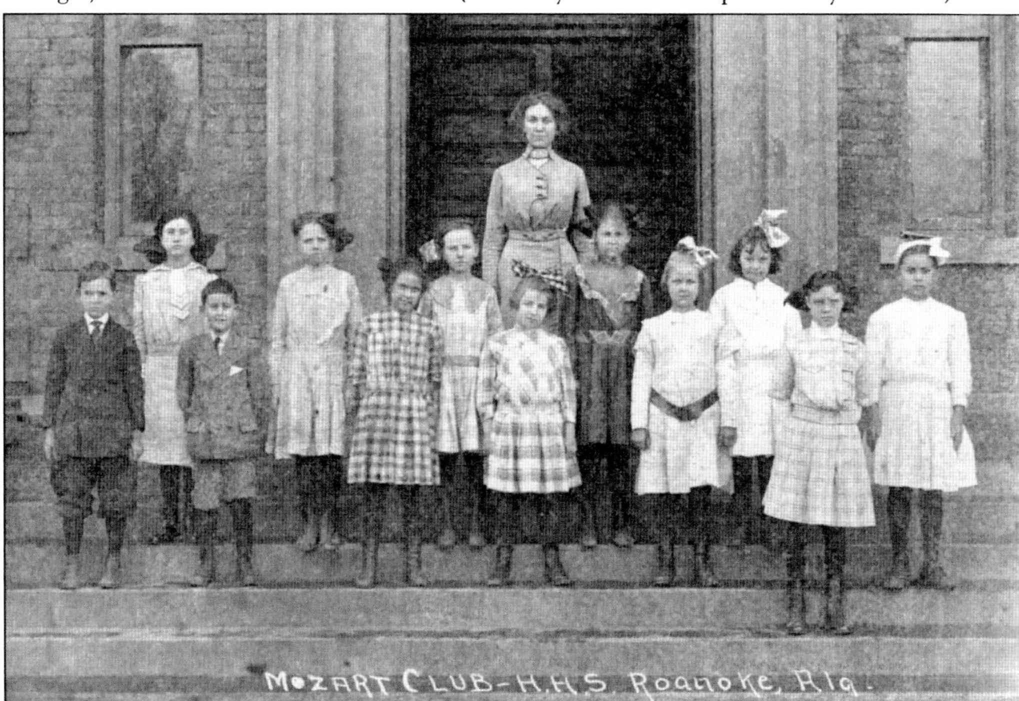

Pictured is the Mozart Club of Handley High School around the year 1915. The boy with the white handkerchief has been identified as W. T. Belcher. (Courtesy of W. T. [Bill] Belcher III.)

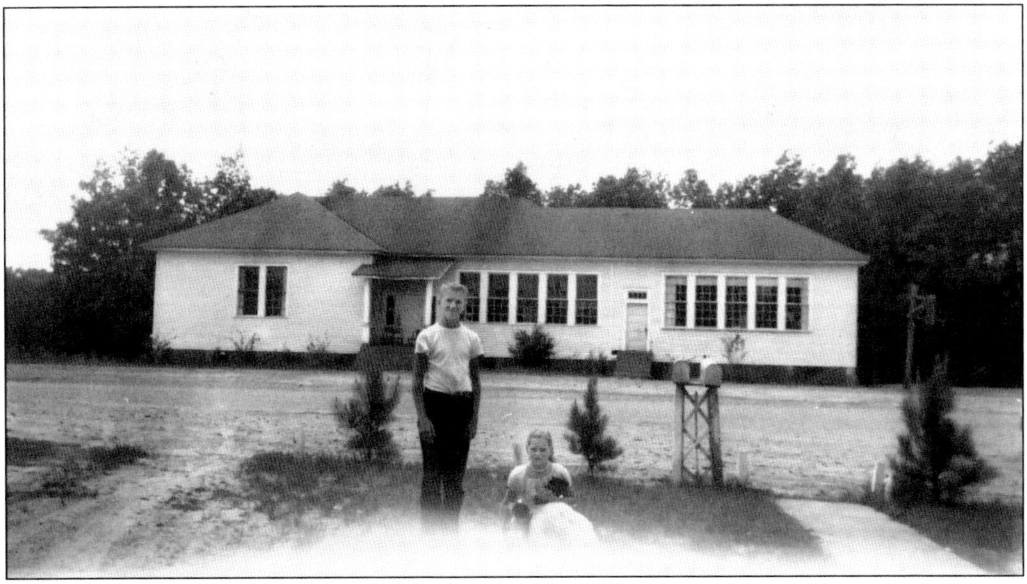

A little log schoolhouse known as "Phillip and Hurley" was used from 1850 to 1900. Crusoe Robinson built a one-room plank building with an open fireplace and the name changed to "Friendship School." When a post office was established in the community, it was necessary to choose a name for the school, post office, and community. The name selected was Napoleon, after Napoleon Robinson, a local resident. A two-story school building served the community until a tornado destroyed it in 1920. This one-story building was built and used until 1964, when many county schools were closed due to consolidation of the schools. Standing in front is Johnny Ward. (Courtesy of Janie [Ward] Cobb.)

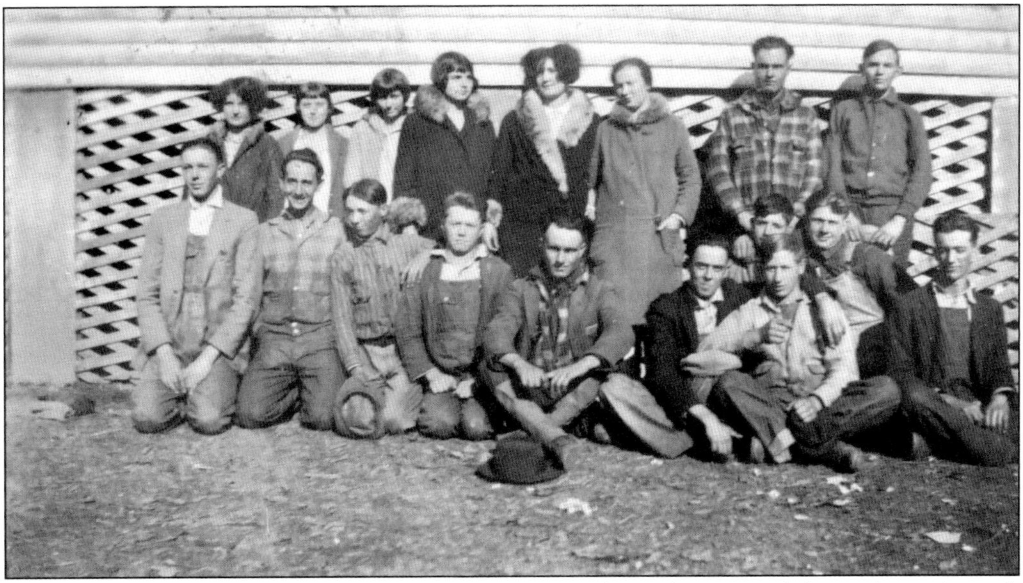

Pictured are the 1925 seventh- and eighth-grade students of Napoleon. From left to right are (seated) Howard Bowen, Arnold Huey, Amos Wilson, Emmitt Bowen, Hoke Edmondson, Arthur Langley, Lawrence Huey, ? Burke, Ivious Nickols, and Earl Laney; (standing) Eva Edmondson, Udell Bailey, unidentified, Wilma Davis, Betty Lou Scott, Enie Hester, Perry Edmondson, and Tuerman Wilson. (Courtesy of Bernice [Wilson] Burson.)

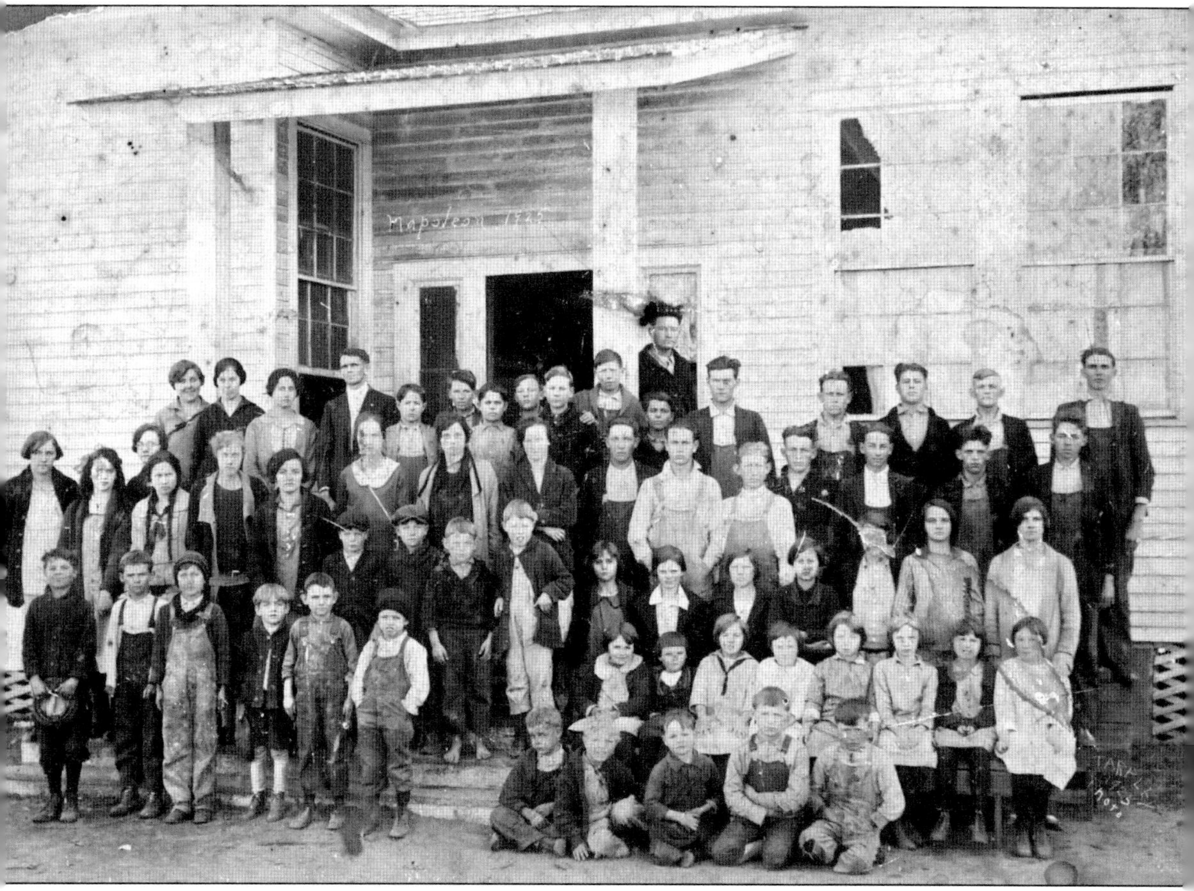

Pictured is the entire student body and faculty of Napoleon school in 1925. From left to right are (first row) Charles T. Chase, Amos Smith, Clarence Hester, Talmadge Bailey, and Junior Huey; (second row) ? Hill, Mebane Wilson, Gillis Prince, Robert Hurley, J. B. Shaw, A. J. Richardson, Ruby Lee Wilson, Brooksy Shaw, Velma Nickols, Dovie Hester, Ellie Mae Langley, Mamie Langley, Betty Ida Hill, and Daisy Hester; (third row) Lois Wilson, Annie Kirby, Rudell Prince, Eunie Langley, Eukel Moses, Coyt Hester, Clyde Laney, Byron Bailey, Joe Smith, ? Hurley, Bernice Chase, Vivian Prince, Mary Will Huey, Eudell Bailey, ? Hill, and Eura Wilson; (fourth row) Clyde Wilson, Bursie Thurmond, Eudell Langley, Evie Hester, Eulas Laney, Ted Huey, Chester Prince, Terell Bailey, Oliver Kirby, Erwin Chase, and Lonnie Wilson; (fifth row) teachers Annie Huey, Ora Wilson, and Palmer Prince, principal Clyde Hester, Guy Hester, Homer Wilson, Reedy Hill, Kermit Hester, Reed Laney, Travis Laney, George Scott, Earl Laney, Garvis Prince, Hazel Hill, Ridley Bailey, Stanford Moore. (Courtesy of Bernice [Wilson] Burson.)

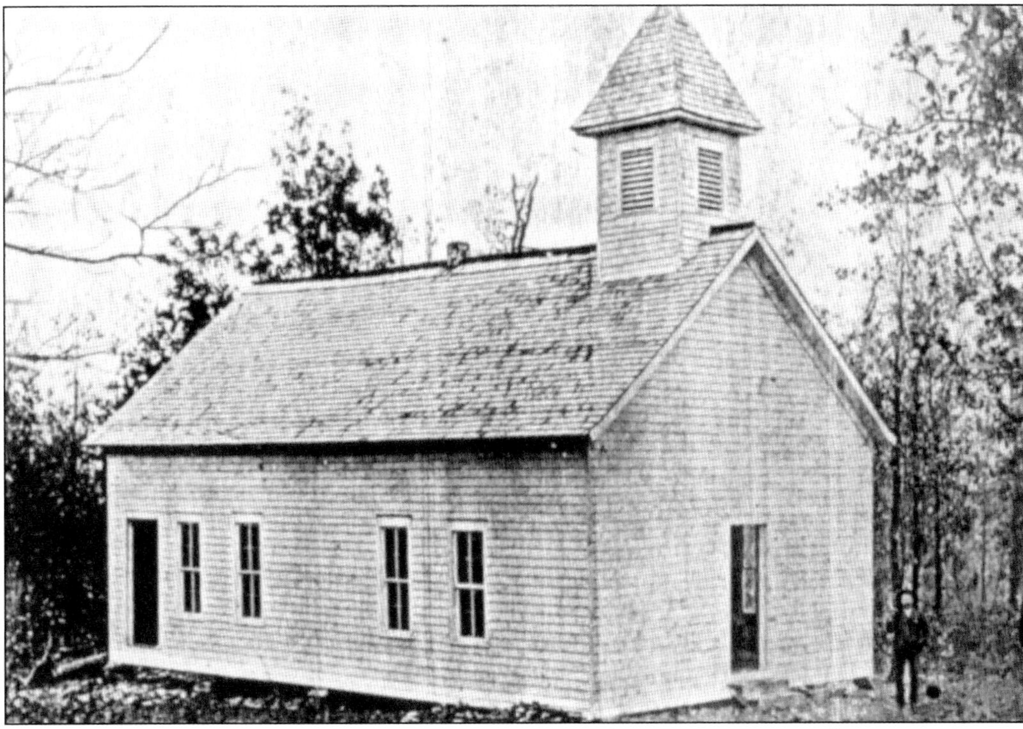

The old Burson School is shown here. Some of the teachers were Mattie Wilson, E. N. Burson, Ruth Sharman, and Essie Edmondson. Omie Hester, a Roanoke resident who was 87 in 2006, stated she attended second grade there before it closed about 1927. (Courtesy of Paula [Burson] Lambert.)

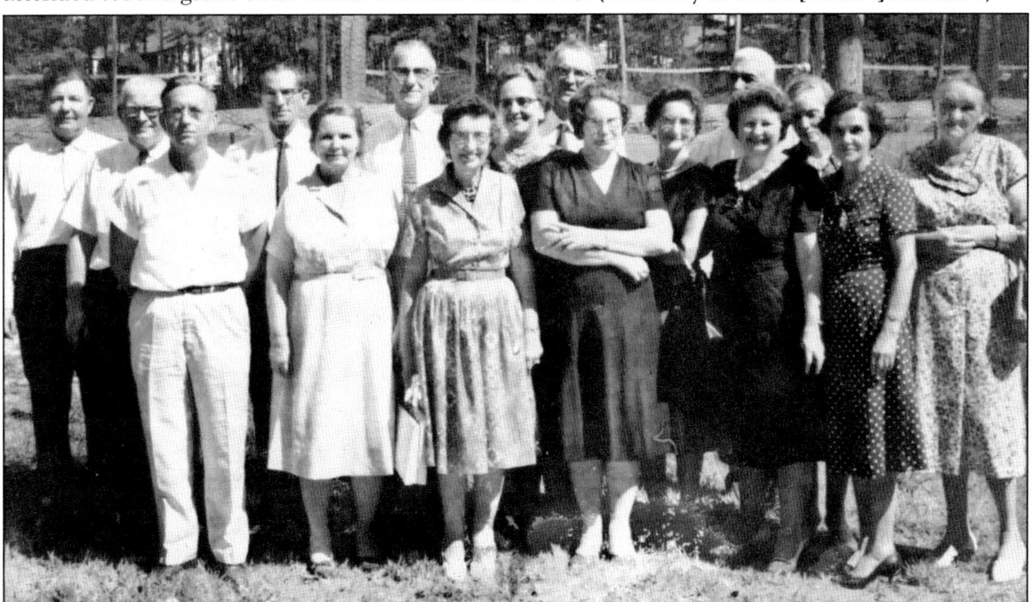

The Randolph County High School class of 1928 gathered for their 30th class reunion. Among those in attendance were Stell Benefield, fourth person from the left on the back row; Eunie Langley, last person on the right on the back row; ? Sikes, first person on the left on first row; and Lois Ward, the last person on the right on the front row. (Courtesy of Janice Ward Cobb.)

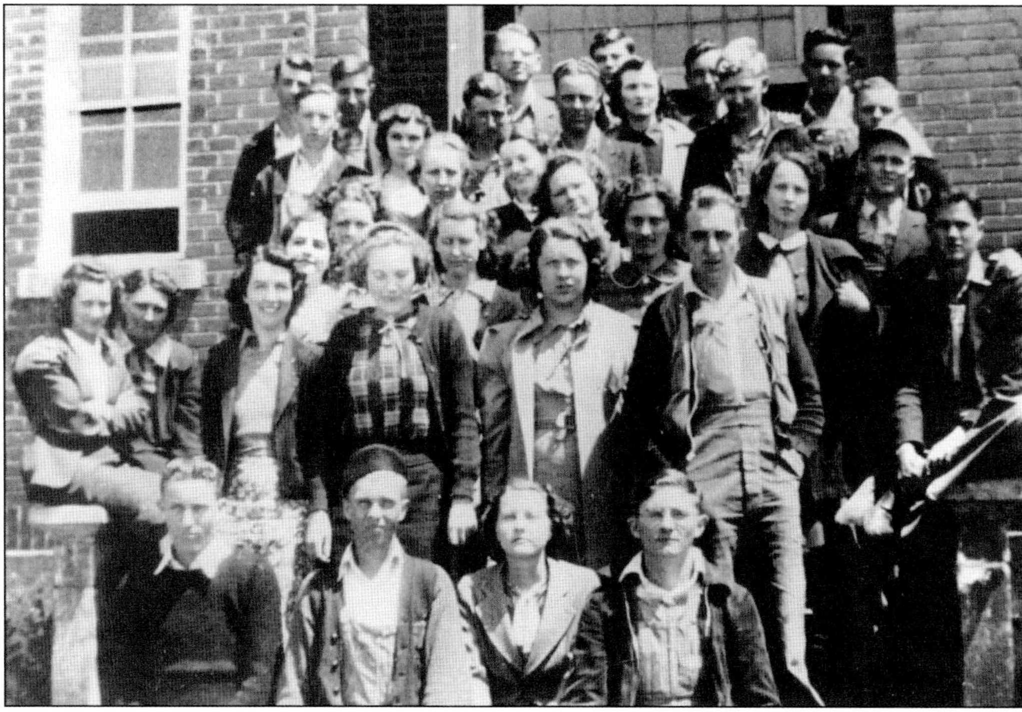

Pictured is the Woodland High School graduating class of 1939. From left to right are (first row) Ocie Yarbrough, Joe Bob McManus, Lonnie Will Tomlinson, and T. C. Wilson; (second row) Isabelle Rampy, Ruby Wilson, Bernice Wilson, Myrtice Strickland, Marie Brown, Gatha Yates, and George Lovvorn; (third row) Omie Hester, Burdie L. Reeves, Helen Reeves, Margaret McCarley, Burnedean Strain, Roy L. Fincher, Arlis Sears, Marvoline Prince, and Julian Lowe; (fourth row) Unid ?, Brooksie Shaw, Lewis Smith Henry Stribbling, Novis Calhoun, Dausey Irvin, and ? Stewart; (fifth row) Joe Wilson, unidentified, Curtis Traylor, J. C. Wilder, Dorsey Prince, and Elton Harris. (Courtesy of Bernice [Wilson] Burson.)

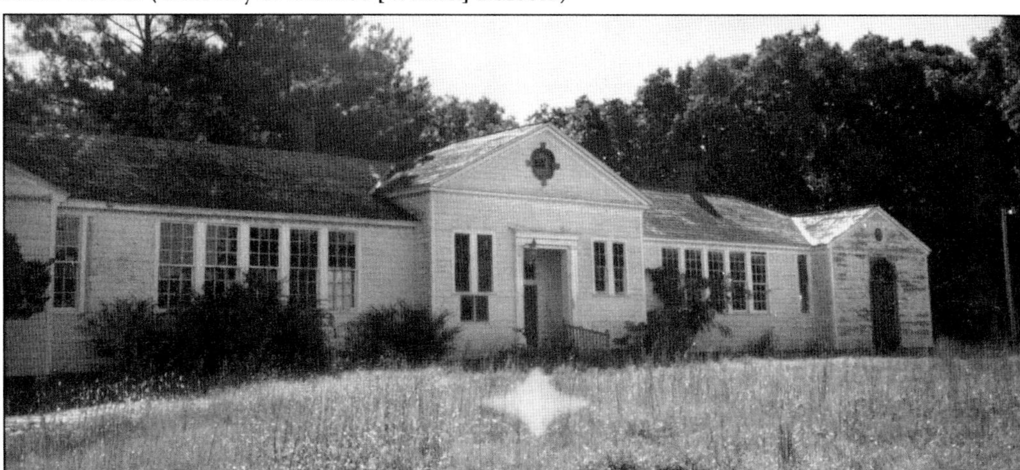

Big Springs School opened in the fall of 1926. W. B. Lipham was the first principal. In 1938, the original school burned. School continued with classes held in several nearby churches, the Masonic lodge, and other places until the school could be rebuilt. The halls are now silent. (Courtesy of Paula [Burson] Lambert.)

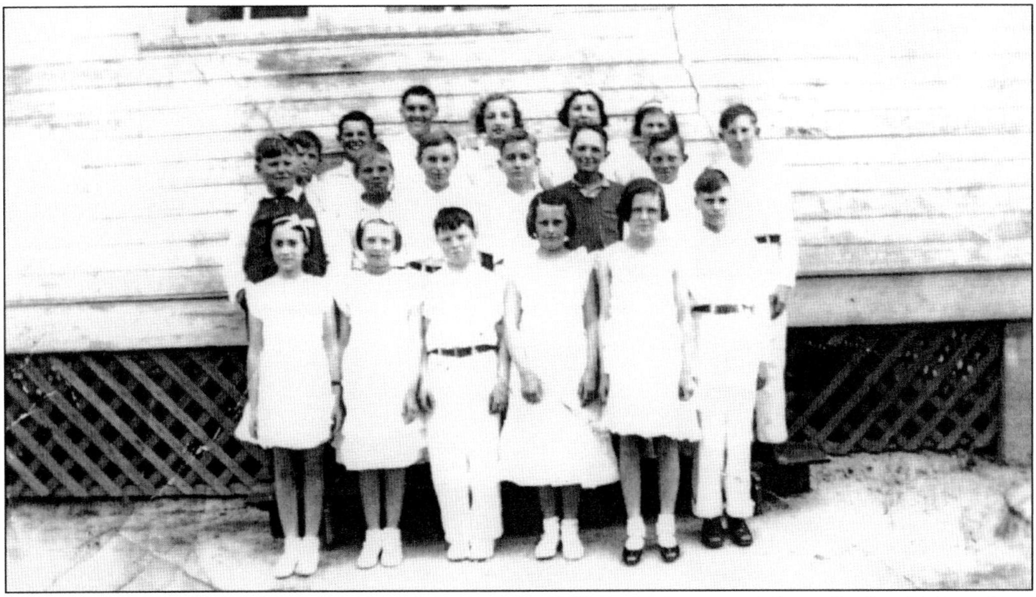

Included in this 1934 class of Big Springs are the following: Lura and Lora Bailey, Eulete Gay, Gilbert Moore, Lee Burson, Elliot Heard, Jean Bailey, and Almond Mitchell. (Courtesy of Connie [Jackson] Osborn.)

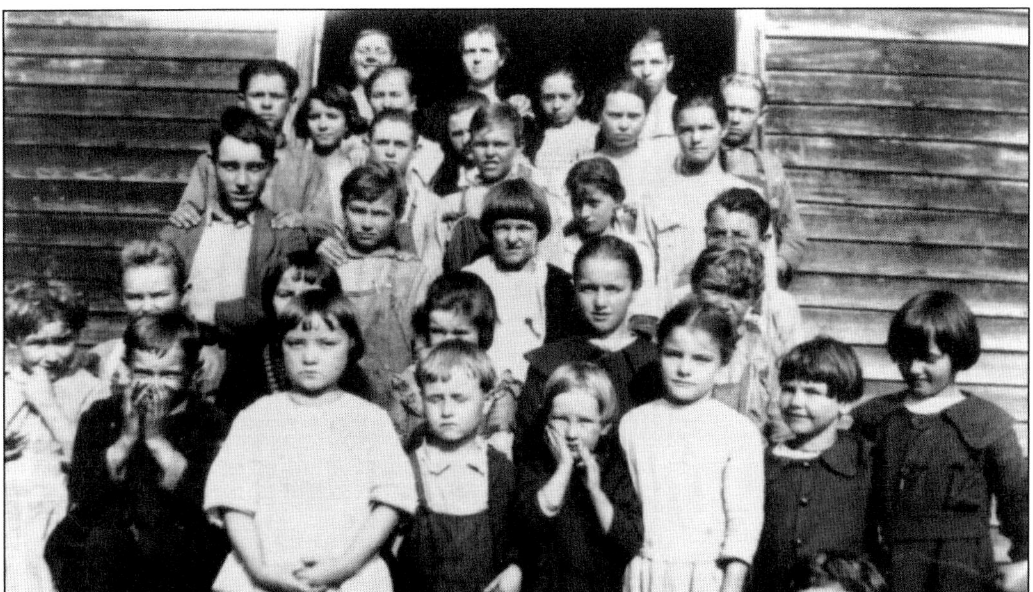

This group is the entire student body of Rock Springs Academy in an unknown year. Among those shown are Mitt Mickle, Ethel Waldrep, Roy Bailey, Minnie Lee Bailey, Flossie Mae Hendon, Docie Harmon, Buster McClendon, Winnie Mae Broach, Ann Mickle, Myrtle Waldrep, Corrie Harmon, Taft Tarver, Rupert McClendon, Floyd Mickle, Jim Tarver, Flossie Mae McClendon, Ida Jackson, Annie Maude Tarver, Roy Tarver, Grady Bailey, Velma Bailey, Lemerle Broach, ? McClendon, Wallace Waldrep, Annie Maude Henry, Troy Baily, Troy Tarver, ? McClendon, Mary Kate Jackson, ? Henry, ? Henry, and Buster Waldrep. (Courtesy of Camilla Jackson.)

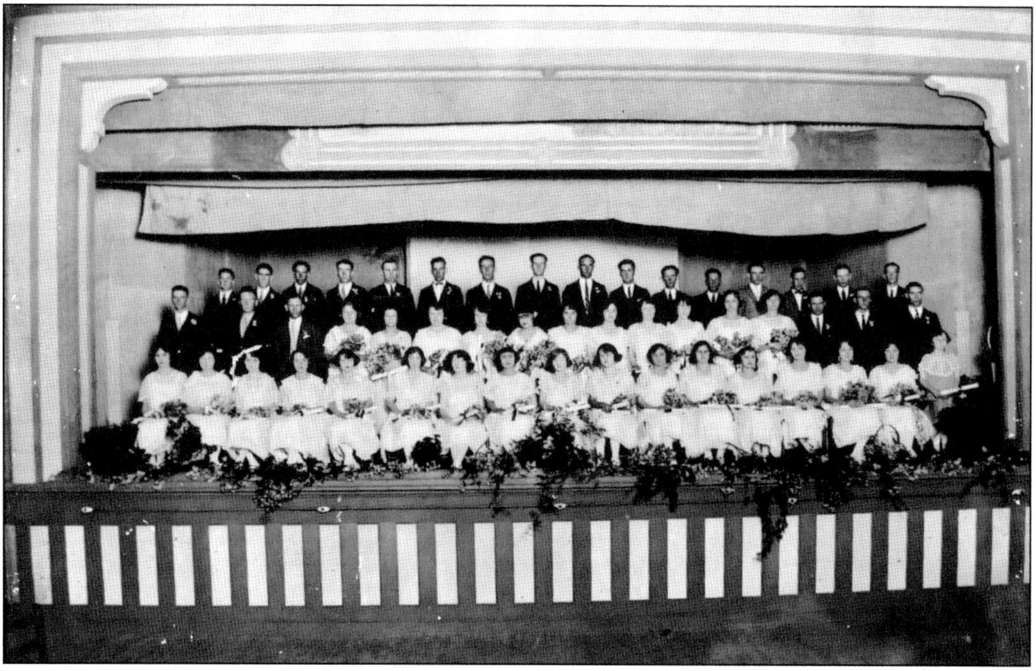

Handley High School's class of 1923 is shown at graduation exercises, which were held at Lowell Auditorium. Constructed in 1921, the Lowell Auditorium was the only building in Roanoke with a stage large enough to hold this number of people. (Courtesy of Harriett Manley.)

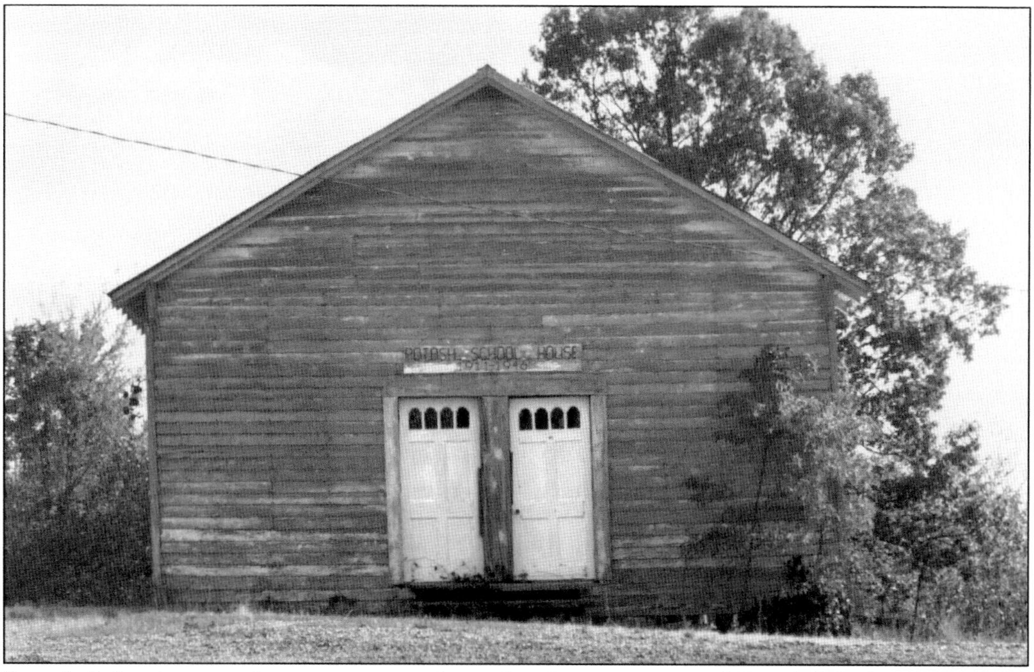

Potash School was a three-room, wooden school in east central Randolph County. It was in use during the years 1911–1946 for grades one through eight. It stood vacant until 1993, when a group of alumni set out to preserve it. Today it is used as a community building in the Potash community. (Courtesy of Camilla Jackson.)

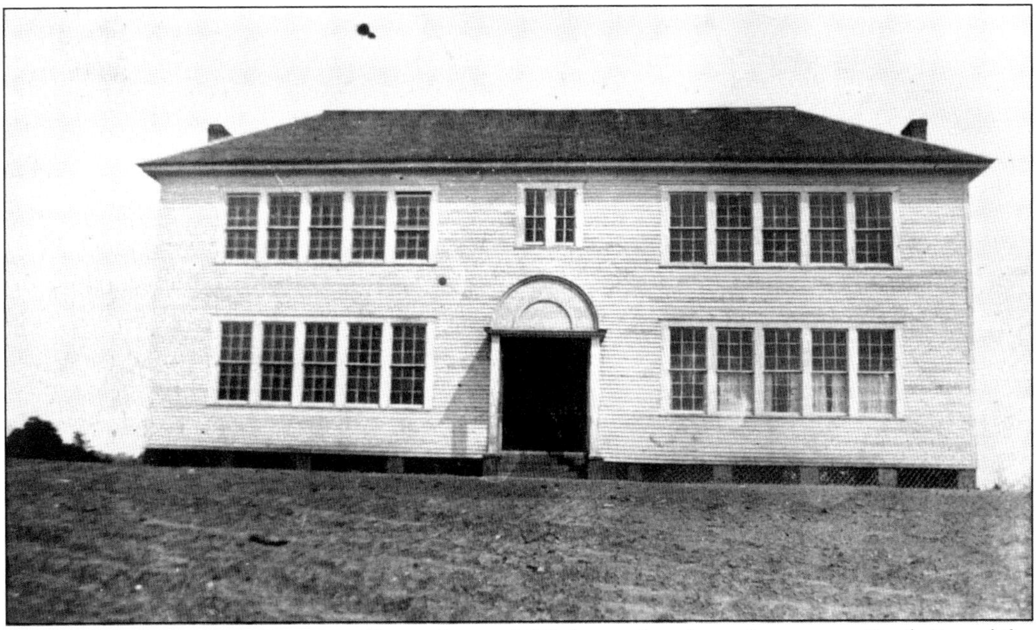

A country community between Roanoke and Wedowee has been known as Rock Stand for approximately 150 years. Hunters had stacked rocks to create an elevated stand to give them a wide view of the area, thus its name, Rock Stand. Pictured is the first Rock Stand School, built in 1919. It later burned in 1929. (Courtesy of Dwayne Pate.)

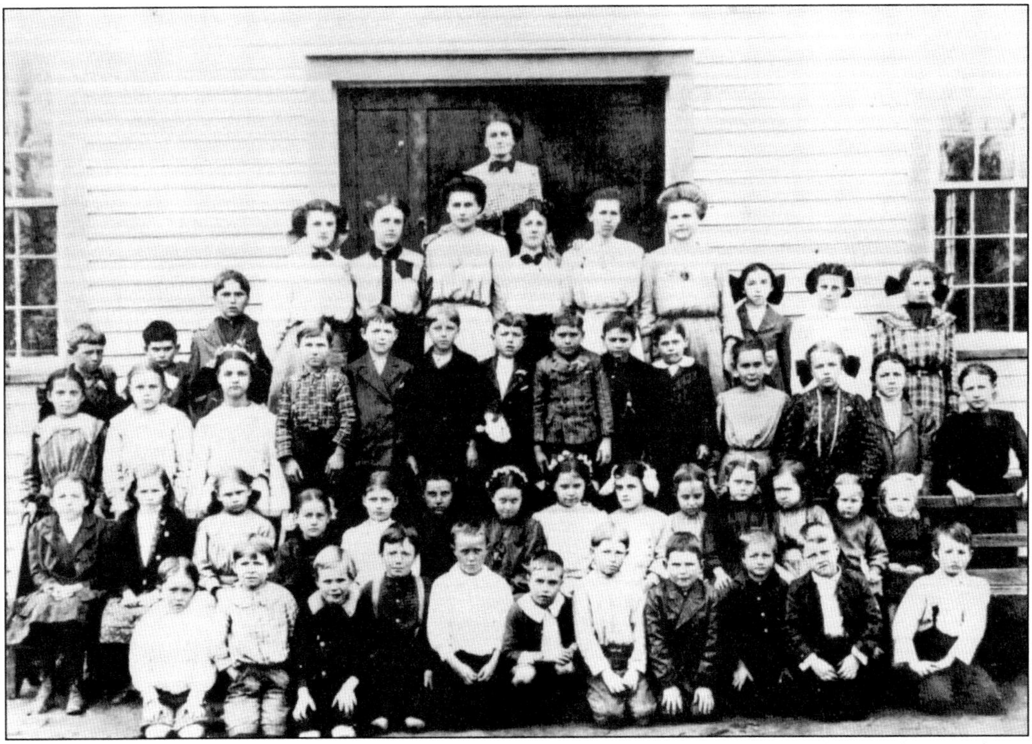

Some time before 1929, this picture of the student body and faculty was made standing in front of the double doors of the first Rock Stand School. (Courtesy of Dwayne Pate.)

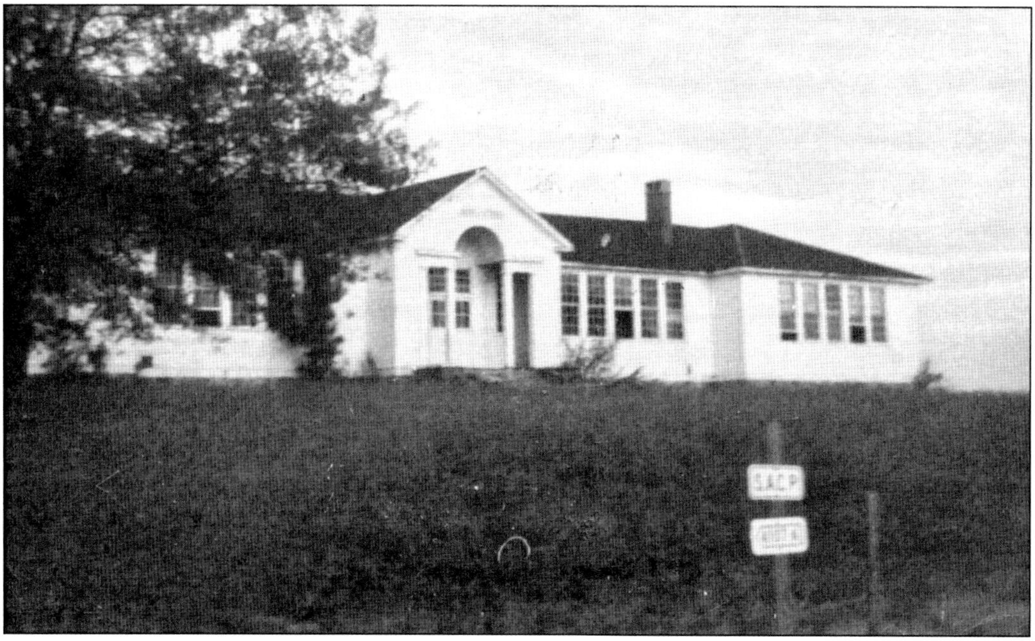

Pictured is the school built to replace the former Rock Stand School after it burned. (Courtesy of Dwayne Pate.)

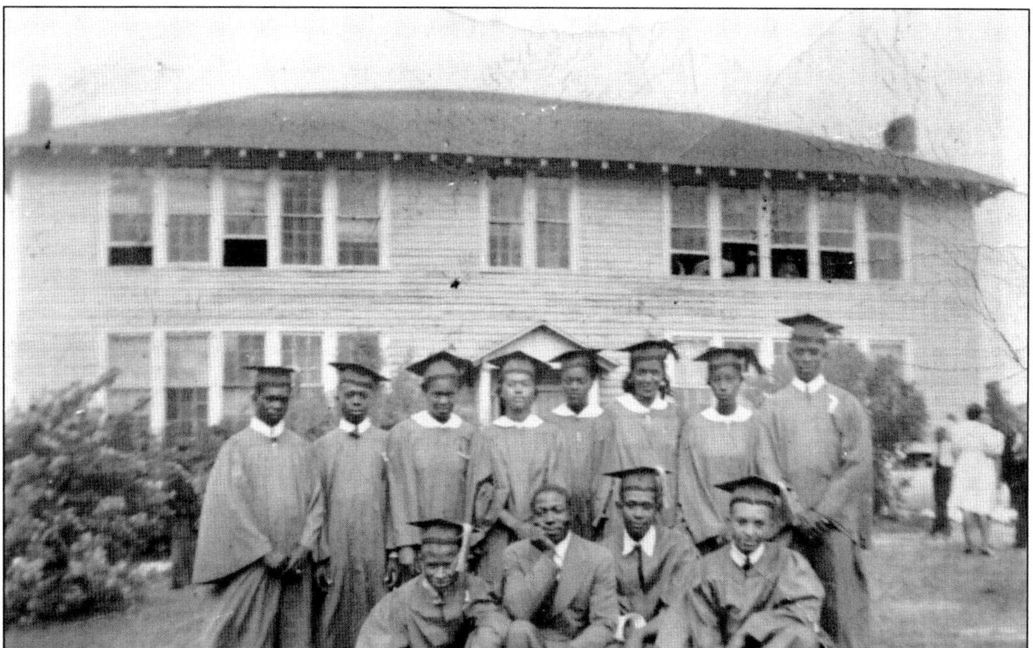

The 1942 graduating class at Randolph County Training School, Roanoke, is shown. From left to right, they are (kneeling) Junior Strickland from Bacon Level, Hezakiah Carstarphen (instructor), Samuel McLain from Malone, and James T. Marable from Malone; (standing) two unidentified, Texanna Marable Royston from Malone, Precious Glenn from Wedowee, Myrtis Wilkes from Wedowee, Thelma Stevens (Minnifield) from Anniston/Roanoke, Emma Kate Hand from Wehadkee, and unidentified. (Courtesy of Gene Thornton.)

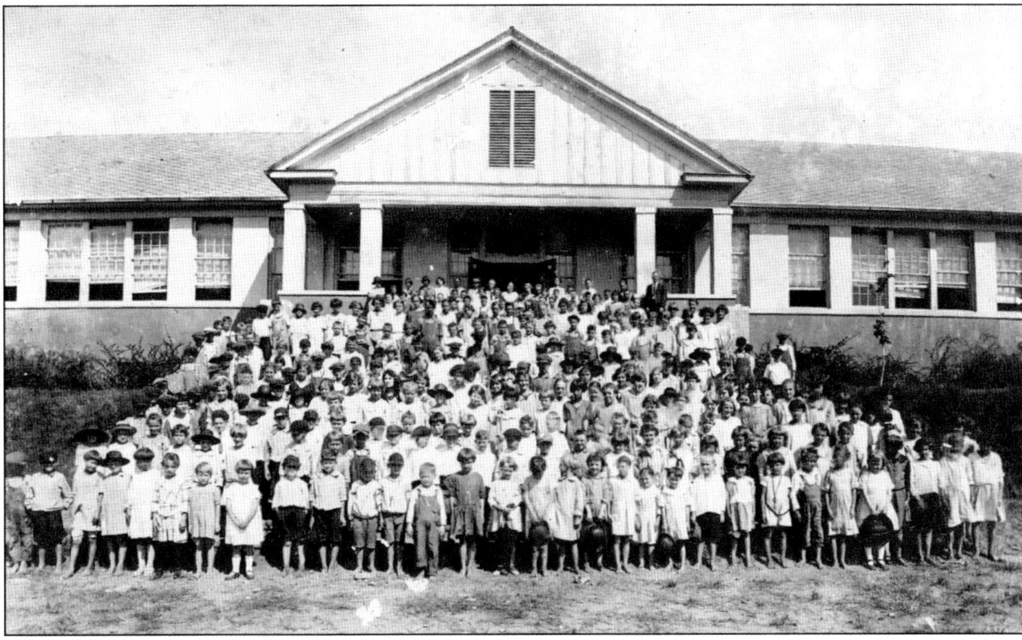

Shown are Knight-Enloe School students around 1930, grades one through six. It is worth noting that only a few have on shoes. (Courtesy of Squat Yarbrough.)

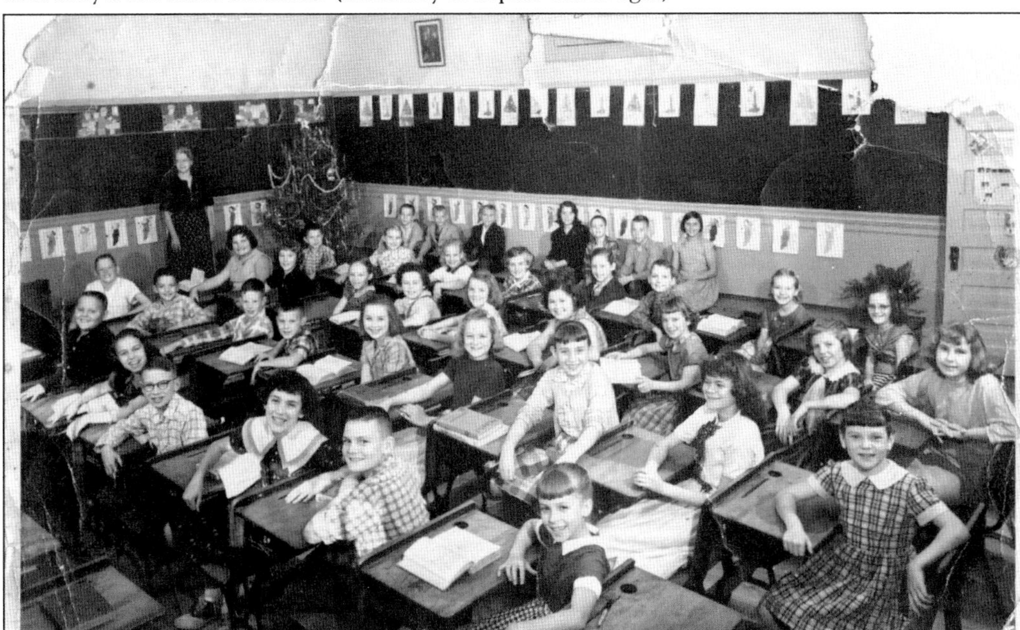

Myrtle Pinckard presents her 1957–1958 fifth-grade class of Knight-Enloe School. Some of the students are Wesley Spears, Jane Rowe, Mike McDaniel, Stanley Daniel, Gloria Rowe, Donny Brown, Linda Wilson, Dianne Arrington, Janice McDonald, Carroll Sandra Gann, Beth McClurg, Janice Robinson, Janice Turner, Joyce Cottle, Carylon Sheppard, Dianne Perry, J. D. Hester, Jerry Fetner, Ronnie Gray, Gerry Burke, Camilla Smith, Betty Ann Smallwood, Gail Gilliland, Opal Farr, Joyce Robinson, Dannie Daniel, Shirley Brown, Larry Puckett, Betty Jane Nix, Kenneth Cole, Juanita Whaley, Larry Lamon, and Waymon Taft. (Courtesy of Camilla Jackson.)

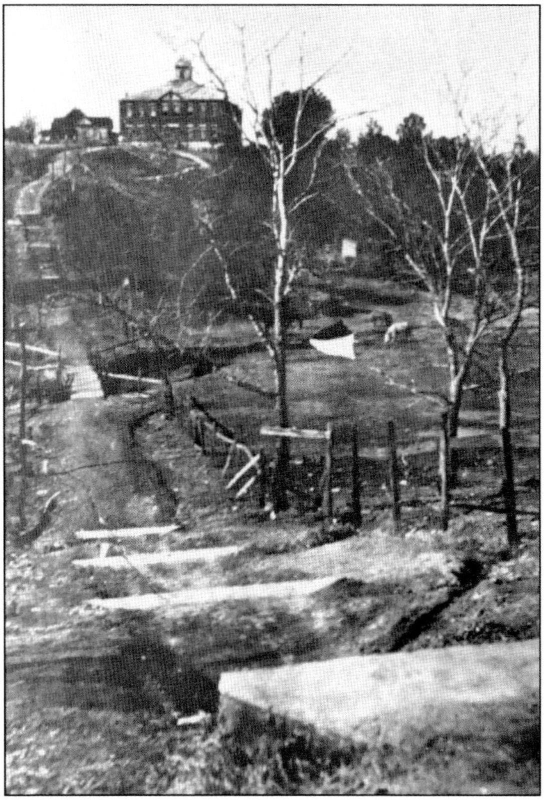

In 1907, the Alabama Legislature passed a bill requiring each county seat to have a high school. Randolph County High School was built in 1910 but burned in November 1910. Probate Judge A. J. Weathers donated 10 acres of land on a hill north of town, and the building pictured was constructed in time for the fall of 1912. The concrete steps and the bridge across the creek were constructed for the benefit of the students who walked to school, as they all did in that day. (Courtesy of Eva Barfield.)

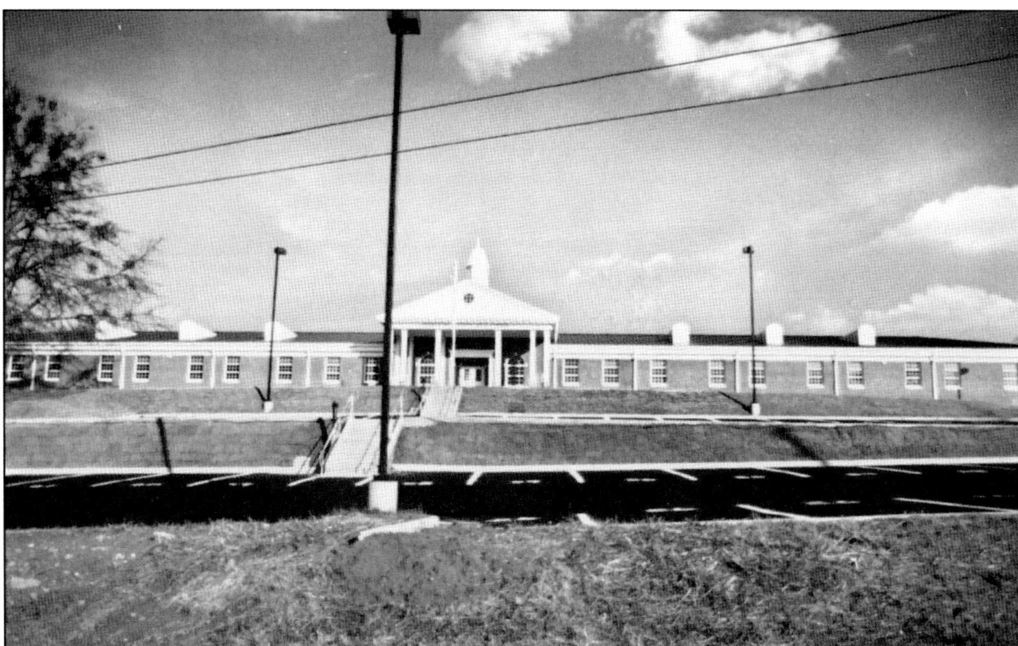

Pictured is the present Randolph County High School. Construction was completed in January 1997 after the unfortunate arson of its predecessor. (Courtesy of the *Randolph Leader*.)

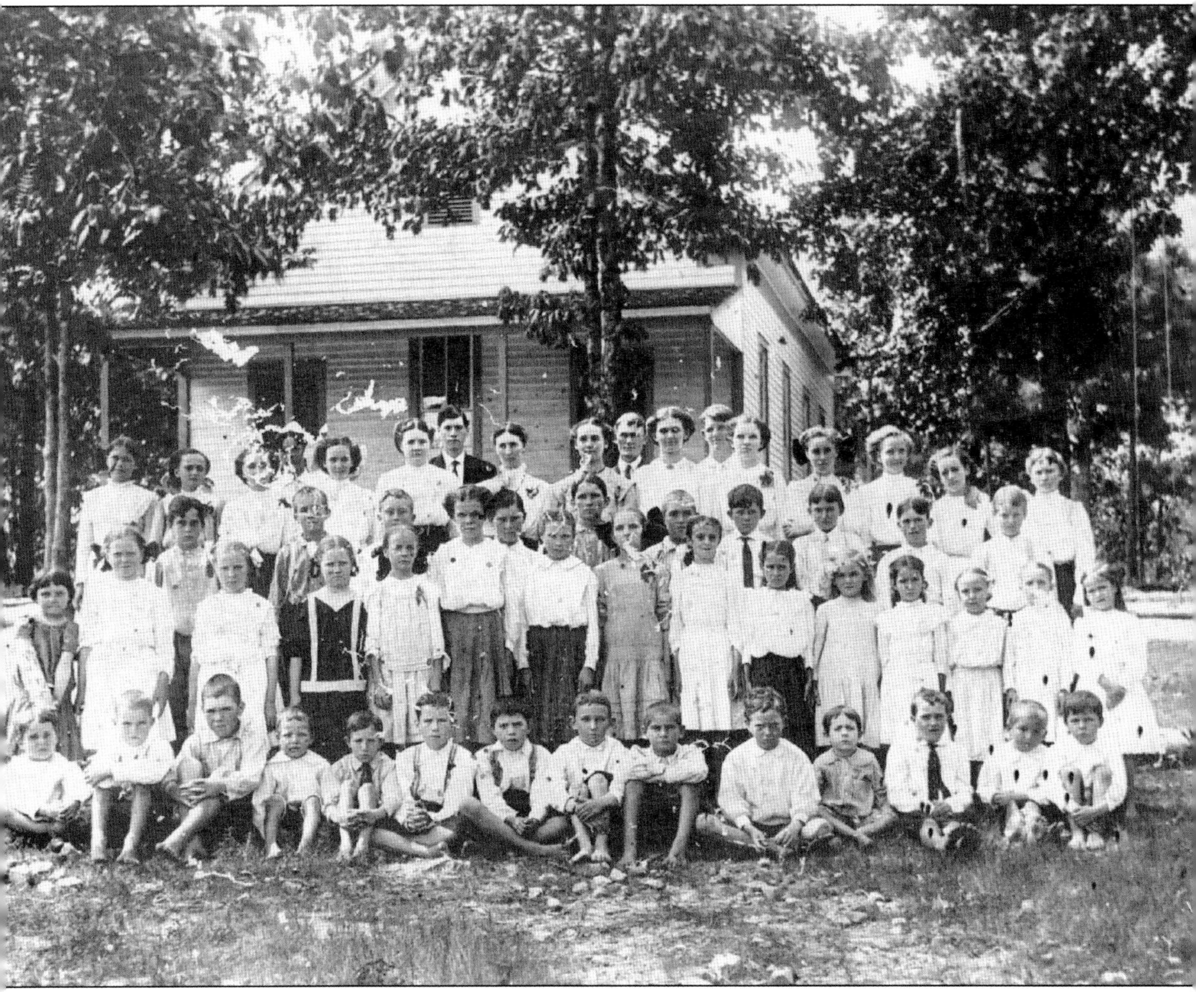

The student body of Lime School gathered in front of their school in 1911 for this picture. Some of the students pictured here are Odell Adamson, Lewis Smith, Gladys Hester, Carrie Hester, Bettie Lou Stitt, Rosa Marshall, Loette Caswell, Daisey Allison, Claudia Prather, Mina Pitts, Lizzie Prather, Annie-Pearl Rushton, Ethell Adamson, Lunar May Sheppard, Radney Adamson, Bernard Adamson, Willis Hester, Otis Caswell, Leonard Vineyard, Herbert Pitts, Gordon Hester, Lane Adamson, Roy Smith, Durell Stitt, Leaonard Adamson, George Sheppard, Pete Sheppard, Leon Adamson, Autrey Adamson, Ben Prather, Little Jeorge Prather, Ben East, Eric Pitts, Cecil Bonner, John Allison, Len (Cap) Smith, Olin Pitts, Willie Caswell, Lurline Vineyard, Edna Smith, Addie Adamson, Earnest Smith, May Hester, Roddie Sheppard, Marion Sheppard, Ora Sheppard, Era East, Bob Muldrew, Lucile East, Melvin Caswell, Mattie Caswell, Carrie Pitts, Ethel Bonner, Bertha Allison, and Murfie Adamson. (Courtesy of Harold Breed and Jeff Towler.)

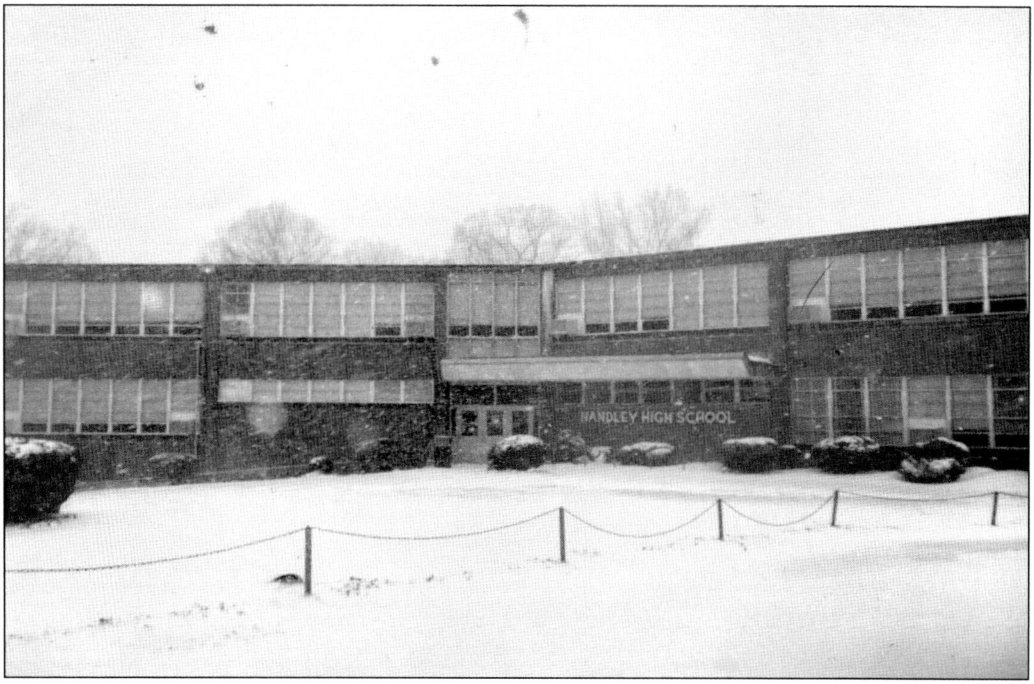

Pictured here is the Handley High School building after 1963. This picture was taken in what was known as the blizzard of 1993. (Courtesy of De Lambert.)

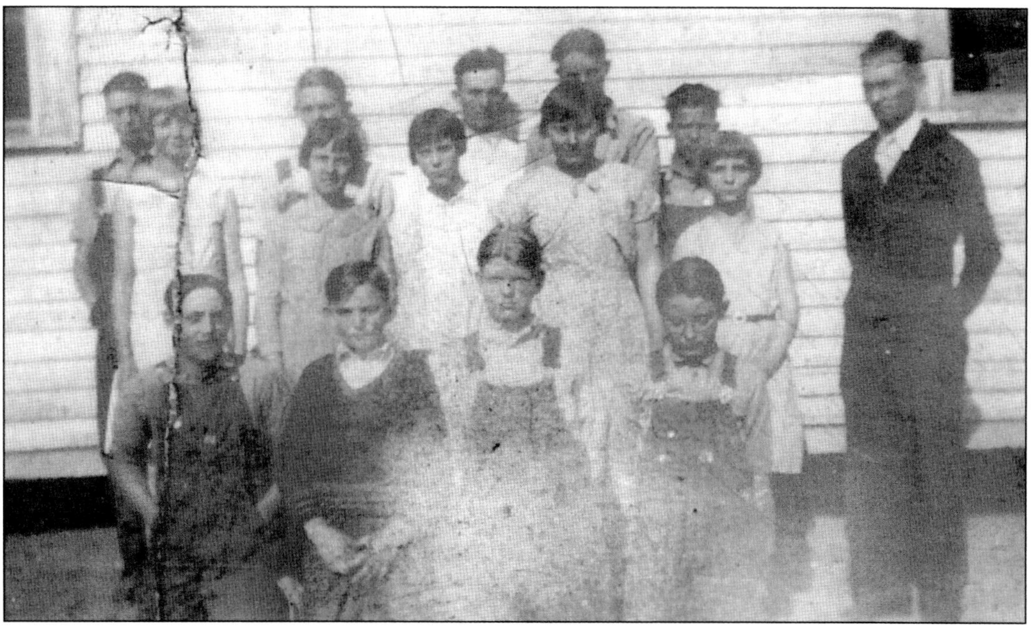

Pictured here are the seventh- and eighth-grade students at Swagg School with Principal C. C. Haynes in 1932. From left to right are (first row) E. B. White, Curtis Williamson, Alvie Rice, and Hershel Bolt; (second row) Mary Ann Bailey, Bernice Williamson, Vera Lipham, Jessie Bean, and Wilma Williamson; (third row) Braska White, Dave Kitchens, Jim Wortham, Snug Holmes, and John Bolt. (Courtesy of Deborah Gabriel.)

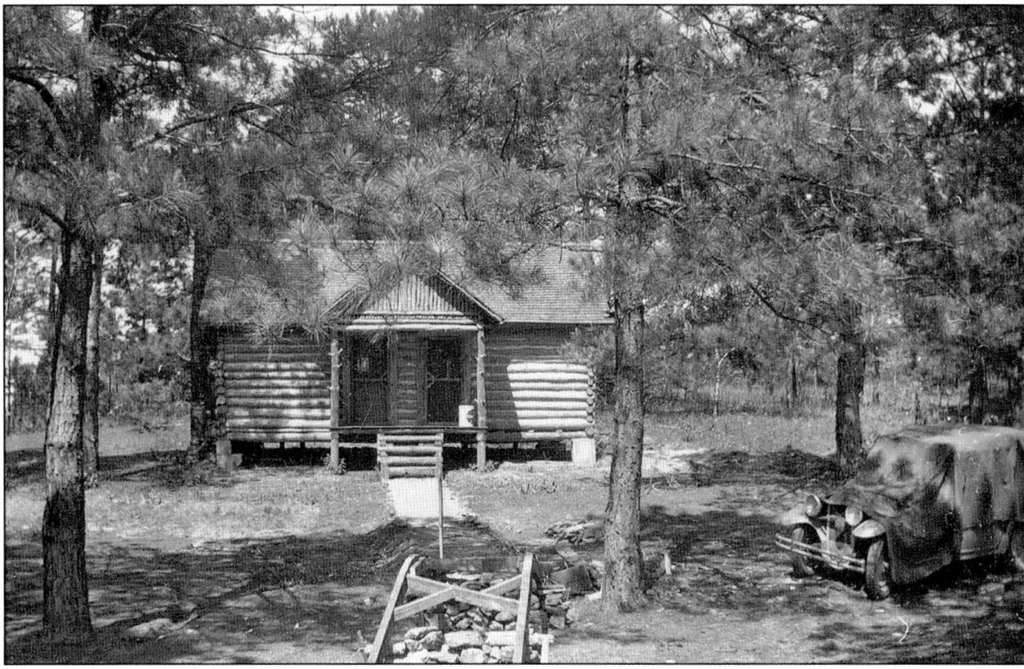

The little log structure was the first building on Bethlehem College campus, now known as Southern Union State Community College. It was moved away for several years, but based upon its historical significance, it was returned as a reminder of yesteryear. (Courtesy of Southern Union State Community College.)

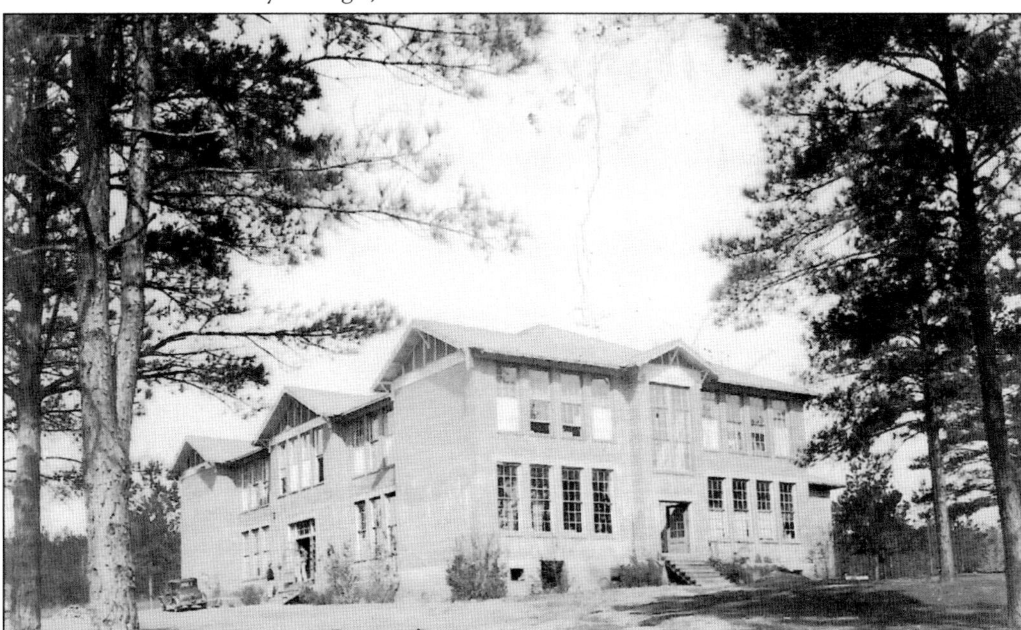

Southern Union College's Elder Hall was an academic building constructed about 1926 that served the students for 40 years. After Southern Union became a state college, a new building was constructed under the presidency of Dr. Walter Graham, and that building was replaced in 2006. (Courtesy of Southern Union State Community College.)

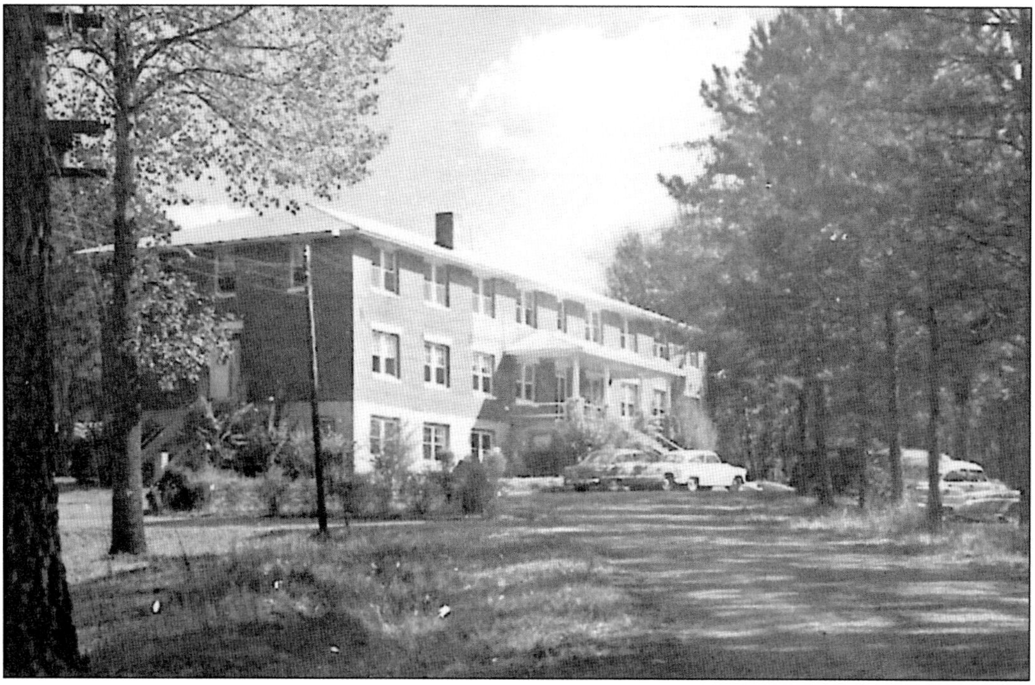

Kimball Hall was Southern Union College's oldest academic building. The basement housed the kitchen and dining room as well as chemistry and physics laboratories. The second floor served as living quarters for the president, classrooms, and library. The third floor was the dormitory—the east section for women and the west section for men. The original structure burned in 1935, and this is the way it looked after rebuilding. (Courtesy of Southern Union State Community College.)

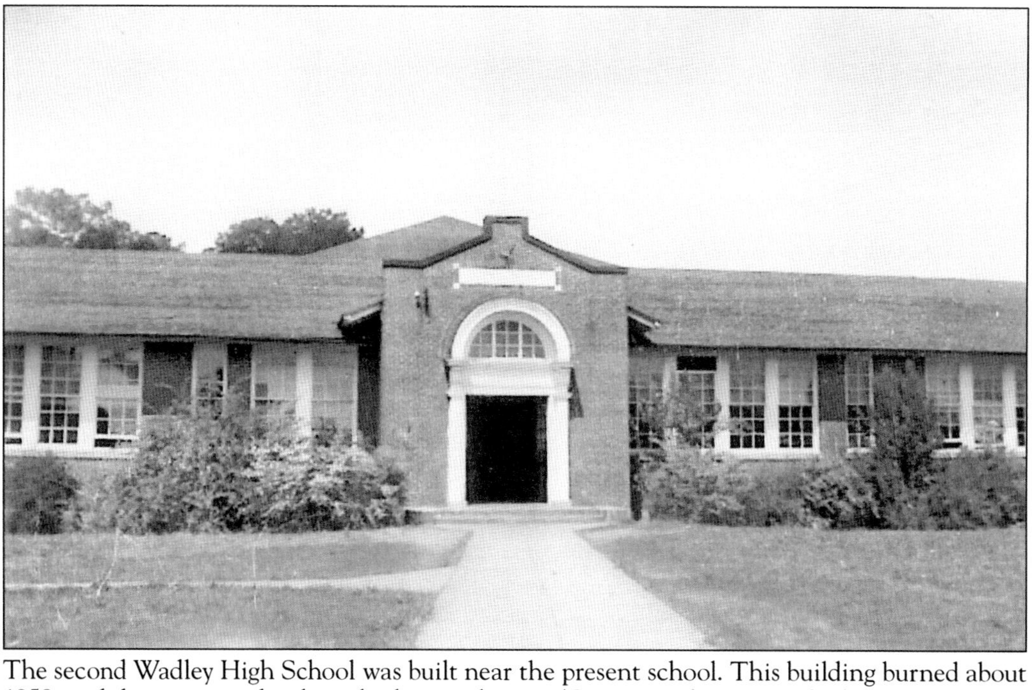

The second Wadley High School was built near the present school. This building burned about 1958, and the present school was built to replace it. (Courtesy of Marian Edge.)

Three

CHURCHES

From the earliest days of settlement, Randolph County migrants brought with them a basic need for the Christian religion to be a major part of their lives. Wherever they settled, within a short time they congregated for religious services, initially in what were called brush arbors. Perhaps because winter weather conditions made brush arbors uncomfortable or perhaps because their reading of the Bible gave them an urgency to have a "house of worship," crude, rustic log buildings were built, usually with large fireplaces and chimneys for heat on cold days. The early rural churches were served by itinerant preachers and held services monthly rather than weekly.

In the more heavily populated towns, denominational churches were built. Baptists built a log church in Roanoke in 1835, and Benager Goss was the first pastor. The Methodists were given a lot with a small frame house that was converted into a church by Wiley White, and it was located where Cedarwood Cemetery now is. The Baptists and Methodists have always had the largest churches and largest number of members. The present First Baptist Church was built in 1901 and the First Methodist Church in 1906.

In 1921, there were 62 churches representing 10 denominations in Randolph County. They were Baptist, Primitive Baptist, Missionary Baptist, Methodist Episcopal, Methodist Episcopal South, Methodist C. M. (Congregational Methodist), Christian Cambellite, Christian Elderite, Holy Roller, and Presbyterian. By 1932, the number of churches had increased to 78.

Through the years, names of churches and names of denominations have changed. Current names are United Methodist, Congregational Christian, Church of Christ, and Church of God. Other churches have come in such as A.M.E., Episcopal, Nazarene, Roman Catholic, and Jehovah's Witness, and many churches are non-denominational. In the present day, there are approximately 150 churches in Randolph County.

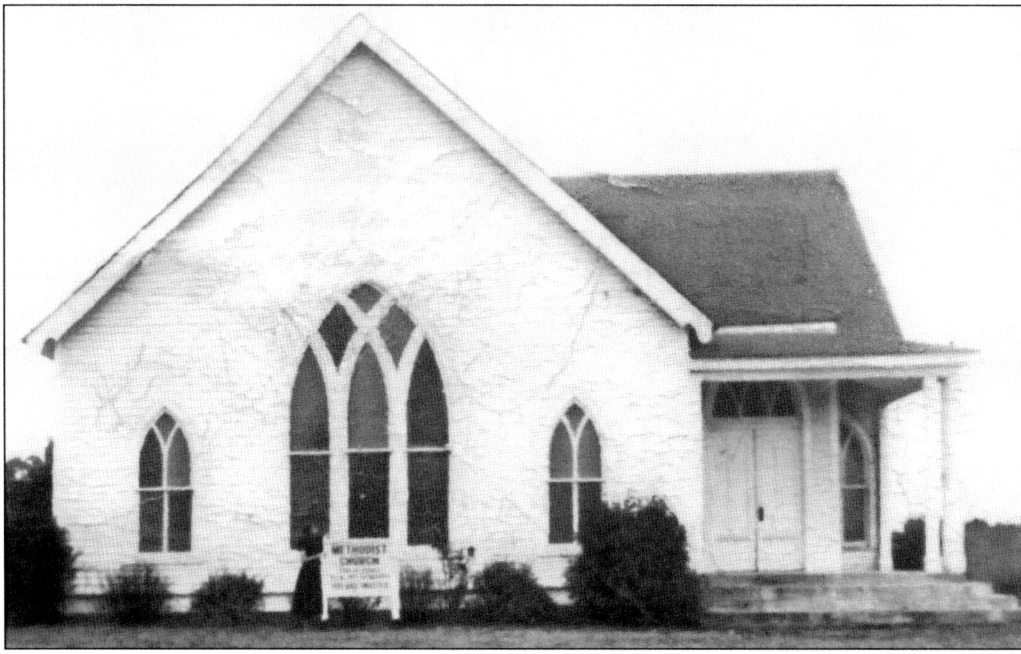

In 1871, Wyatt Harper donated the lumber to build the Methodist church in Rock Mills. In July 1884, a growing congregation required a new building. In 1909, a third church was completed, wood-frame and painted white like the other two. On March 14, 1954, the third church burned. Eight months later, the current building was ready for services on November 21, 1954. (Courtesy of Harold Breed and Jeff Towler.)

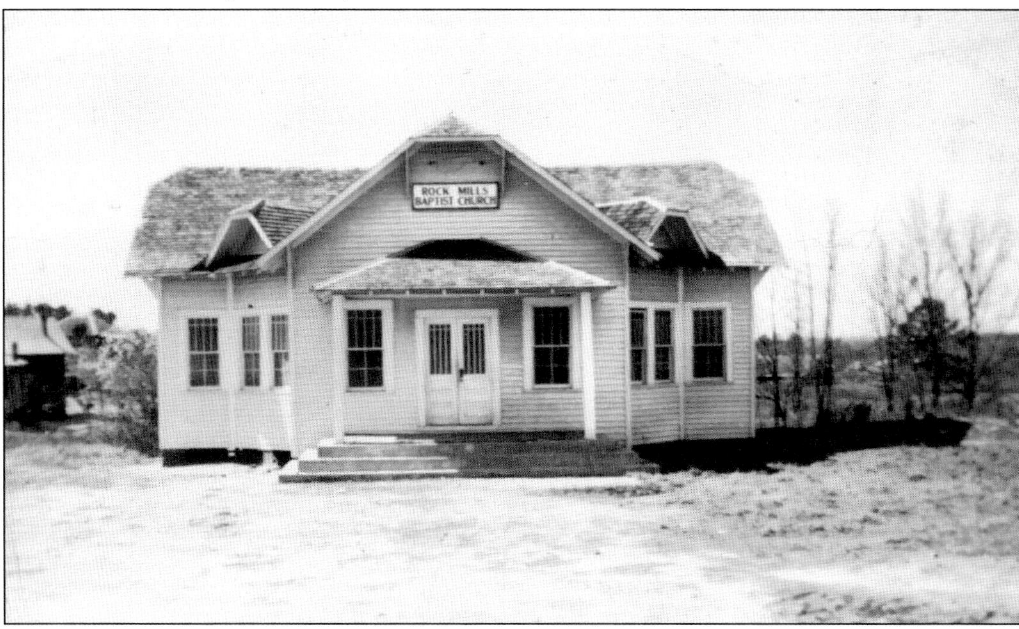

Rock Mills First Baptist Church erected its first house for worship in 1883. The first was torn down in 1934, and a smaller one erected and used until 1949, at which time it was torn down and replaced by the current building. There have been many additions and improvements over the years. (Courtesy of Harold Breed and Jeff Towler.)

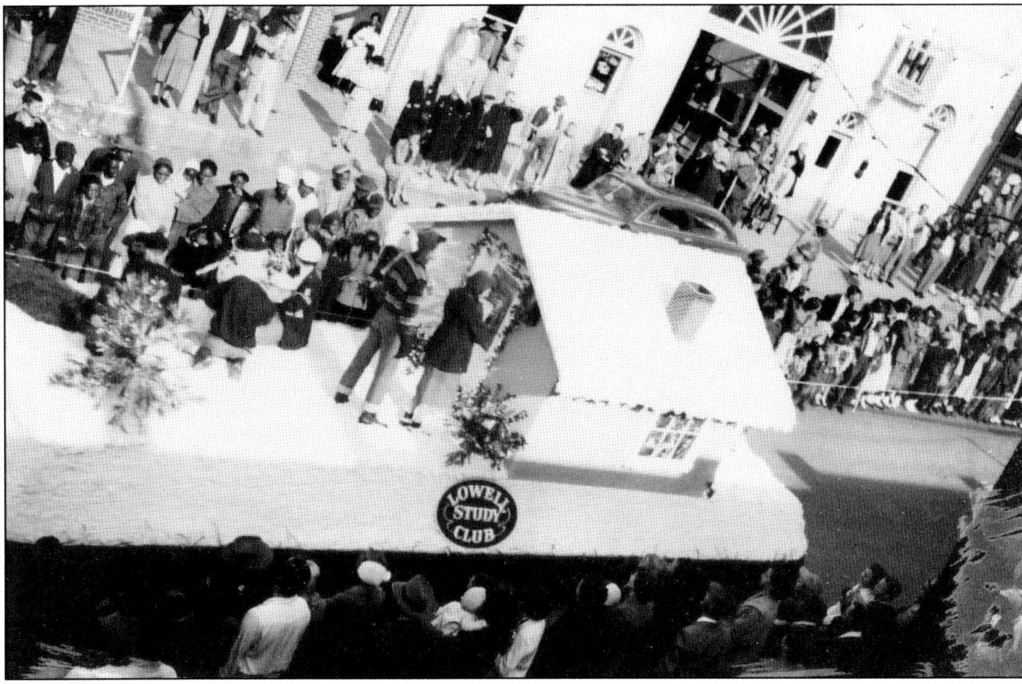

It was common for various businesses and groups to create their own floats. It was great advertisement for the organization and much fun for its members to build and then display in Christmas and other parades in the county. (Courtesy of Iva Cunningham.)

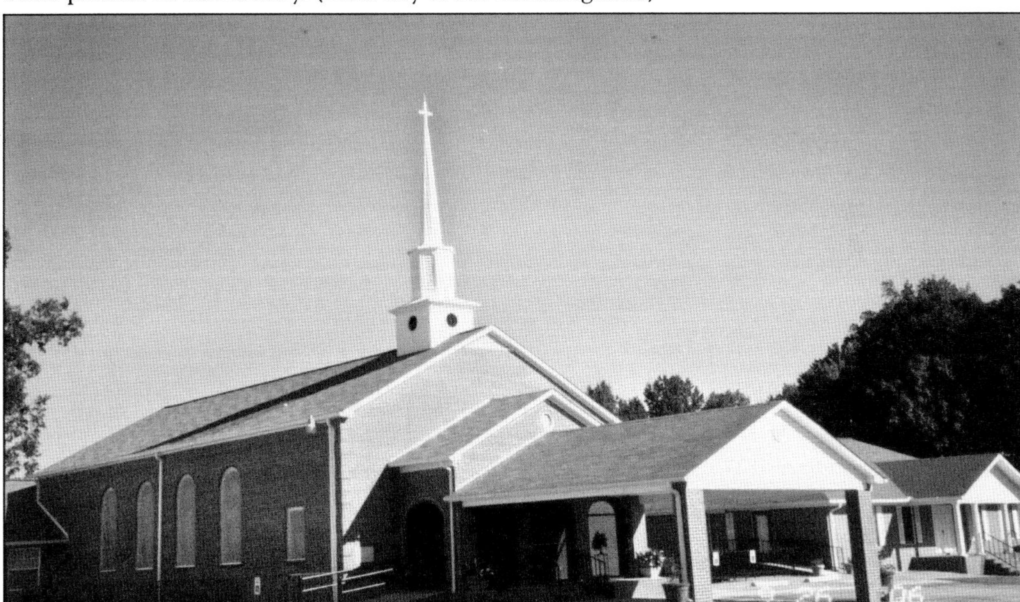

In the early days, a trading post was near Big Springs, and the springs became a place for weary travelers to rest. Under a brush arbor, pioneer preachers brought the word to travelers and nearby settlers. By 1850, a log building had replaced the arbor. Today Big Springs Church holds a prominent place in the Big Spring community. (Courtesy of Paula [Burson] Lambert.)

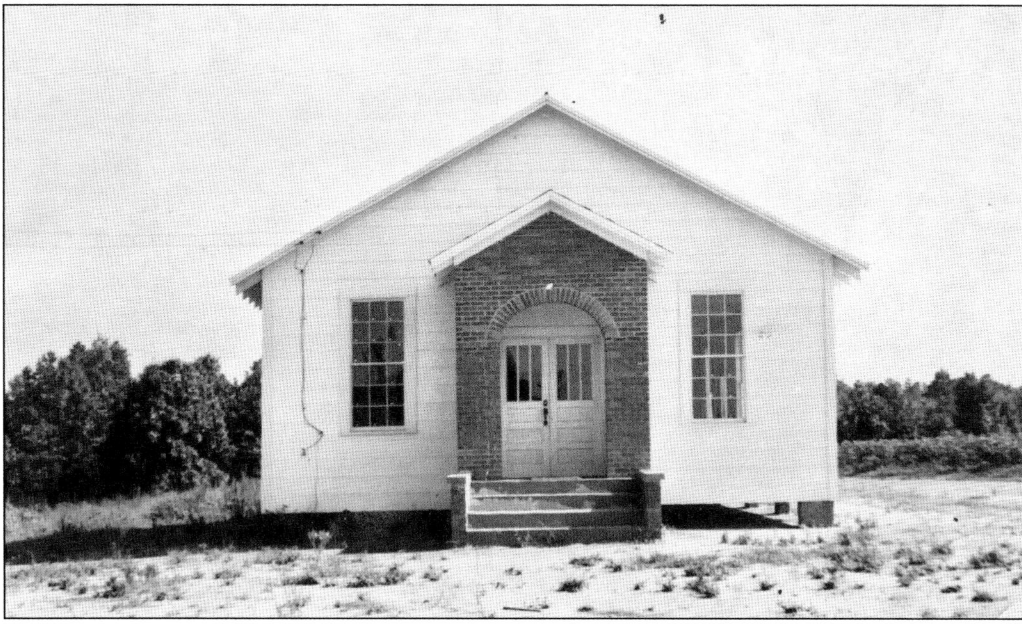

Funerals were held in the school building, and then the deceased was taken across the road and buried in the Old Napoleon Cemetery. A church was built in 1915 but was outside the community. In 1948, another church was built next to the Old Napoleon Cemetery. Both were called Napoleon Church of Christ. The second Sunday in May is Decoration or Homecoming Day, when friends and relatives gather to end a weeklong revival in worship with dinner on the ground and singing. (Courtesy of Napoleon Church of Christ.)

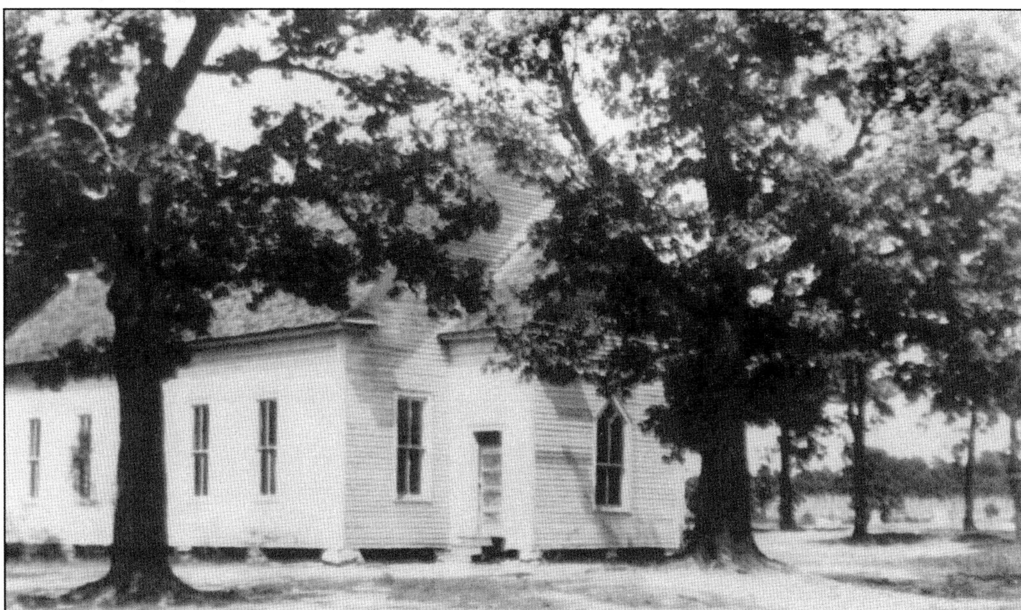

Springfield Church began as the Church of Christ, named and built by Calvin Ussery on his property in the early 1870s. It later was renamed High Shoals and joined the Baptist Association. In 1911, members voted to move the church. In 1912, the newly named Springfield Baptist Church was built on land donated by Mr. and Mrs. W. A. Pittman. (Courtesy of Buck Morris.)

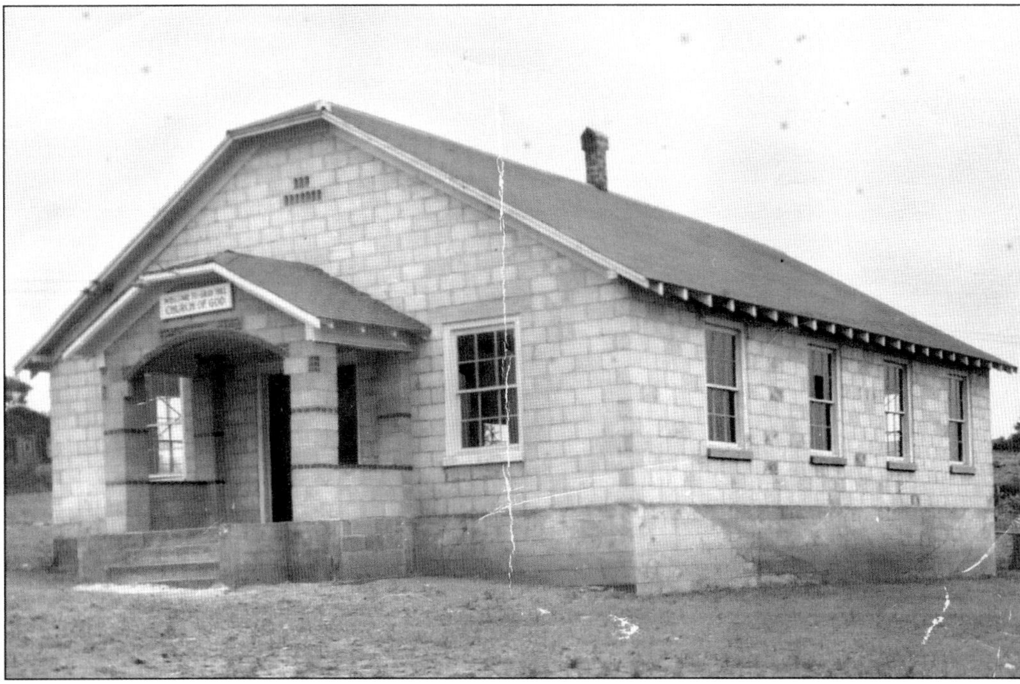

The Gray Hill Church of God was chartered in 1920. It moved from a brush arbor to a tabernacle to its own building in 1944 (shown here) and to its present building in 1981. Among the early leaders of the church were Tom Gilley, Charlie Parmer, Henry Phillips, and Hayden Gosdin. The Mill House Revival was one of the first Pentecostal revivals in this area. Homecoming is the second Sunday in June. (Courtesy of Melissa Moore.)

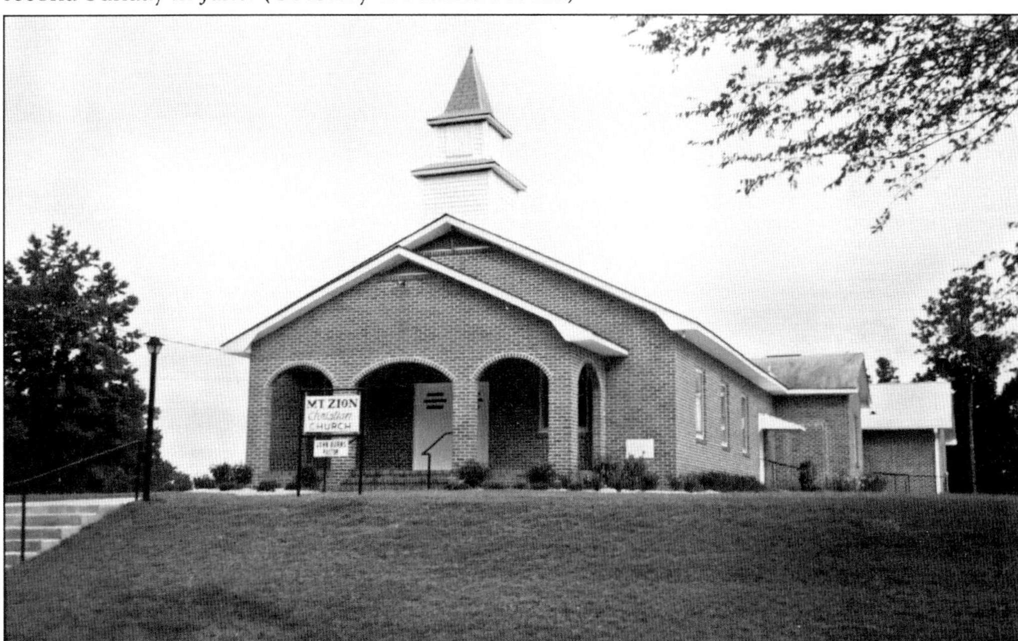

Mount Zion Christian Church on Louina Road was organized in 1890 by W. R. Knight. It was remodeled and brick veneered in 1956. (Courtesy of Helen Blankenship.)

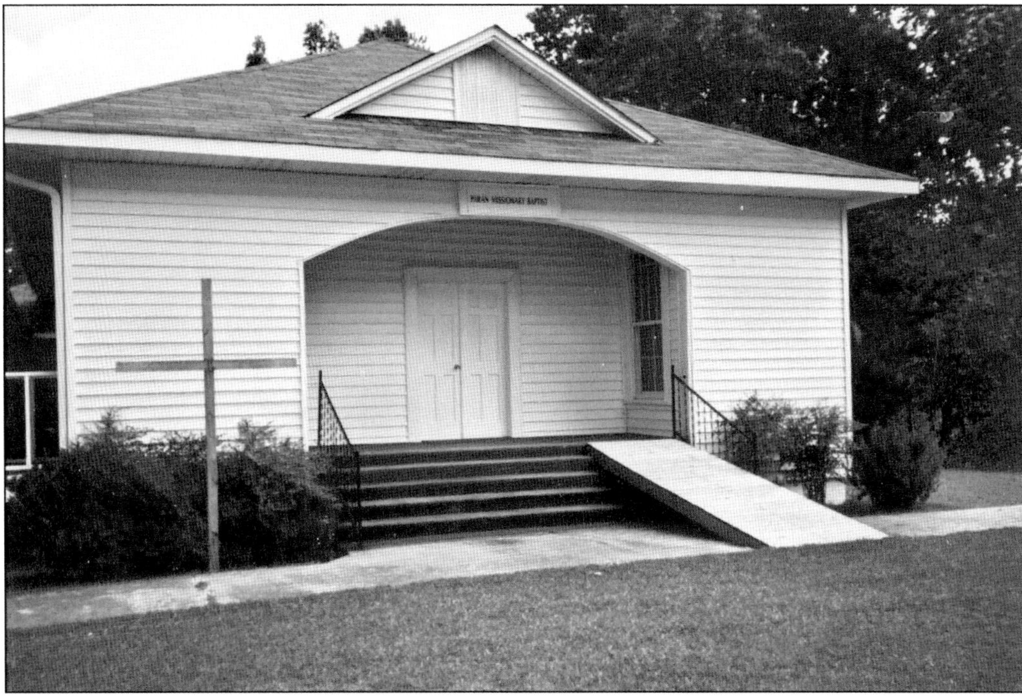

Pictured is Paran Missionary Baptist Church, established in 1846, the second oldest Baptist Church in Randolph County. The existing building was built in 1929 with additions made in 1977 and 1993. (Courtesy of Camilla Jackson.)

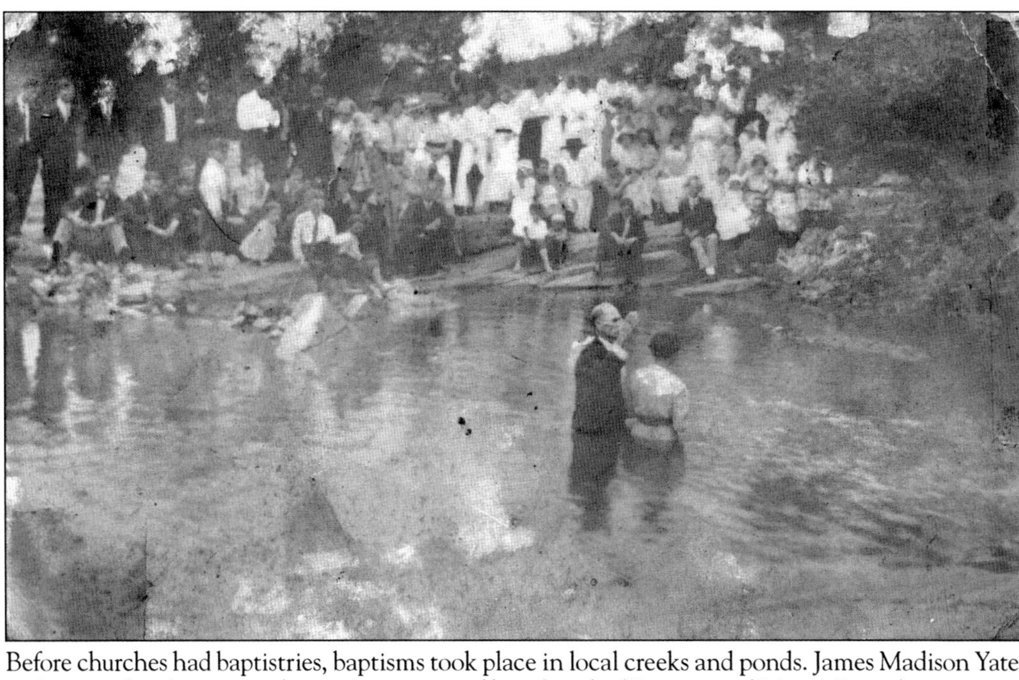

Before churches had baptistries, baptisms took place in local creeks and ponds. James Madison Yates is the preacher baptizing the new converts of his church. (Courtesy of Marty Davis.)

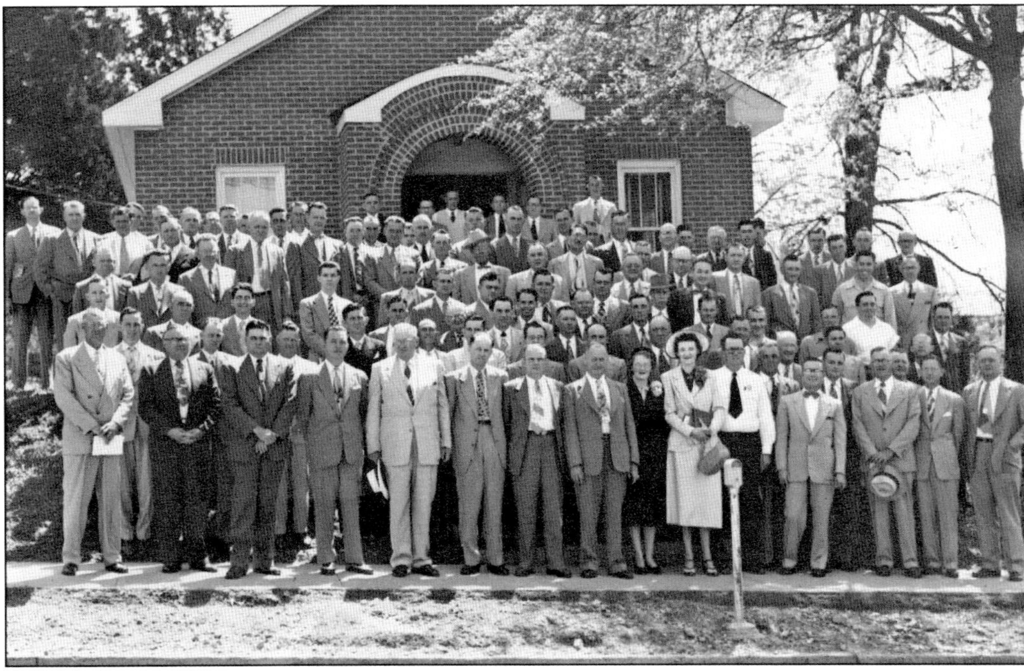

First Baptist Church, Roanoke, erected a white-frame chapel on the eastern lawn beside the church in 1934. In 1951, the chapel was moved to the site of the first church building and has served for small weddings, funerals, prayer meetings, and the men's Sunday school class. On Easter Sunday 1952, with 123 in attendance, the men's class gathered in front of the chapel. The last man on the right on the first row is Earl Cooper, teacher of the class for 40 years. (Courtesy of First Baptist Men's Sunday School Class.)

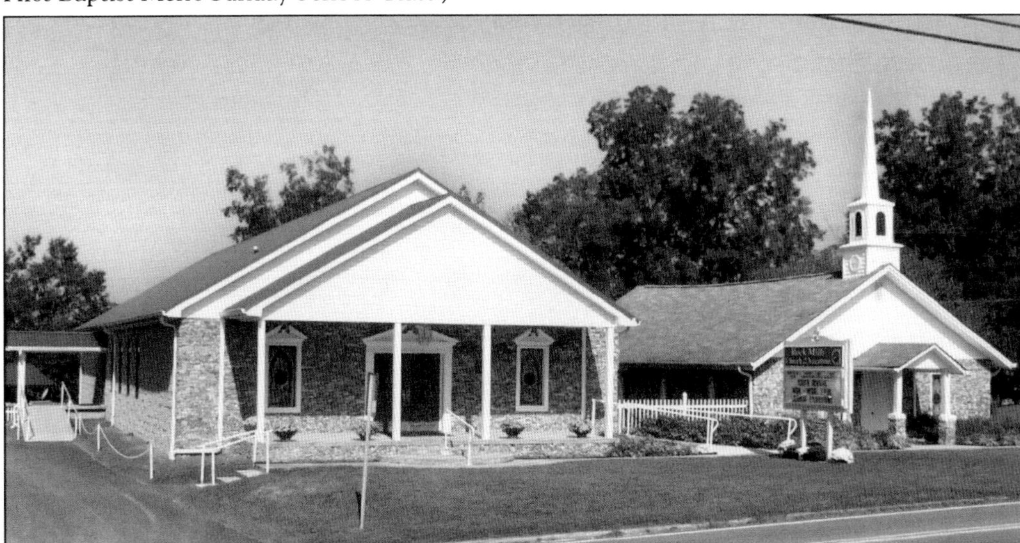

The small church on the right was the first Rock Mills Church of the Nazarene, which was organized on August 2 and 3, 1940, with 51 members. The beginning revival was run by Br. J. T. Dykes and Br. Leon Chambers. Growing in members, a larger church on the left was built in 1996. The front of the new building was made to look like the old. All the stones came from the Rock Mills area. Homecoming is the second Sunday in October. (Courtesy of Barbara Bowen.)

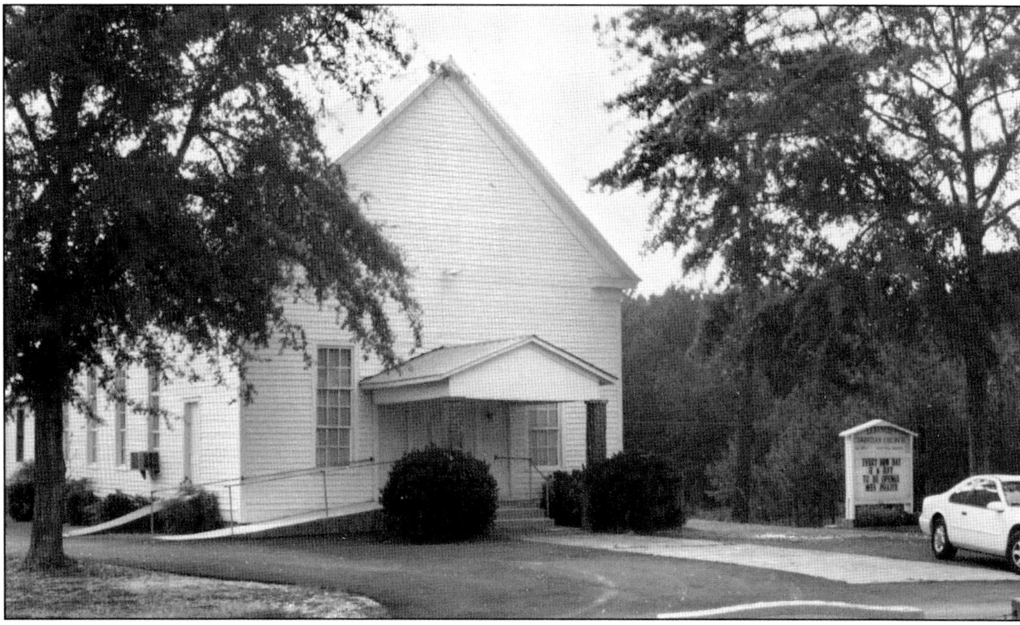

Lebanon Church began as a brush arbor. Moses Park was the traveling preacher. Built in 1864, the original building still stands and is covered with the original pine planks. Inside are still some of the original pews, complete with the divisors, developed to keep males and females separated. The original pulpit is still in use in one of the Sunday school rooms. There have been some enhancements to the building. Homecoming is always the second Sunday in August. (Courtesy of Camilla Jackson.)

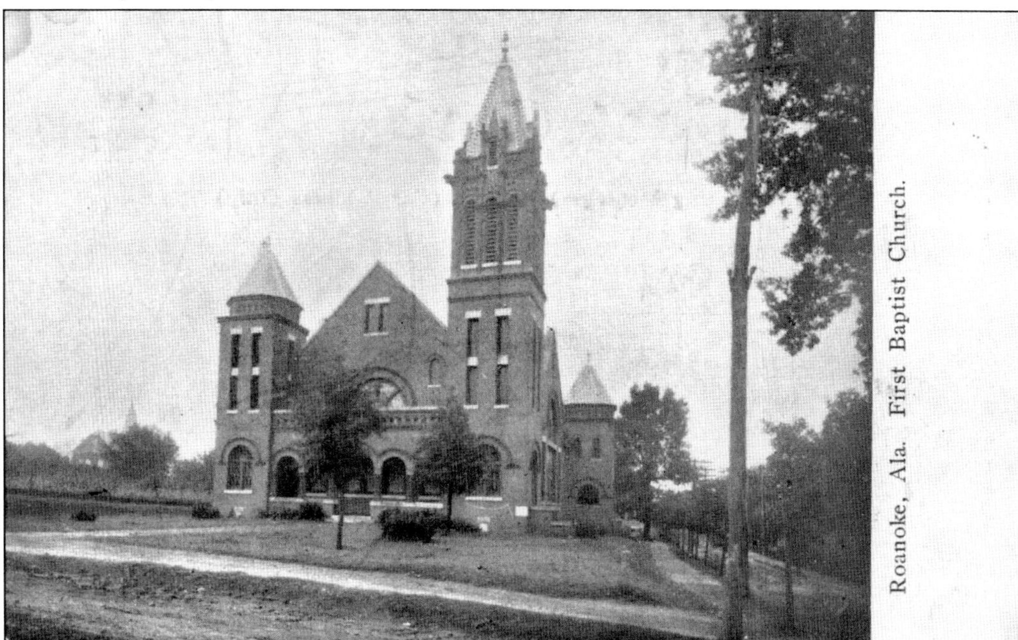

This photograph was taken in the early days of the First Baptist Church, Roanoke, which was built in 1901, when the streets and sidewalks were not paved but the grounds were immaculately landscaped. (Courtesy of Roseann Fuller.)

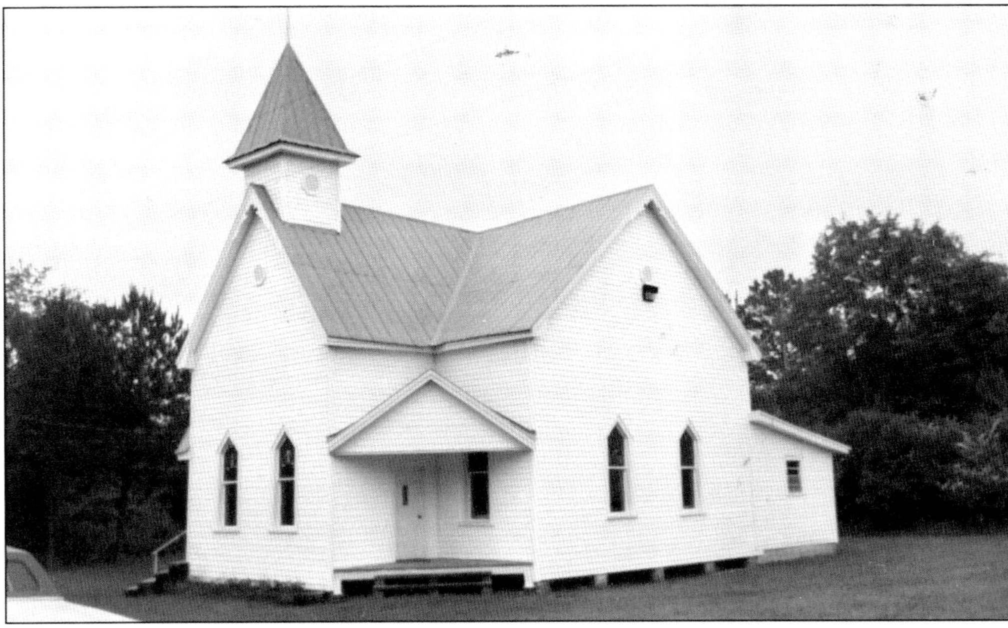

The Malone Baptist Church was built in 1910, with its primary pillar being Nixon Lucas. Ninety-four years later, it is still an active church, even though the only thing left in Malone is the Baptist church, the Methodist church, and a few residences. No businesses remain in the once-bustling community. (Courtesy of Laura [Lucas] Pittman.)

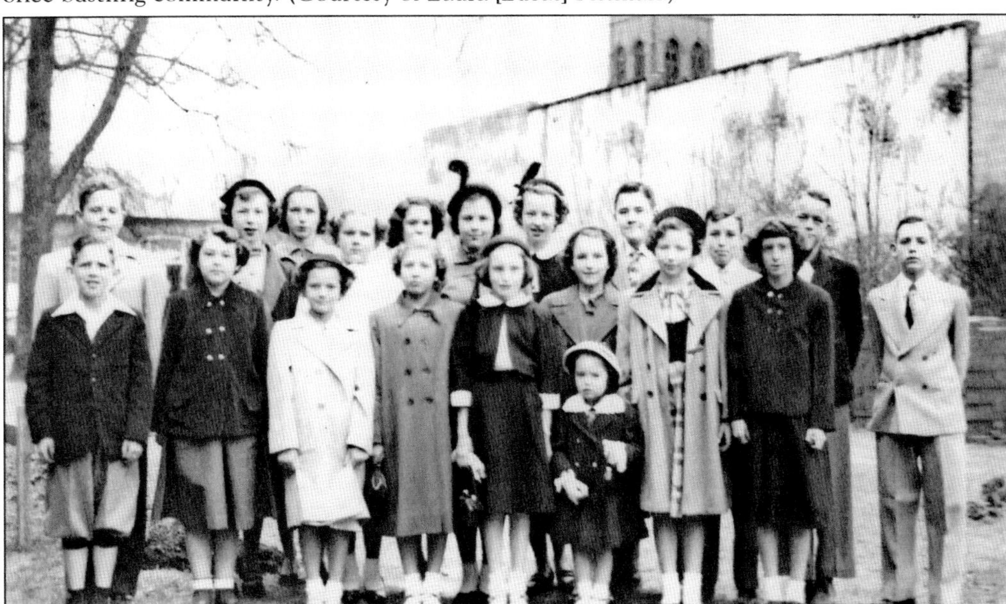

In 1950, the young people with perfect Sunday school attendance at the Roanoke First Baptist Church from left to right are (first row) Jimmy Dunn, Linda Phillips, Janie Jordon, Harriett Landers, Mary Ann Phillips, Jane Phillips, Lucy Jane Dunn, Kay Gilliland, and Jean Pool; (second row) Don Long, Lillian Howell, Sylvia Gilliland, Barbara Vinson, John Ellen Pool, Harriett Jenkins, Barbara Wood, Gordon "Doc" Ussery, Frank Phillips, Billy Jordan, and Wyner Phillips. (Courtesy of Jane [Phillips] Cato.)

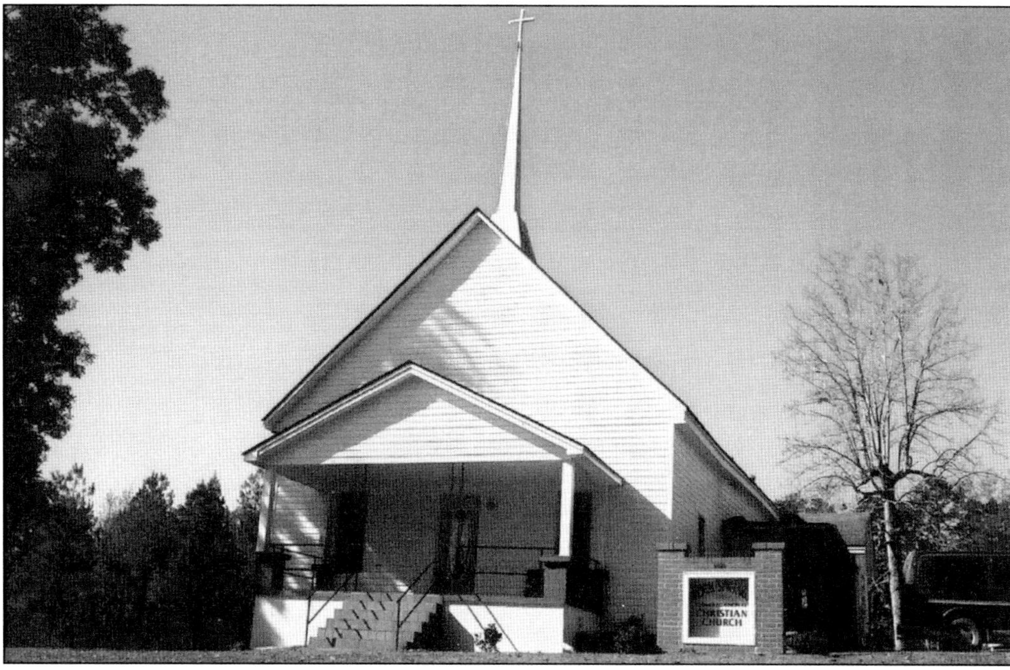

Rock Springs Christian Church is a beautiful country church located on the banks of Cornhouse Creek. It was organized at Rock Springs Academy on September 21, 1884. Land was donated for the church by W. Z. and Ester Meadows and J. W. and Vastie Messer. There were 17 original members, and Rev. James D. Elder was the first pastor. Memorial services are observed the second Sunday in May. (Courtesy of Camilla Jackson.)

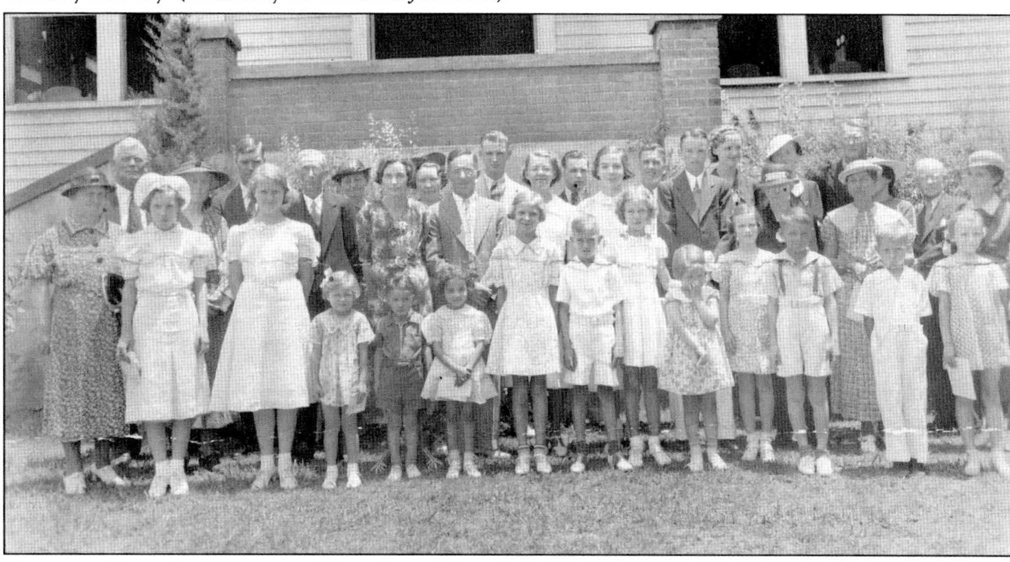

Shown is Roanoke Christian Church on West Point Street, Roanoke, on a Sunday in 1937. Some of the ones pictured are Mary Burdette, Oliver Moore, Atha Collier, ? Perry, Nan Perry, James ?, Kirby Bowen, Allene Bowen, Emily Moore, Willie Faye Allen, Juanita Allen, Dessa Burdette, Ed Shelnutt, Mrs. Perry, Mr. Perry, Frances Rorke, Owen Shelnutt, Mrs. James Brown, Rev. Belt White, James Bowen, Martha Pittman, John Frank Burdette, Pauline Moore, and Bessie Shelnutt. (Courtesy of Emily Knight.)

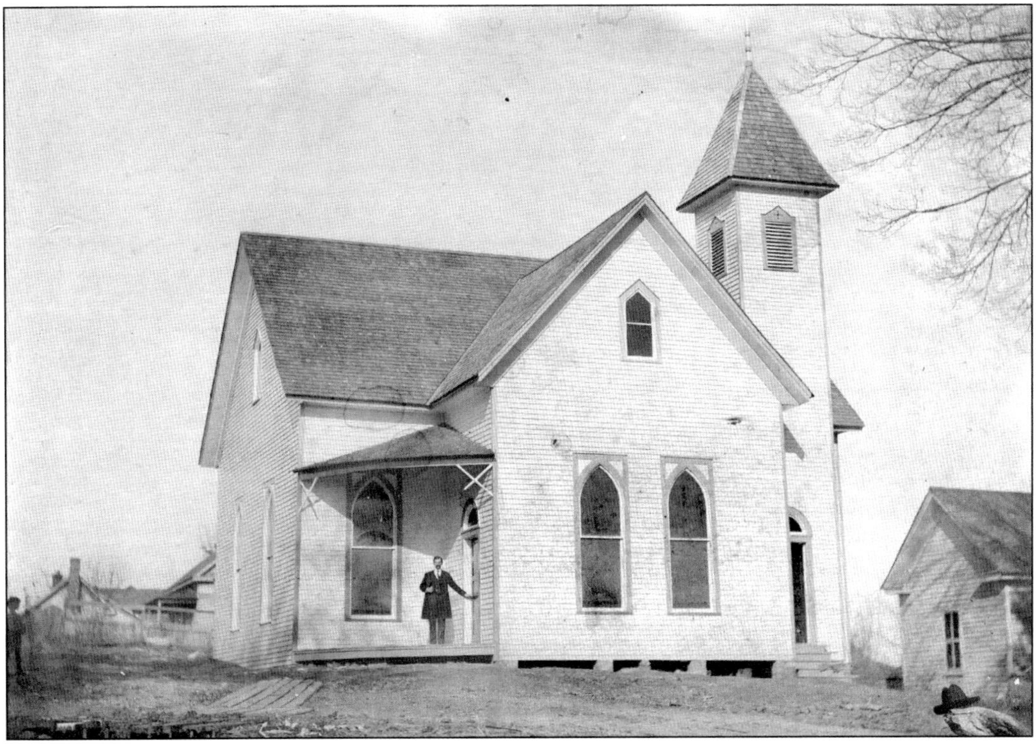

Pictured is the First Methodist Church of Wedowee around 1890. (Courtesy of Glenda Hale.)

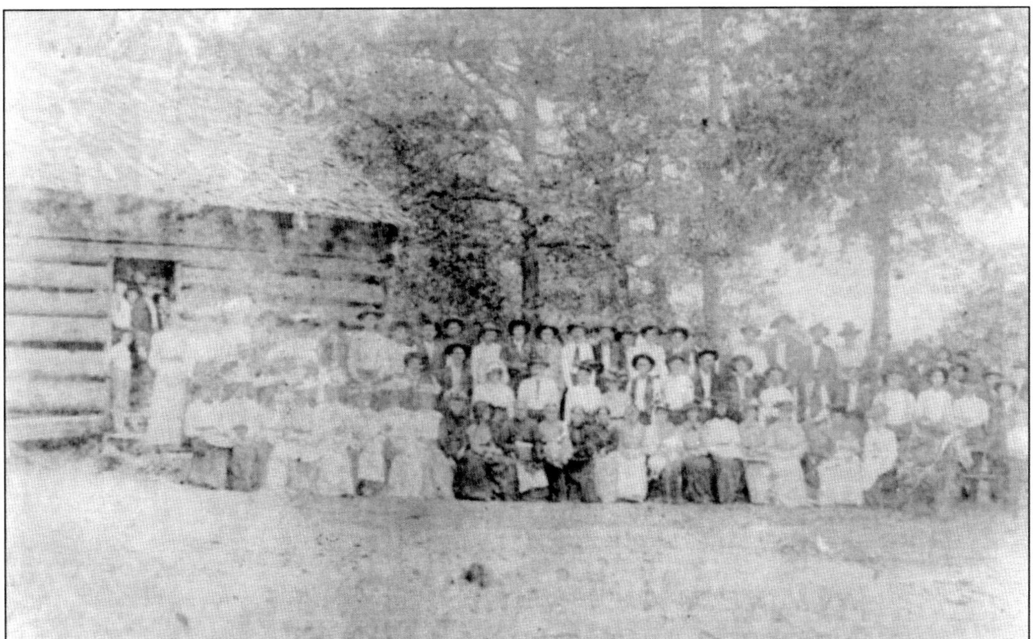

The first building for Union Baptist church was constructed in 1854 out of long-leaf yellow pine logs. The logs do not appear to be chinked to keep cold air out, but such conditions did not keep the members from coming to church. (Courtesy of Byrd Stewart.)

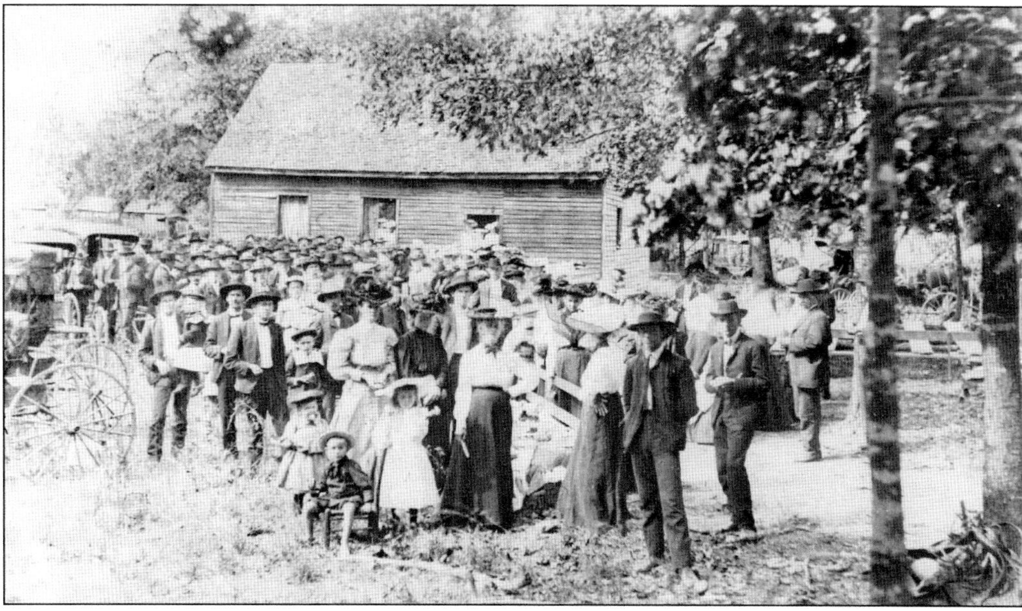

This scene at Union Baptist Church could have been Easter Sunday or Homecoming with "dinner on the ground." Dinner on the ground was at one time a very popular custom. Members brought food to church, and after the service, the women filled the tables that had been set up on the grounds of the church and the congregation ate together. (Courtesy of Byrd Stewart.)

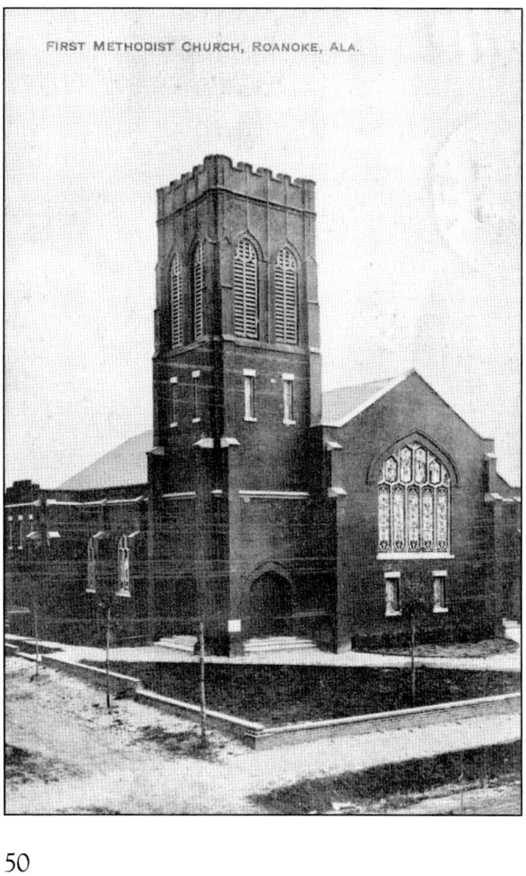

Methodism in Roanoke began as the Methodist Episcopal Church in a small house on a lot in what is now Cedarwood Cemetery. Pastor Wiley White donated it as the first church building. In 1845, the name was changed to Methodist Episcopal Church South, later to First Methodist Church, and in the present day, to First United Methodist Church. The church building was constructed in 1906 and continues, with later expansions, to serve the Methodists of Roanoke. (Courtesy of the Randolph County Museum.)

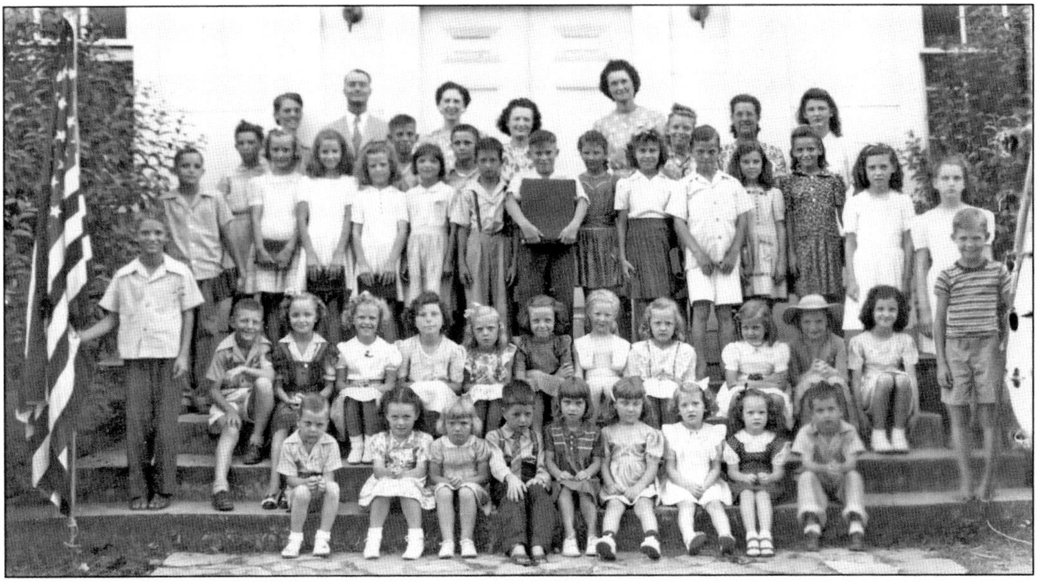

Pictured is the Bible school at Handley Avenue Baptist Church, June 18, 1944. This church became Trinity Baptist Church in the 1970s when it was moved to the bypass. (Courtesy of Mohee Bozeman.)

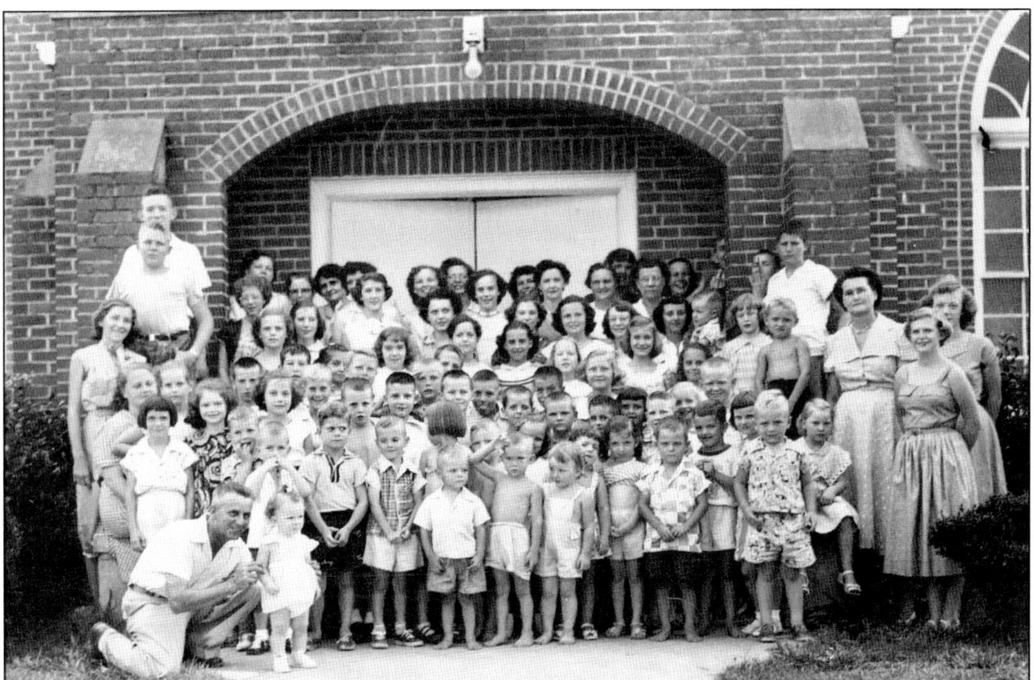

This is Lowell Methodist Church Vacation Bible School in the summer of 1953. Reverend Giddens was the pastor. (Courtesy of Bonnie Sue Knight.)

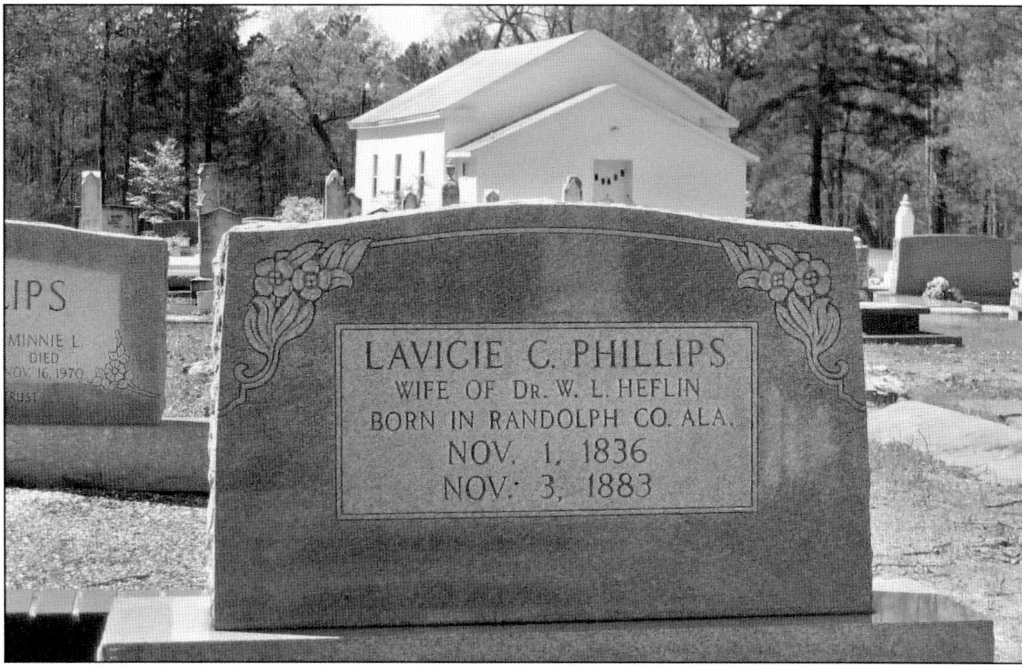

On January 1, 1850, Wyatt Heflin, Peter Mitchell, Harrington Phillips, F. A. McMurray, and John J. Chewning gave a total of 40 acres with the stipulation that the land be used for church and school purposes only. The church Concord was built and continues to be an active church. (Courtesy of Wyner Phillips.)

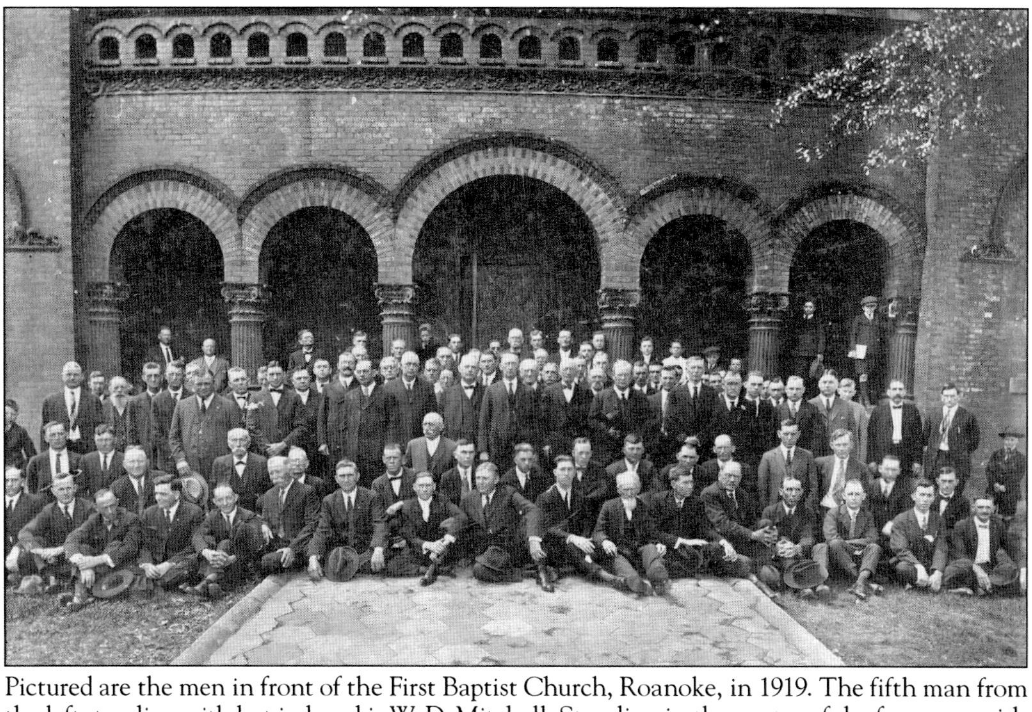

Pictured are the men in front of the First Baptist Church, Roanoke, in 1919. The fifth man from the left standing with hat in hand is W. D. Mitchell. Standing in the center of the front row with a bow tie is Guy Handley, and to his left is J. J. Awbrey. (Courtesy of Carolyn Lane.)

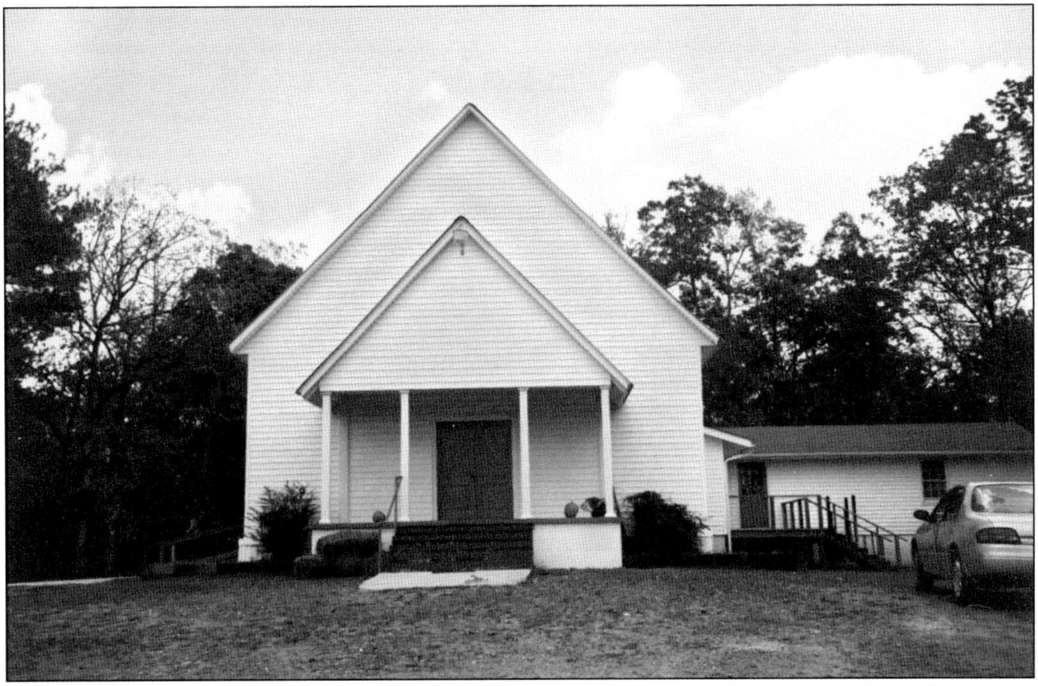

Beulah Baptist Church is located on County Road 631, near the Georgia line. (Courtesy of Helen Blankenship.)

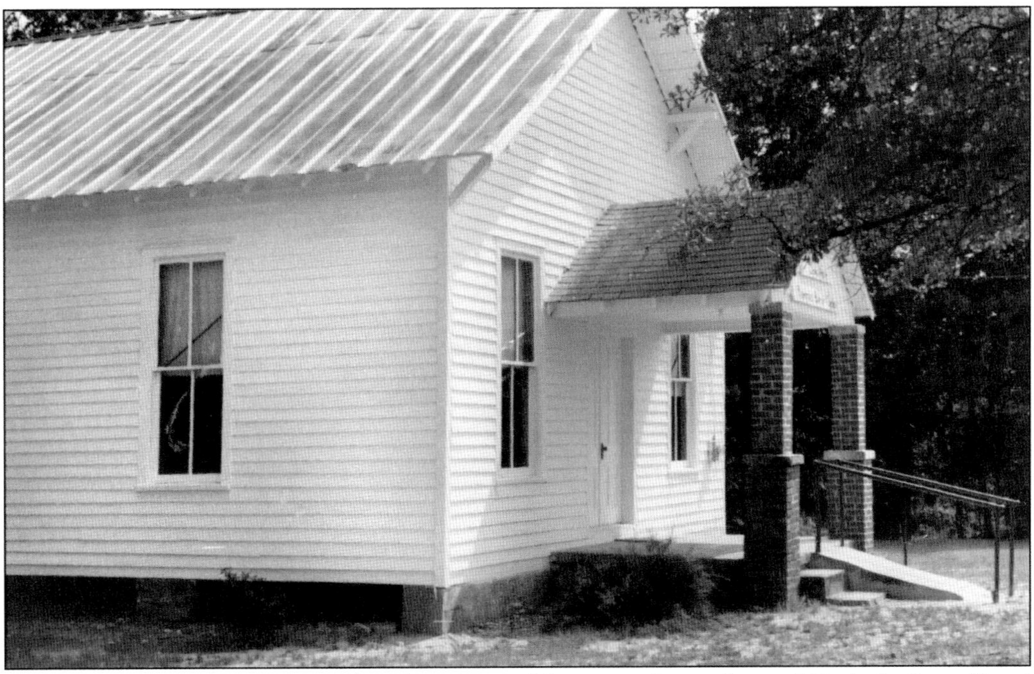

Zions Rest Primitive Baptist Church is located between Roanoke and Taylor's Cross Road on County Road 59. This picture was taken before the church was renovated. (Courtesy of Helen Blankenship.)

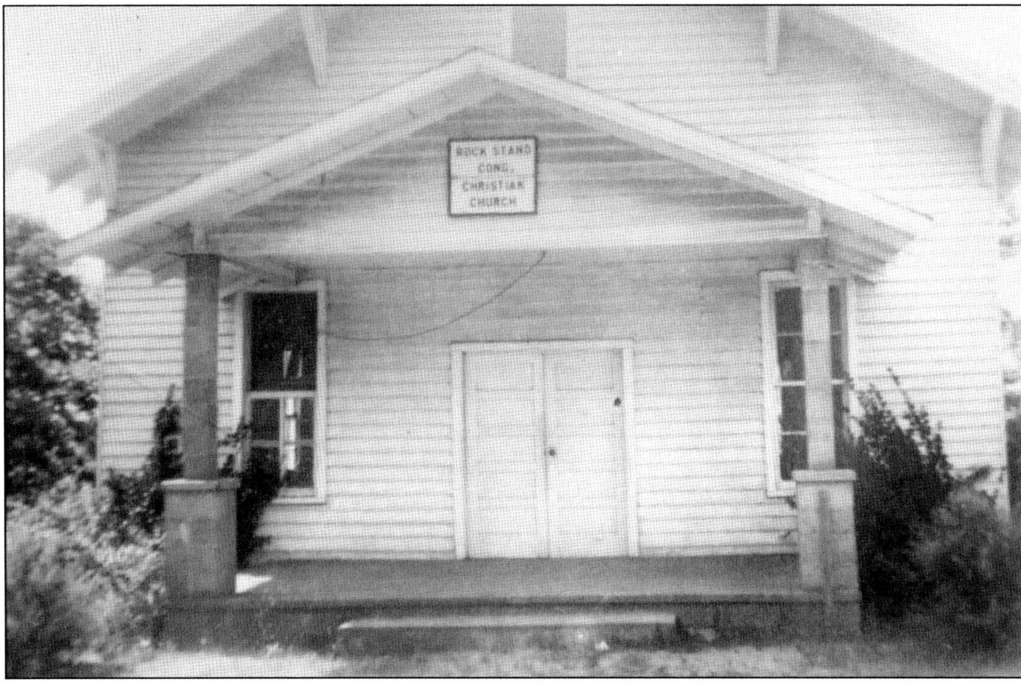

Rock Stand Congregational Christian Church was organized in 1908 by Rev. J. D. Dollar and J. H. Hughes. It was remodeled and bricked in 1953. (Courtesy of Billy Treadwell.)

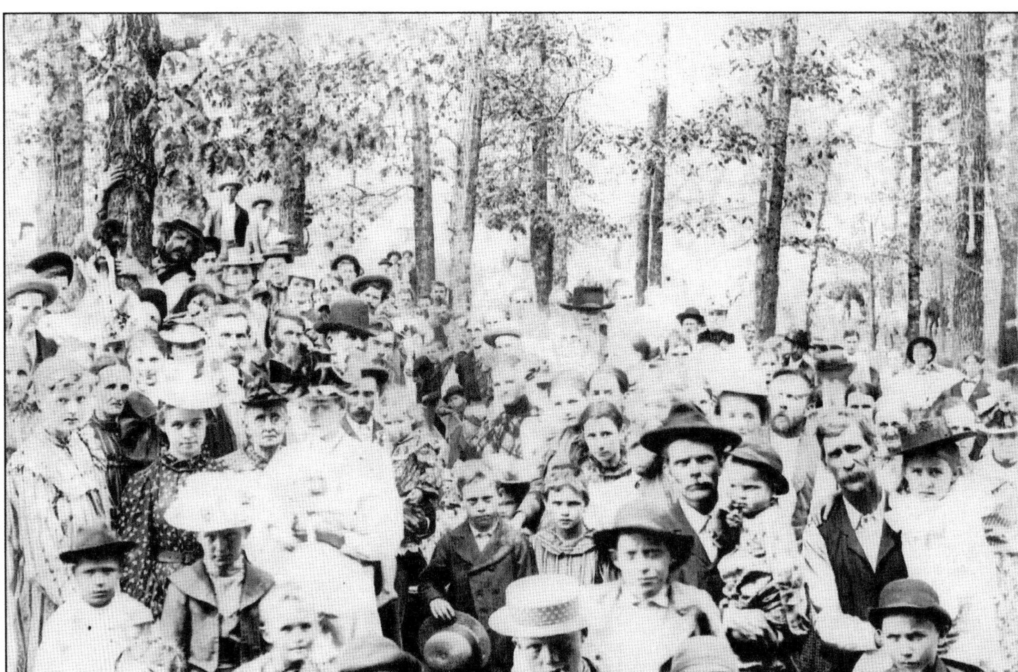

This picture shows a tent meeting across from Beverly's Store in Rock Stand community in the mid-1920s. (Courtesy of Dwayne Pate.)

Four

Business

In the pioneer days of Randolph County, when settlers first began coming in, the only way to obtain goods was either make them or barter with the Native Americans to get them. The settlers' primary purpose in coming to this area was to obtain land to farm, for that was basically all they knew how to do. When more people started coming in, there was always an innovative person who would open a trading post with a two-fold purpose. The first purpose was to supply people in the area with goods they needed, and the other was to do it in a profitable manner as a means of livelihood. As the population grew, one trading post wasn't enough to supply all needs, and another innovative person would open a store, changing the terminology from trading post to store.

Communities developed around the stores because of the convenience, and as the community expanded, more stores came into being and became more diversified. The diversification created a higher demand for goods, and towns developed from what formerly were communities.

The pace of those early residents was steady but not hurried. The farmer could travel by mule and wagon three or four miles to purchase supplies at a country store for incidental needs, but he could take a whole day and travel six or seven miles to town where he could shop around and completely fill his shopping list. And then came along the motorized transportation, which made his trips to town quicker. With this new development in transportation, another innovative fellow bought a truck and created a rolling store, going from farmhouse to farmhouse, and this gave the farmer's wife and children the opportunity to shop. The rolling store even had exotic merchandise such as bananas.

As towns grew and more stores were opened and more families acquired automobiles, going to town on Saturday became the farmer's ritual. Most Randolph county businesses were locally owned, and store owners even traded with other store owners to keep the money at home and circulate it over and over. Such practice made Randolph County business feasible.

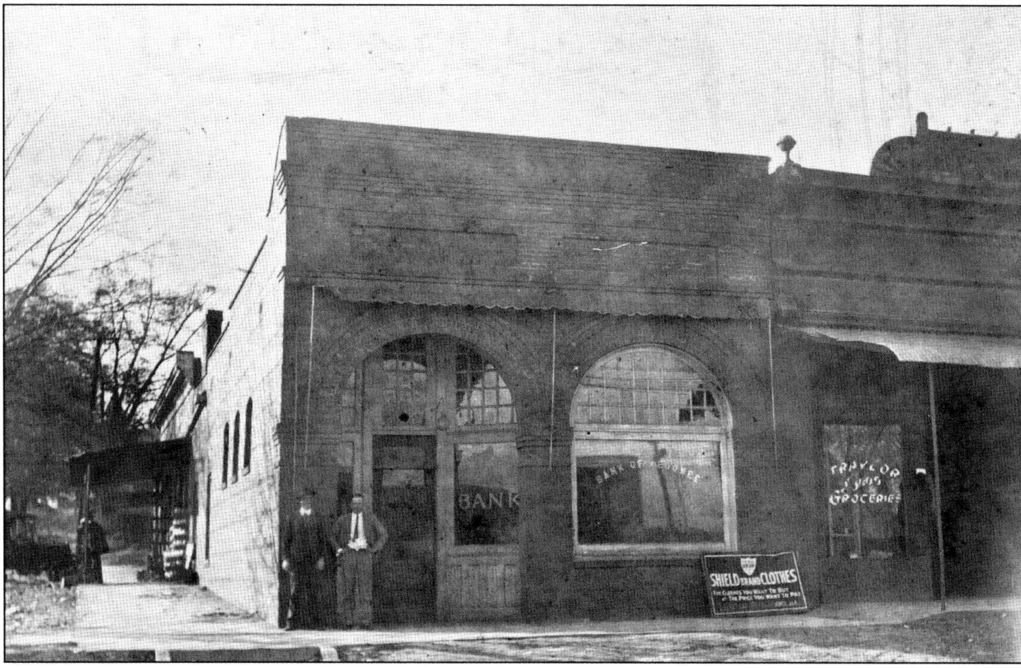

The Bank of Wedowee was organized by Dr. J. C. Swann in 1906. It occupied this building on the corner lot for more than 50 years and built larger, more modern buildings in the 1960s and again in the 1990s. This photograph is *c.* 1935. (Courtesy of Glenda Hale.)

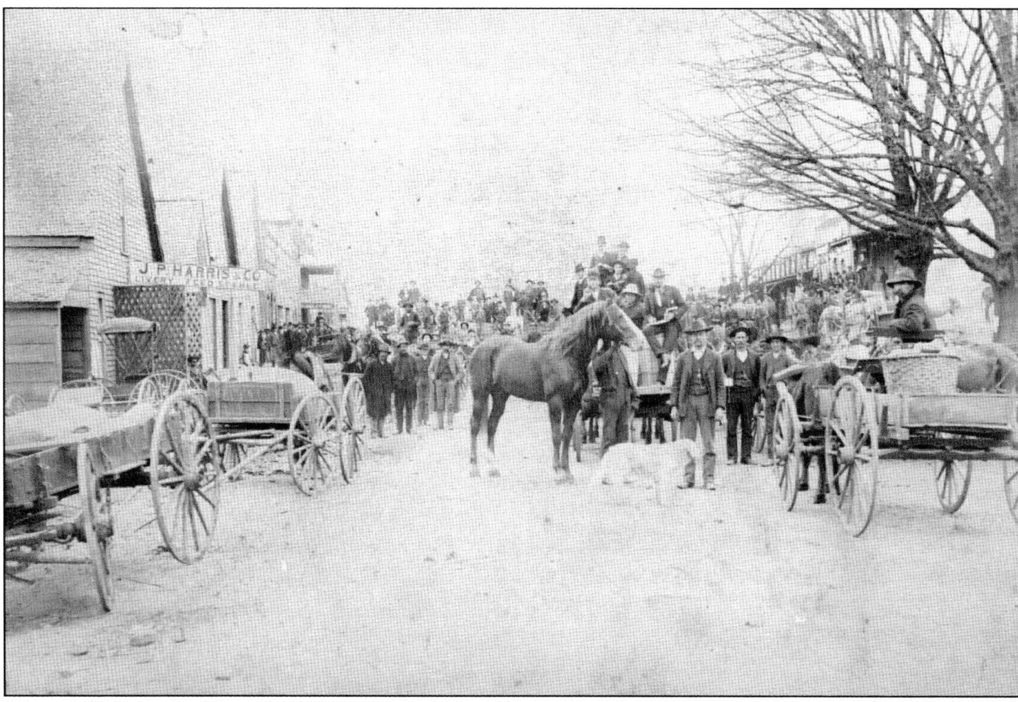

This is the main section of downtown Roanoke in the mid-1880s, well before the days of the auto. The two-story building on left, with a second-floor porch, is the Handley Hotel. (Courtesy of the Randolph County Museum.)

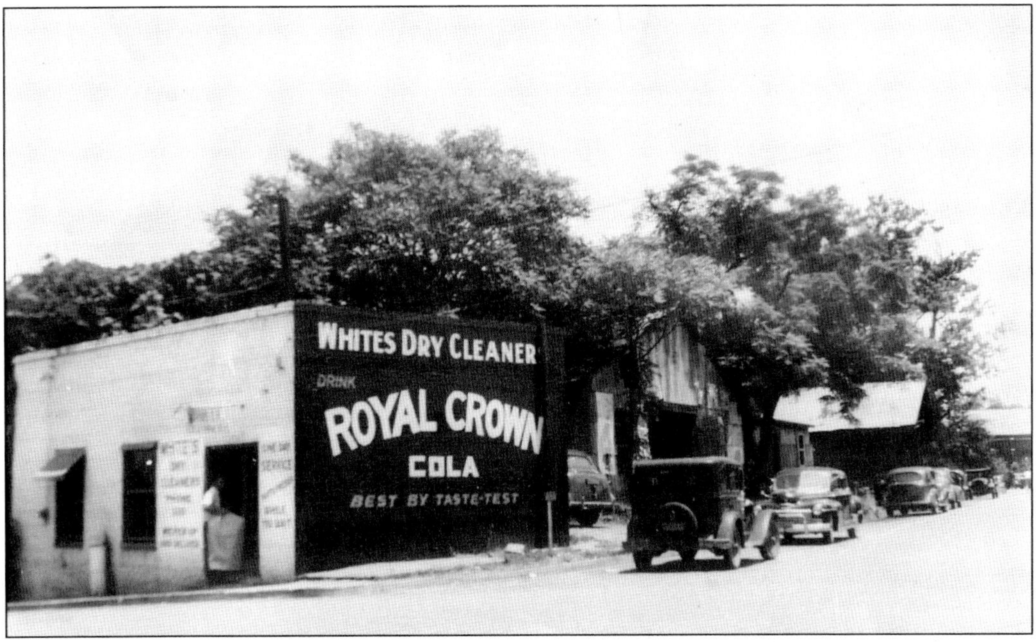

The scene is White Street, Roanoke, *c.* 1942, at the corner of Peachtree Street, where cars ranging from 1920 Model As to Page Enloe's Packard are parked. Behind White's Dry Cleaner is B. E. Satterwhite's storage building and the house of Gen. B. F. Weather's housekeeper. The First Methodist Church can be seen at the end of the block. Big Chik is now located in this area. (Courtesy of Roy Williamson.)

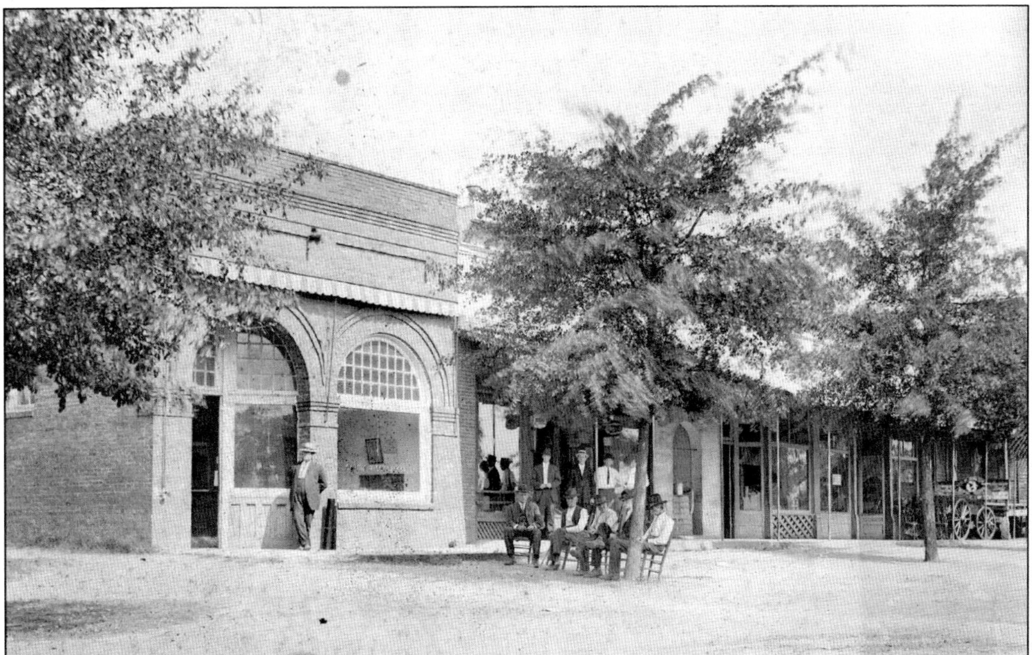

Main Street in Wedowee *c.* 1925 is shown in this view across from the courthouse. Water was provided for shoppers and their horses and mules from a well in the center of the photograph. (Courtesy of Glenda Hale.)

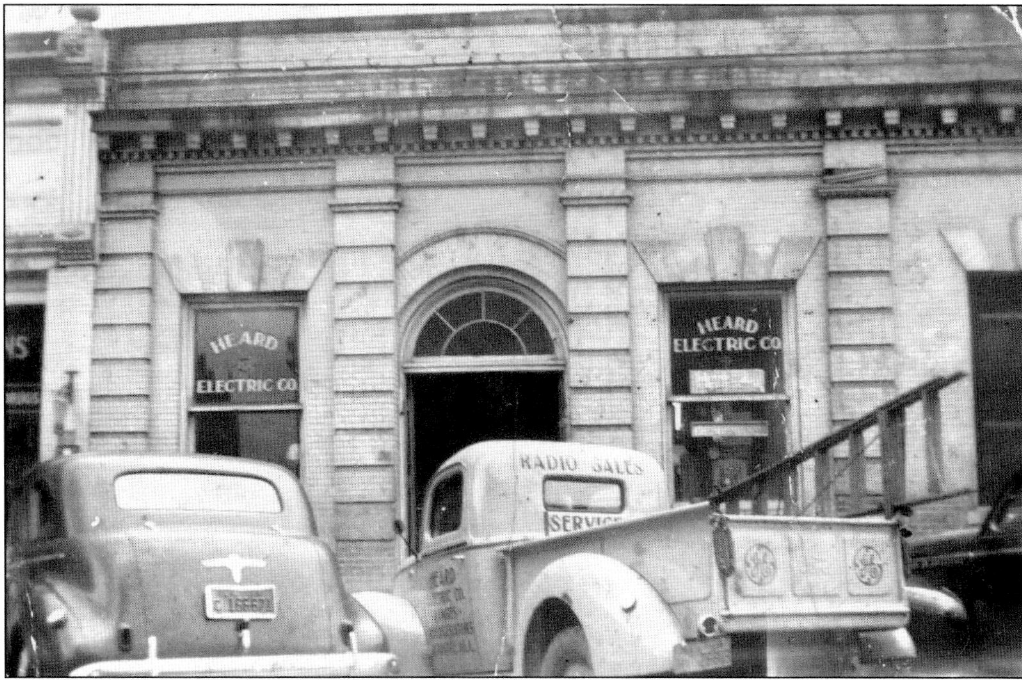

Garfield Heard established the Heard Electric Company in the back portion of the building that originally was Roanoke Banking Company. The service truck is parked in front, *c.* 1942. (Courtesy of Idus Heard.)

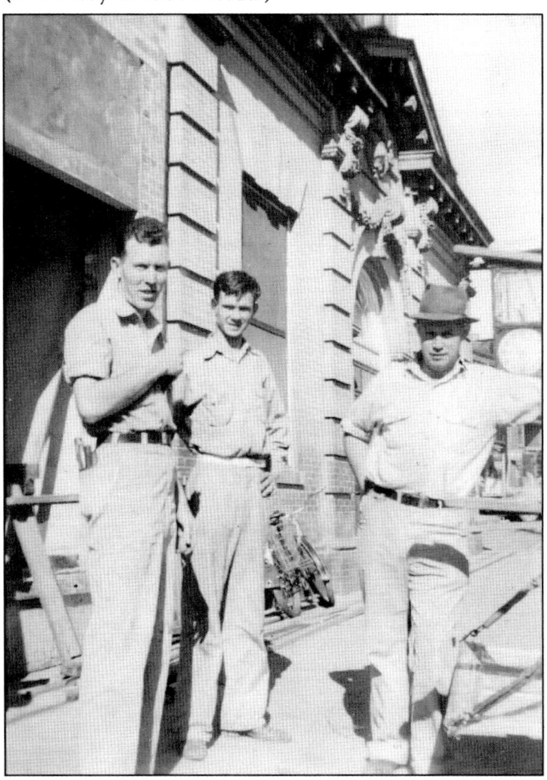

Garfield Heard, on the right; Grover Heard (center), Garfield's son and successor; and electrician Hickman check out the progress of the remodeling of Heard Electric Company. Today Grover's daughter, Janice Fincher, and granddaughter, Angie Mitchem, still operate a family business out of the same store. (Courtesy of Idus Heard.)

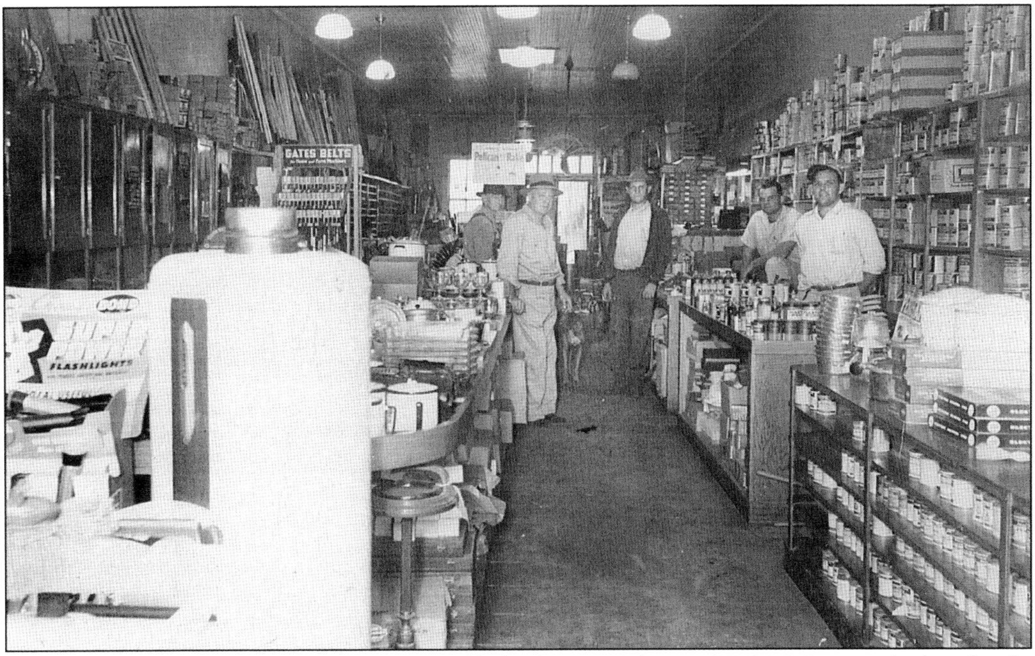

The McMurray Hardware store was established is 1897 by W. H. McMurray. At his death, McMurray's son, Gus (in the middle of the picture), ran the store. His two sons, seen on the right, later took over the store. The building is still in use but is no longer a hardware store. (Courtesy of Jane [MacMurray] Edwards.)

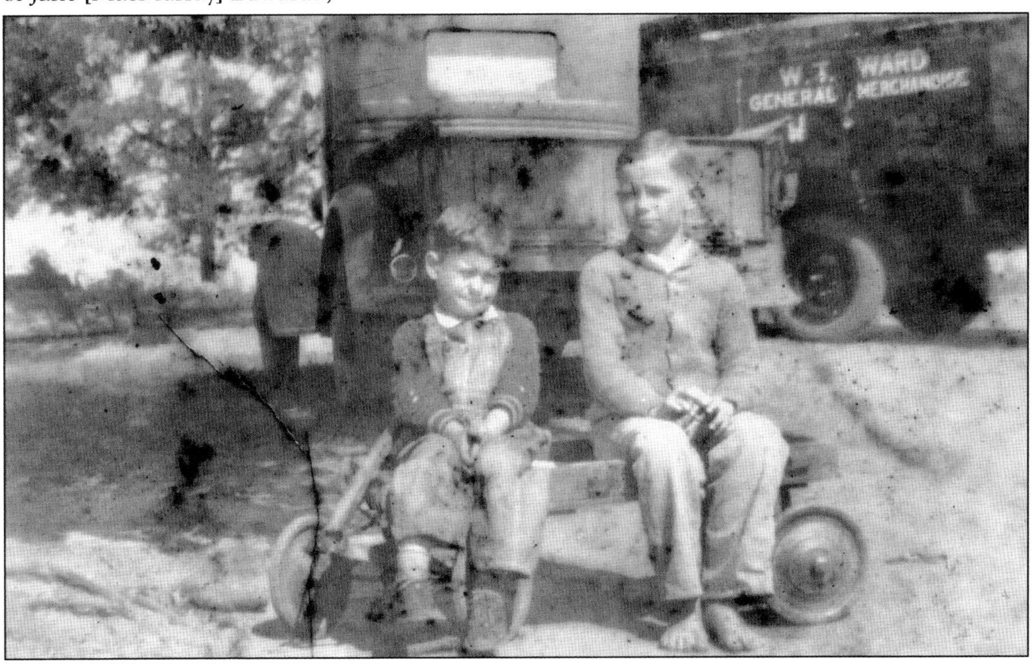

Junior Ward (left) and Linward Wilson (right) sat in their wagon parked in front of W. T. Ward's Napoleon store. In the background is Ward's General Merchandise Rolling Store, which ran for about 20 years. He was known as "The Peddler" and was very important to the rural community he served. (Courtesy of Janie [Ward] Cobb.)

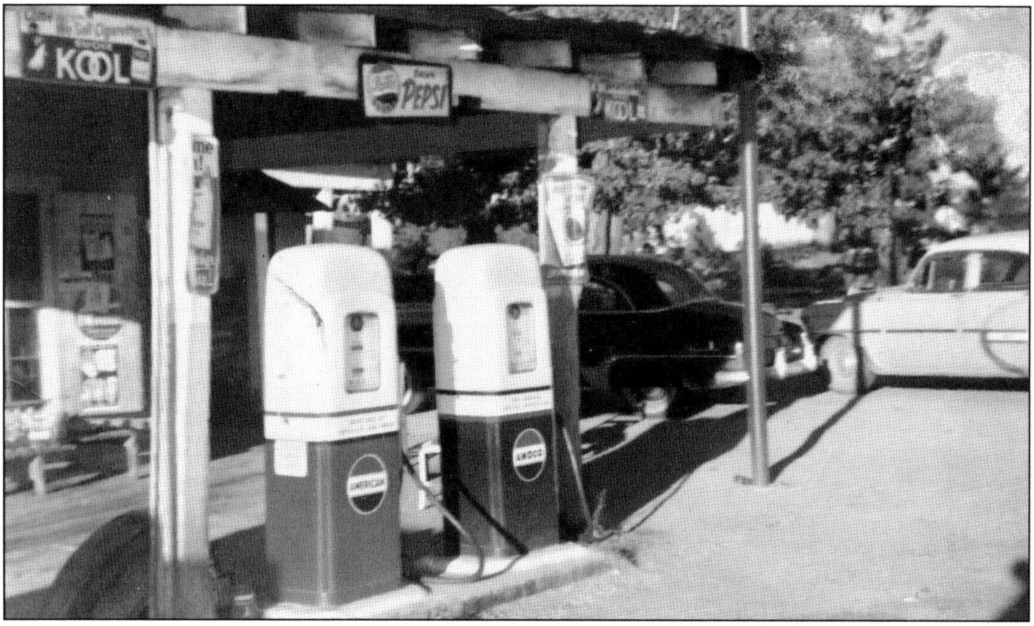

A. J. Prescott built store and gristmill in Napoleon around 1892. Hoyt Enloe was the first caretaker of the store and mill, which used waterpower to grind corn into meal and wheat into flour. In 1929, William T. Ward became owner of the store and operated it until his death in 1958. His wife, Lois Ward, operated the store until her health failed and she closed the store in the early 1960s. Thirty years later, in 1990, the Wards' son Larry purchased the property and restored the building. Once again it was a general store, but this time it held antiques. Upon his death in 2004, the store was left to the Napoleon Church of Christ and is now used as a community center. (Courtesy of Janie [Ward] Cobb.)

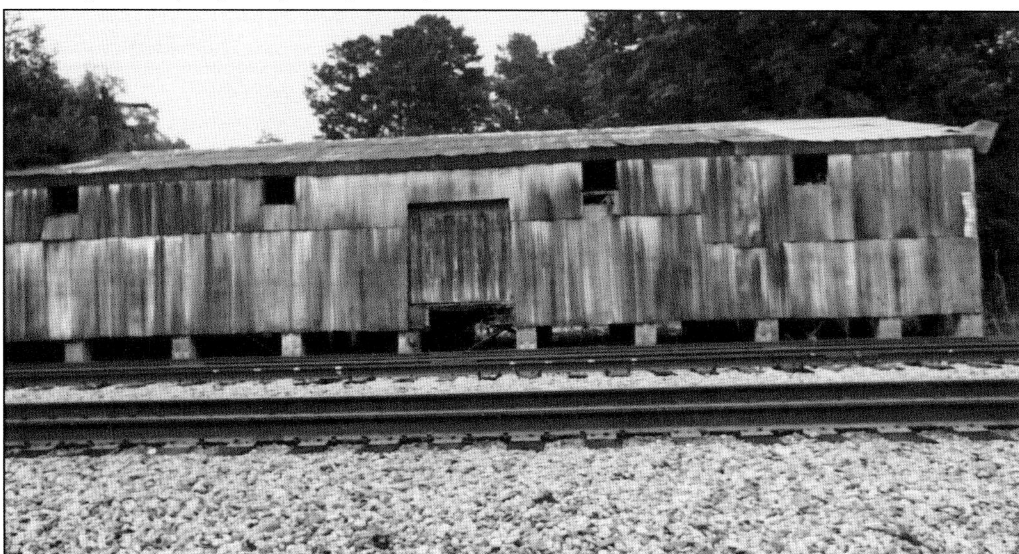

This metal building, dating form early railroad days, was Phillips Brothers Warehouse. Through the wooden sliding door, merchandise was unloaded from the train into the warehouse and then transported by truck to the hardware store uptown. The warehouse was demolished in 2004. (Courtesy of Helen Blankenship.)

Thornton's Motel and Café was located half way between Roanoke and Wedowee on what was called the North–South Fast Route, Alabama 37. It had luxuries such as central hot water, comfortable quarters, delicious meals, a swimming pool, and picnic grounds. Alabama 37 is now called Highway 431. (Courtesy of Camilla Jackson.)

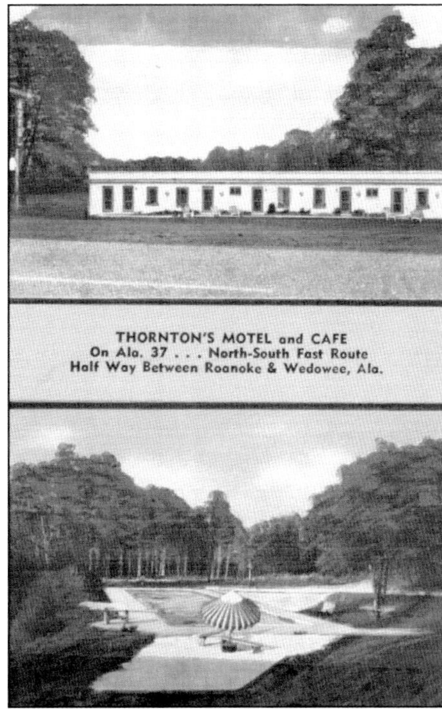

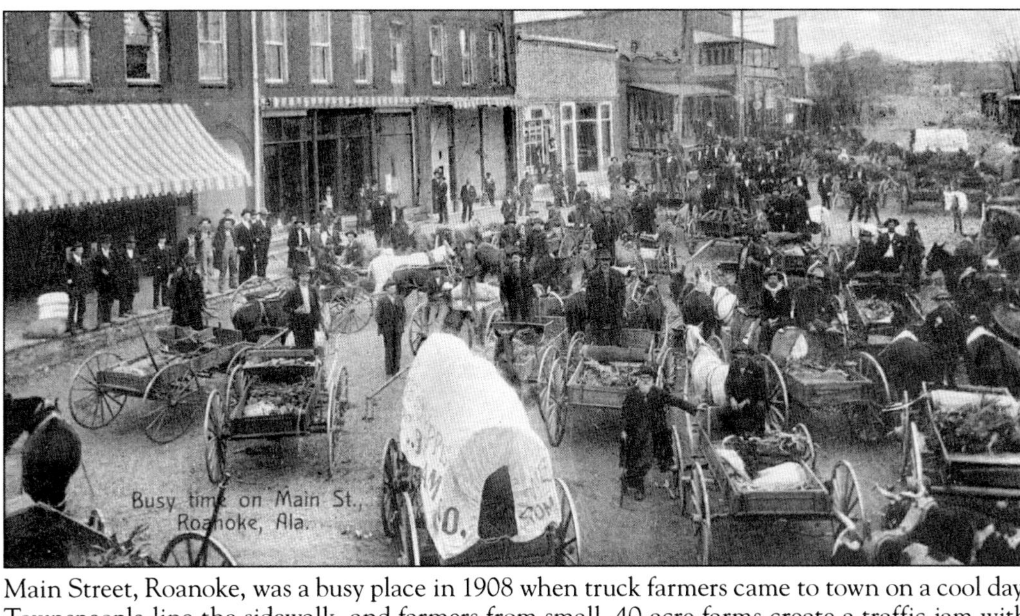

Main Street, Roanoke, was a busy place in 1908 when truck farmers came to town on a cool day. Townspeople line the sidewalk, and farmers from small, 40-acre farms create a traffic jam with their one-horse wagons, having brought their produce and kindling to town for barter or sale to merchants. The last building on the left side of the street with the square belfry is First Methodist Church, which was built in 1906 and remains a very important landmark in the present day. The two-story building with the porch on the top floor was Griffin and Satterwhite Hardware. That building and the two buildings to its left burned in 1946. Phillips Brothers Hardware was built on the Griffin and Satterwhite lot in 1948 and is still there today. (Courtesy of the Randolph County Museum.)

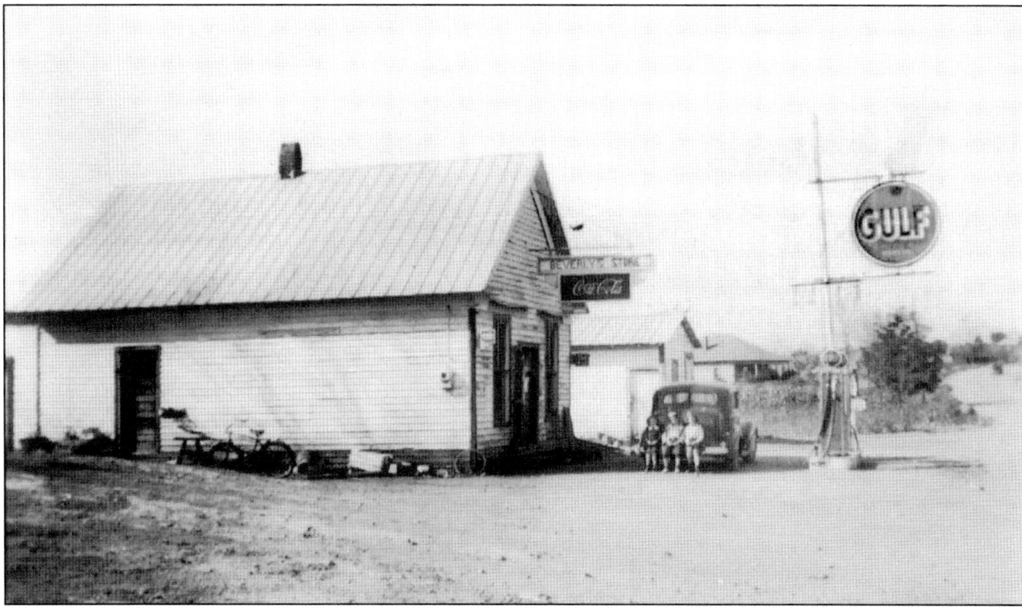

Pictured is Beverly's Store near Rock Stand in 1938. The store still stands and is presently owned by Carlos Beverly's grandson, Dwayne Pate. (Courtesy of Dwayne Pate.)

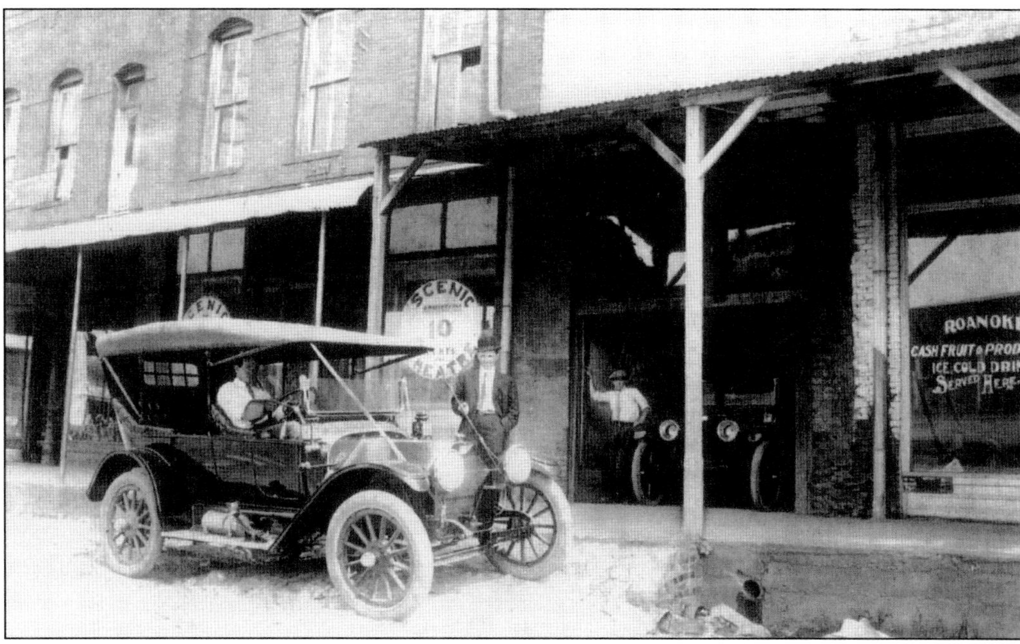

The first automobile dealer in Roanoke was Dr. D. M. Yates, who diversified his primary profession of dentistry into retailing through a music store and the car dealership. This photograph from May 1916 shows Dr. Yates standing beside a blue Cloverleaf Overland Six, which was special ordered for Dr. A. J. Gay as the honeymoon vehicle for his upcoming marriage to Lenda Boulware. The driver of the Cloverleaf, wearing the long-cuffed driving gloves, is Courtney Yates. Zelmer Yates is standing in the doorway leaning on a Willys-Knight, which was ordered for Dr. Gay's future brother-in-law, Milda Boulware. The automobiles were shipped by train from the factory at Toledo, Ohio, at a freight cost of $260. (Courtesy of Sara Jean Harman.)

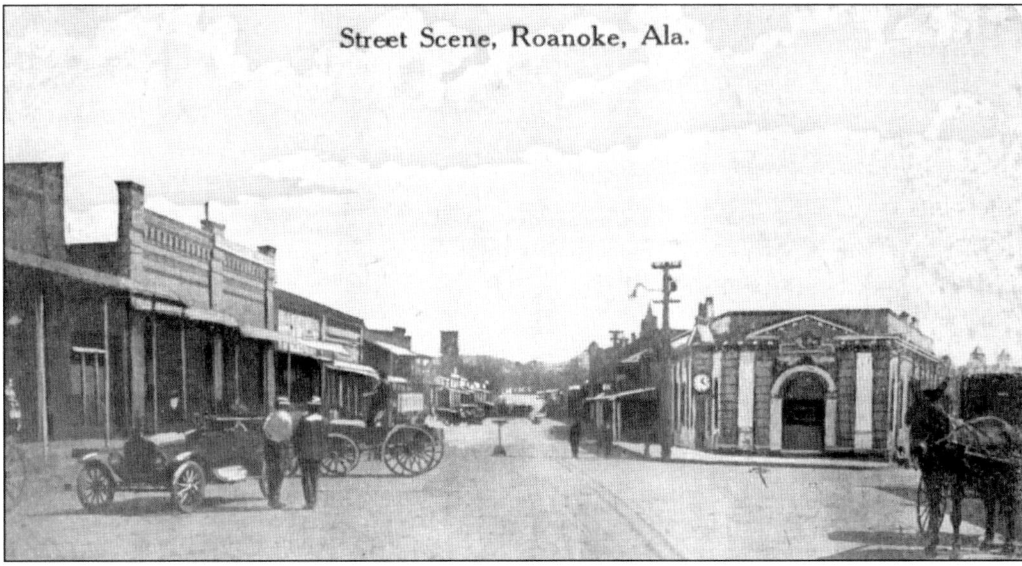

Looking east on Main Street in 1917 Roanoke, there were few automobiles in the city. The dominant, ornate building in right center was the Roanoke Banking Company. To the extreme right can be seen the spires of the Roanoke Normal College, which burned in 1923. The fixture in the middle of the dirt street was a well, which furnished water for horses and mules. This area was the hub of downtown Roanoke, with six streets at this point. The photographer was situated at the fork of Louina Street and Wedowee Street to his rear. At the right side of Roanoke Banking Company is West Pont Street. Chestnut Street is at a 90-degree turn on the right side of the photograph. All six streets were filled with businesses that were thriving at this time in Roanoke, and all were locally owned. (Courtesy of the Randolph County Museum.)

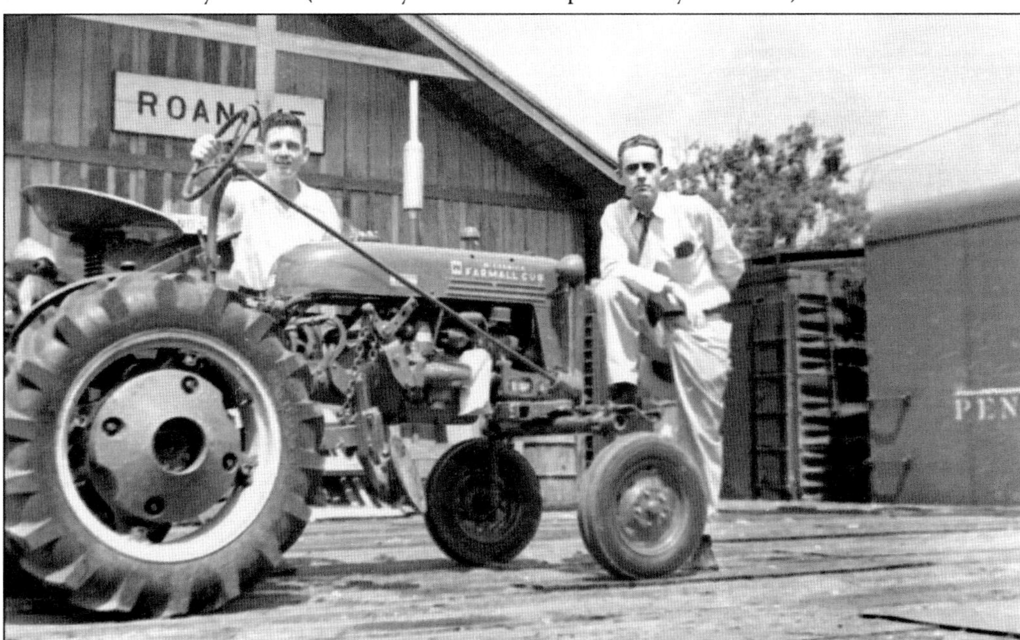

W. T. Belcher Sr. (right) seems to have just unloaded an International Farmall tractor at the depot in Roanoke with the help of Gordon Sharman. (Courtesy of W. T. [Bill] Belcher III.)

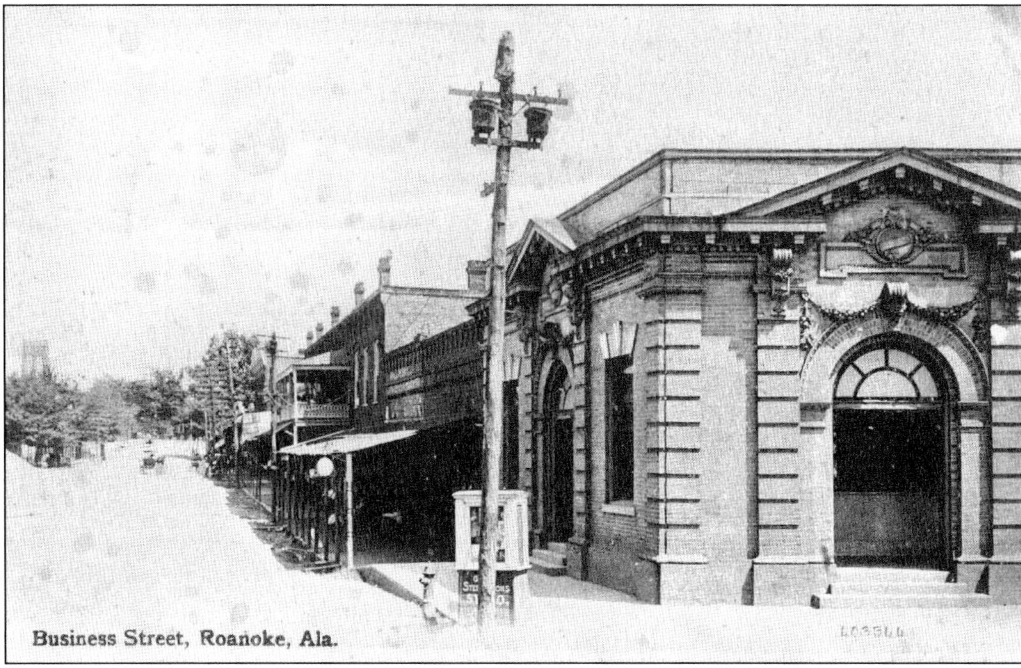

Roanoke Banking Company, organized in 1906, was the second bank in Roanoke. This photograph from 1908 gives a view of the ornate structure of the Campbell and Wright Banking Company, its original name, when it was enjoying the prosperity of a growing Roanoke. In 1930, it became a statistic of the Great Depression, and the bank was closed. (Courtesy of the Randolph County Museum.)

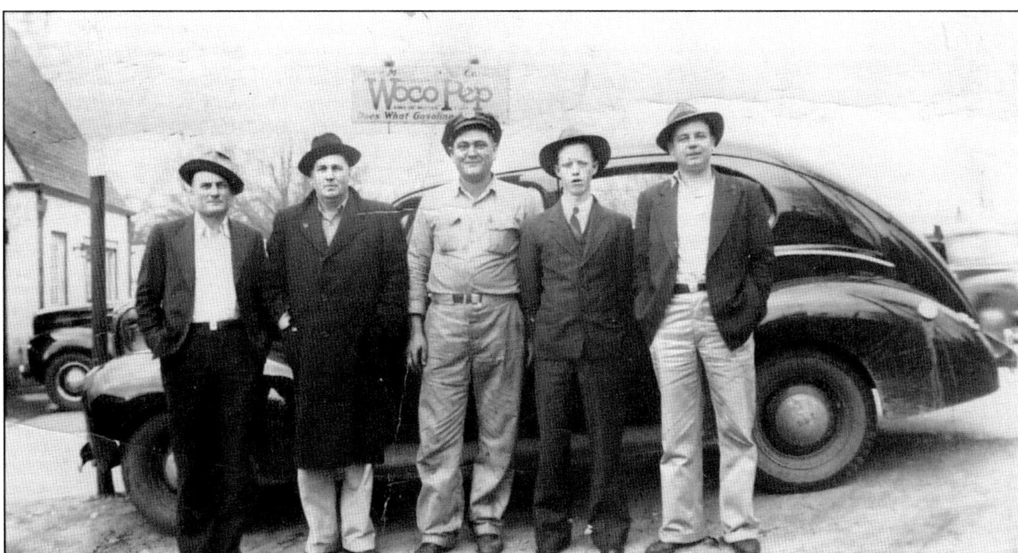

In the mid-1940s, there were many taxicabs in Roanoke, because a large percentage of the citizens did not own cars. This group of four taxi drivers, pictured with George Weaver (center), operator of the WocoPep Service Station on North Main Street, from left to right is Colonel Caldwell, Dewey Nolan, Red McDow, and Arthur Siggers. The WocoPep building, with the right side showing in the photograph, still stands on Main Street. (Courtesy of Squat Yarbrough.)

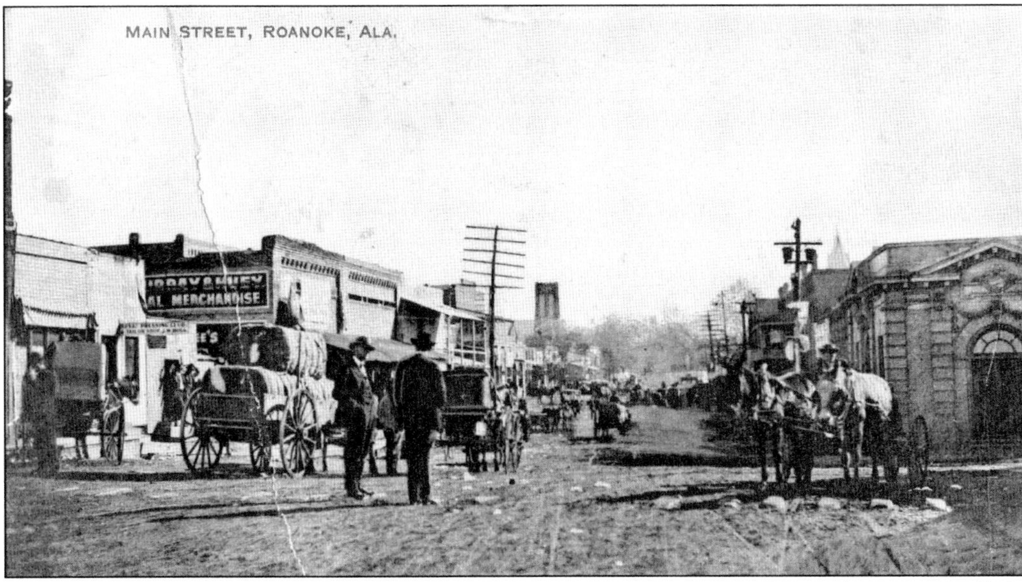

In 1908, dirt streets were common, and rocks were used for crosswalks to keep mud off the businessmen's shoes. It was the day when cotton was the primary crop and was transported to market by mule and wagon. The wagon with three bales of cotton indicates that this farmer had picked at least three acres, provided that 1908 was a good crop year, for every farmer's ambition was to produce one bale per acre. (Courtesy of the Randolph County Museum.)

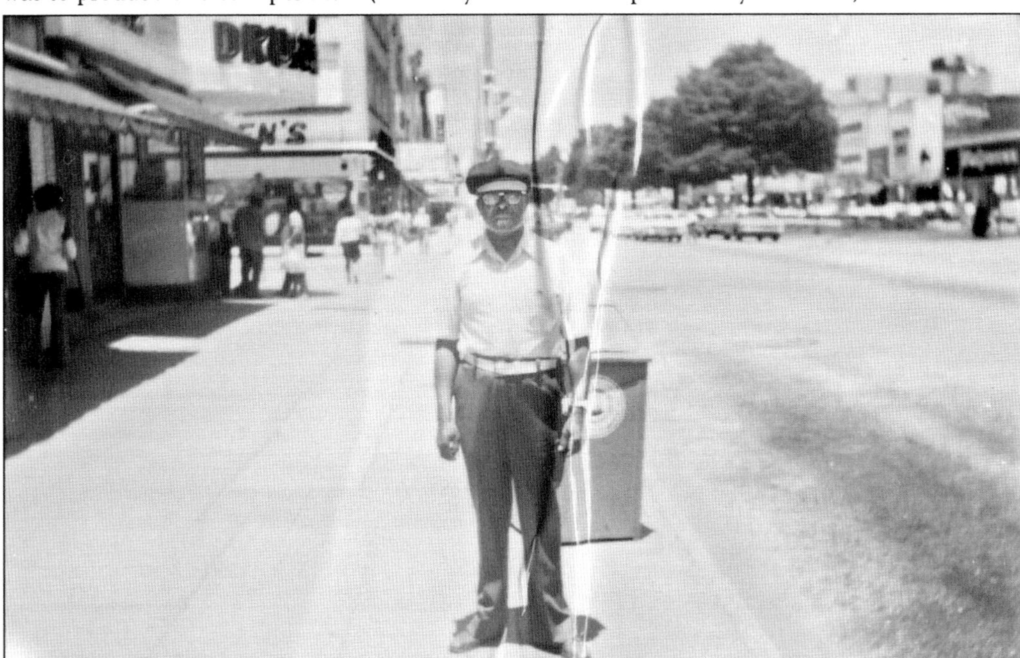

H. T. "Lighting" Rosser owned and operated the Colored Cab Company in Roanoke for many years. Everyone in Roanoke knew and respected Lighting, and few people knew he had another name other than Lighting. He and his wife, Susie, built the Rosser Nursing Home in 1967 for the care of the elderly and personally operated it until their demise. The Rosser Nursing Home still cares for the elderly citizens under the name Roanoke Health Care. (Courtesy of Alberta Ester.)

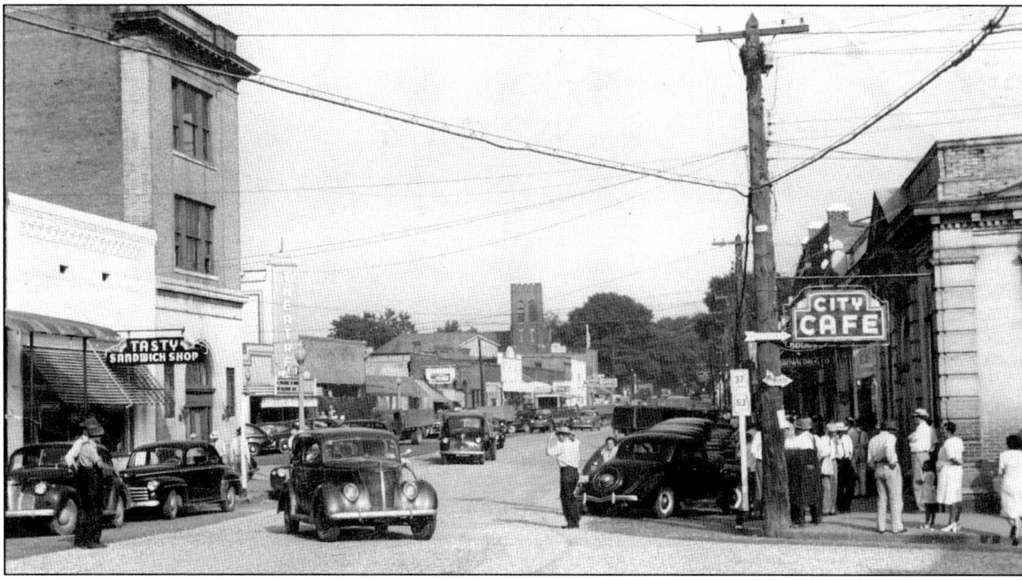

Shown is Main Street in Roanoke, *c.* 1946, and it is most certainly on a Saturday because the African Americans gathering on the corner at the café are dressed to visit and socialize rather than work. On a weekday, fewer automobiles would have lined the street, and the Martin Theatre marquee would have had only one movie, since listed double features were only on Saturday. Standing beside the coupe with the spare tire on the rear is Lucy Rombokas. She and her husband, Sam, owned and operated the City Café for years. Next door was Heard Electric Company, and then Brown Drug Company, which had recently been purchased from Teddy Walker by Cecil Brown. Next to the Martin Theatre stood the Griffin-Satterwhite Hardware building that burned in 1946 and was rebuilt by Phillips Brothers Hardware in 1947–1948. (Courtesy of Betty Ziglar.)

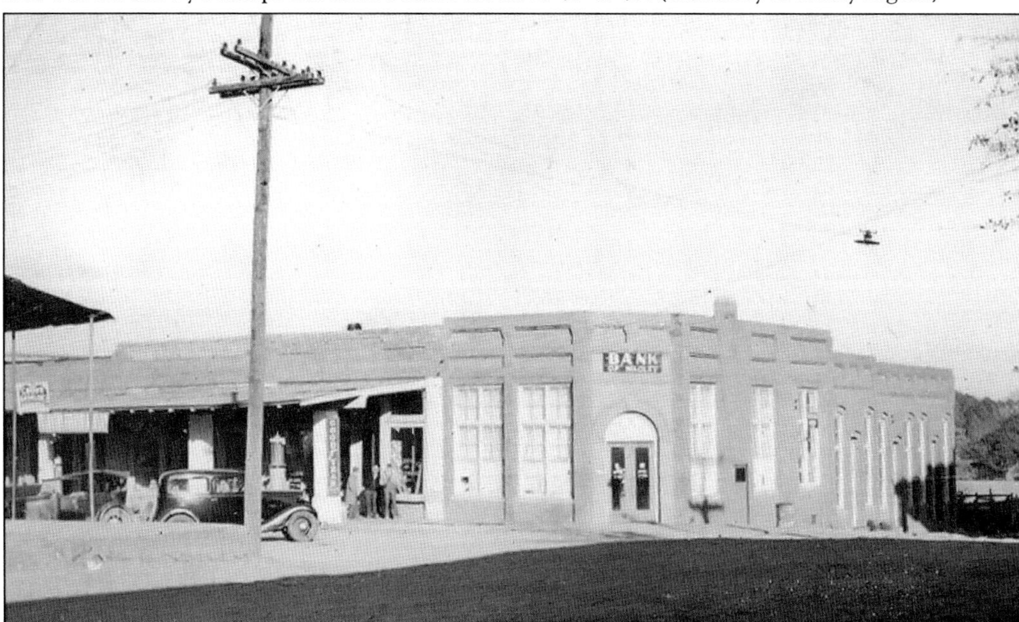

This picture shows the original look of the Bank of Wadley, some 15 years after it was constructed. (Courtesy of Southern Union State Community College.)

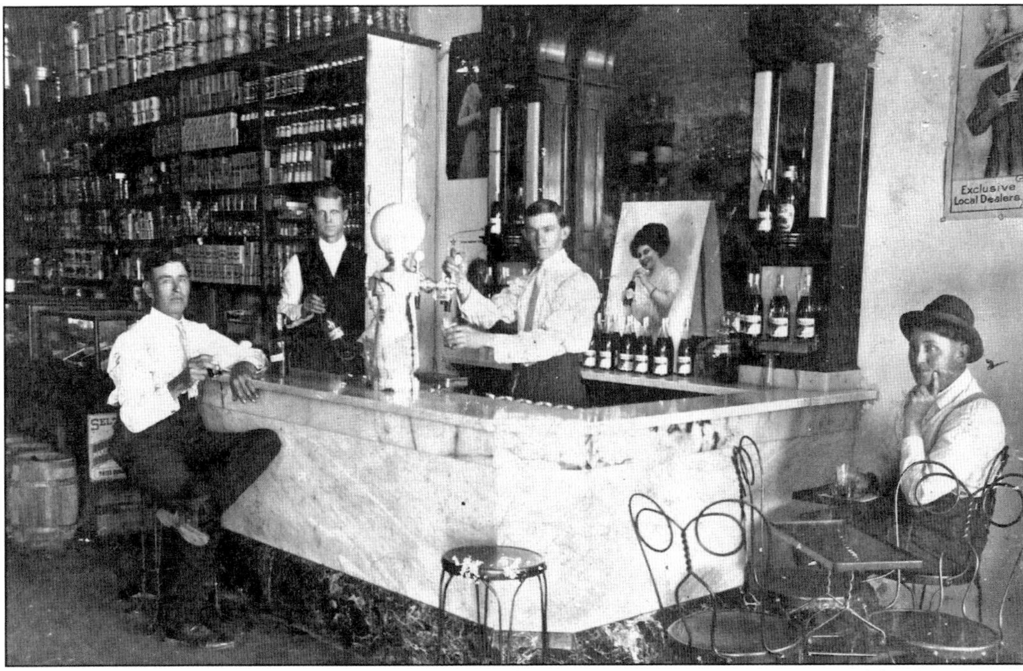

The Rock Store at Rock Mills in 1910 was a thriving enterprise. It was owned by Dr. Gerson Bonner, M.D. The soda jerk is Charles H. Vinson, and his customers are Jess Whitaker, seated on left; Sam Yates, standing; and Jess Harry, seated on right. (Courtesy of Charles Vinson.)

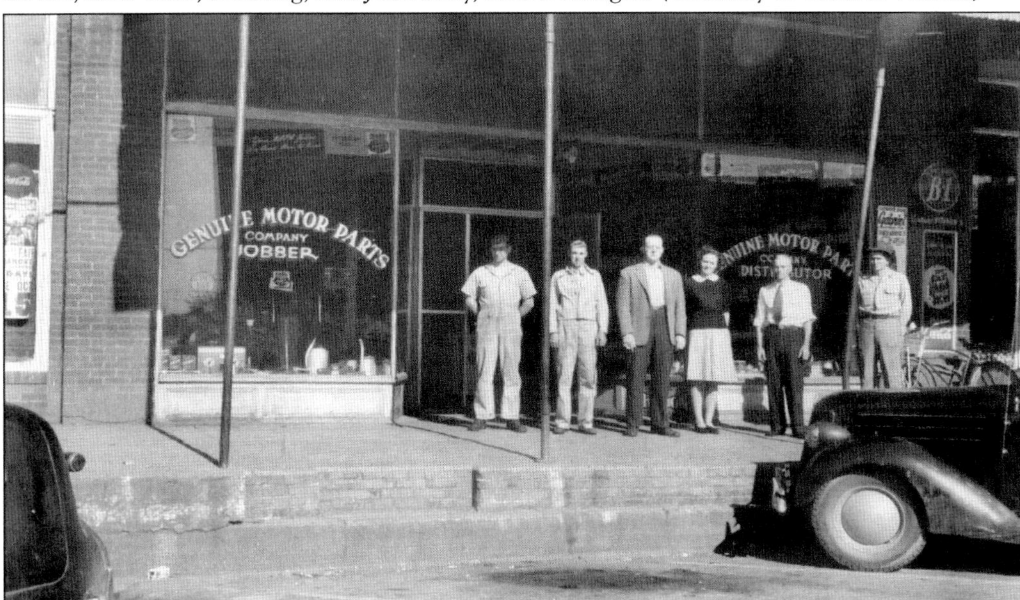

In the late 1930s, Genuine Motor Parts was on Main Street, Roanoke, where Cotter Furniture is now located. Standing out front for the picture are all employees. From left to right are Ralph Benefield; Walter "Buck" Still; Robert "Woody" Woodman; Demaris McCullars, bookkeeper; Robert Durham, owner; and "Bud" Yates. The store to the right was Washington's Grocery, and the bicycle was used by Sam Burpee, Mr. Washington's delivery boy who could do wonders on a bike. (Courtesy of Jack Still.)

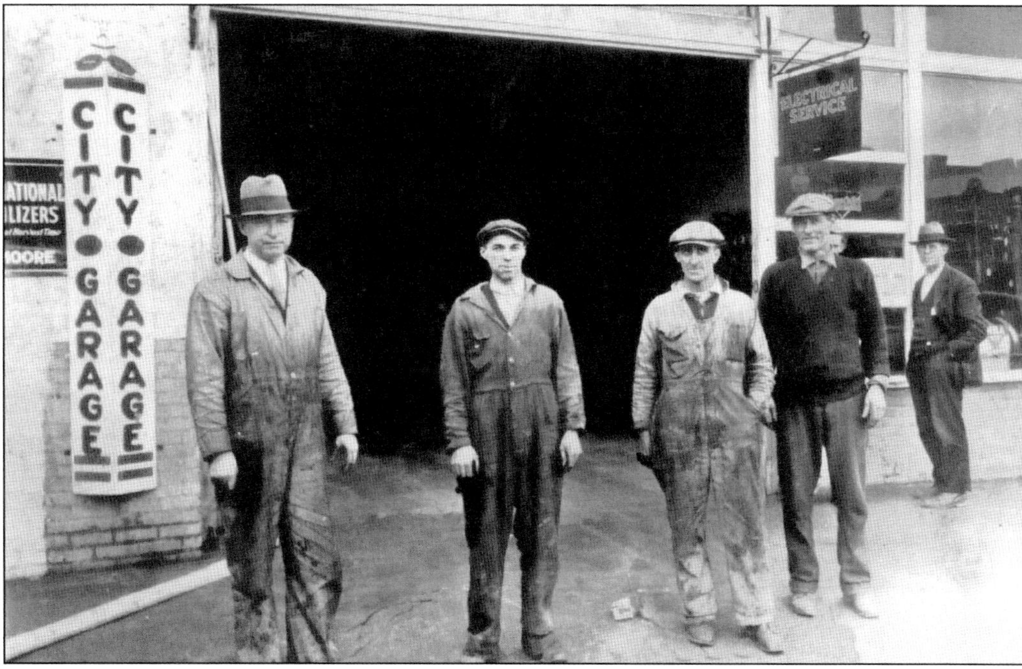

City Garage had both mechanics and body repairman. From left to right are mechanics Tom Still, Walter "Buck" Still, and Dewey "Nemo" Jones; next is Cliff Wallern, who did the bodywork. The bystander in the rear is Howard Myhand, a nearby resident. (Courtesy of Jack Still.)

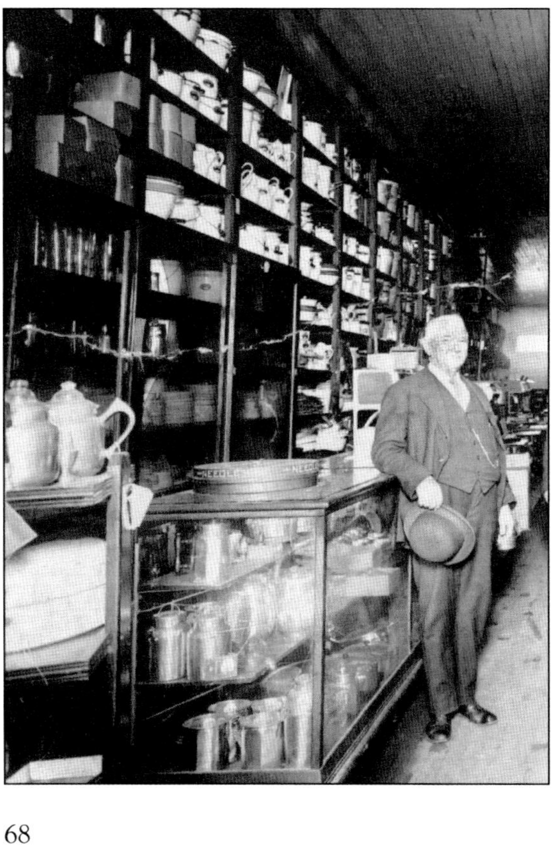

Photographed inside the Handley Hardware store is Dr. W. A. White, whose dental office was located in the building next door, which was occupied by Baker Shoe Shop after 1930, the year of Dr. White's death. The Handley Hardware was purchased by J. P. and Leon Phillips in 1937, shortly after Guy Handley's death, and became Phillips Brothers Hardware. (Courtesy of Mohee Bozeman.)

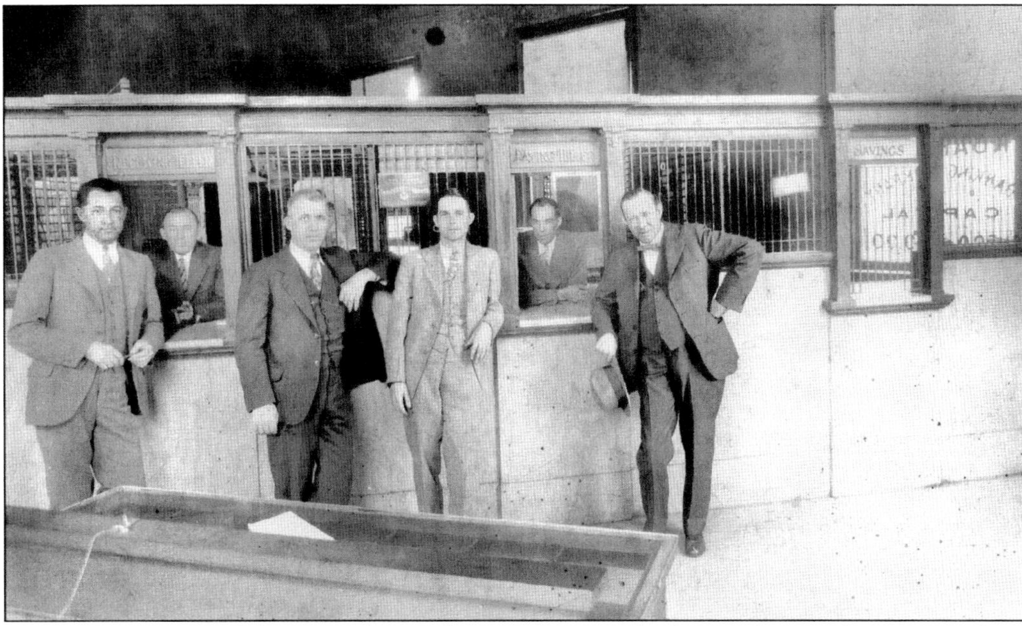

This is the interior of the Roanoke Banking Company, which was chartered in 1906 and was very instrumental in the industrialization and growth of Roanoke and was one of the primary factors in Roanoke becoming the largest city in Randolph County. The marble counter, brass grille, and the decorative finish on the walls indicate its prosperity. The gentleman standing on the left is banking official Tom Still, and the teller on the right is his brother, Walter "Buck" Still. The other gentlemen are unknown. (Courtesy of Jack Still.)

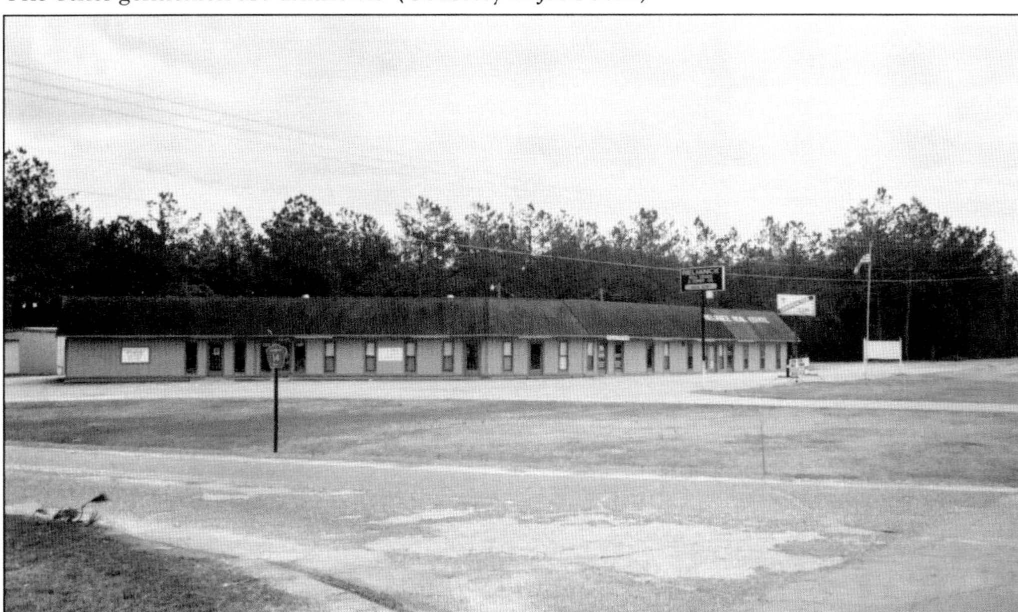

Reliance Real Estate opened for business in 1980 owned and operated by Joe Lambert and Jerome Bowen. Reliance expanded their building in 1986 and housed other businesses such as Dr. Brazeal's Optometrist, Dr. Pacelli's Chiropractic, and Alabama Oxygen and Medical Equipment. (Courtesy of De Lambert.)

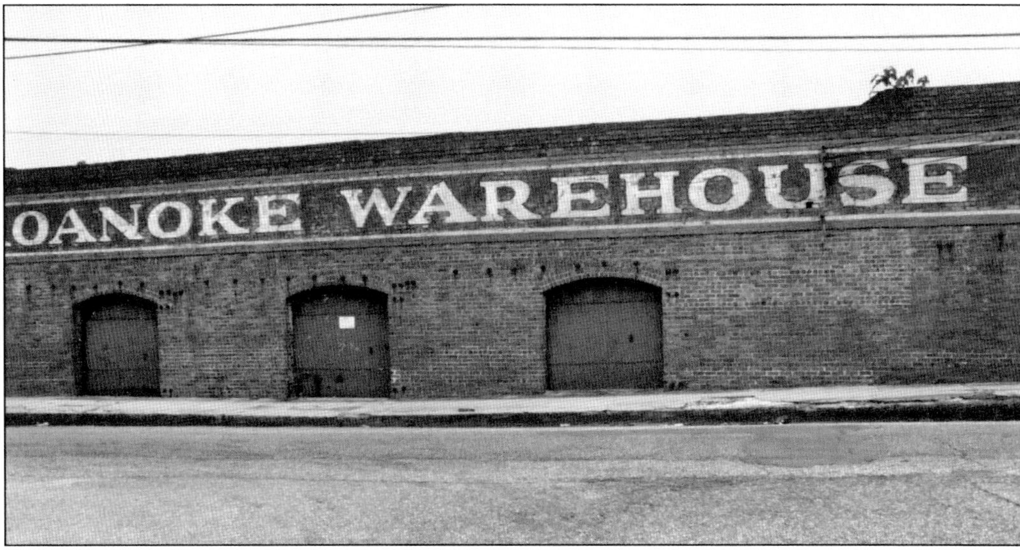

Roanoke Warehouse Company was built by Bedford Ponder *c.* 1908 on Back Street. Roanoke Banking Company purchased it in 1928, and it continued as a cotton warehouse until the 1950s. Master Door Company manufactured doors there during the 1960s and 1970s. Roanoke Manufacturing Company made men's shirts in one section, and Roanoke Material Company made aluminum windows in another section. All companies eventually phased out, leaving the building vacant, and it was demolished. Today Roanoke Justice Center occupies the location. (Courtesy of Helen Blankenship.)

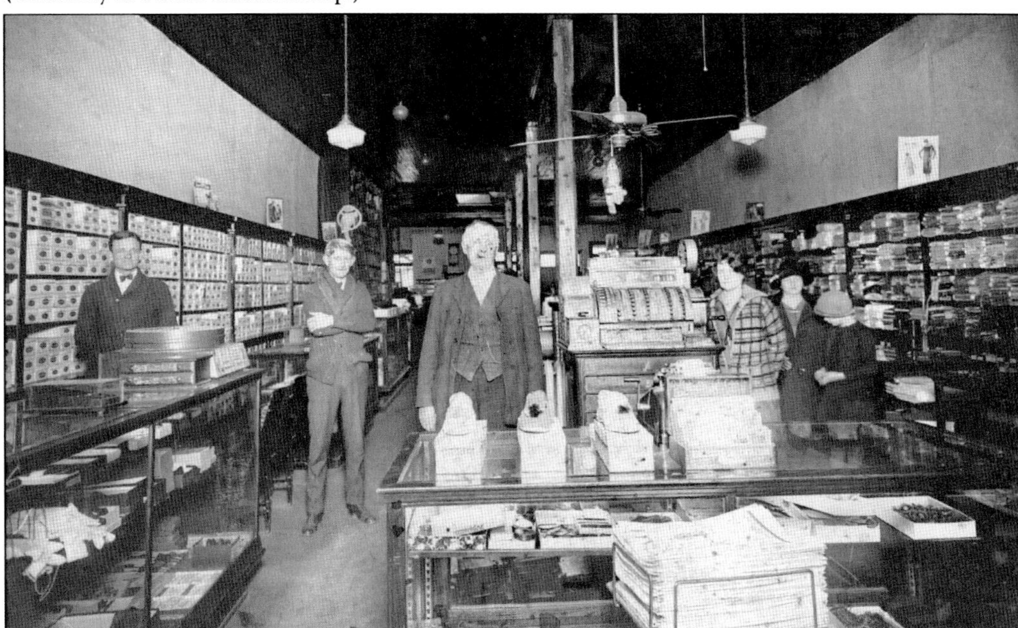

In 1931, retail stores did not have to be large in order for the proprietors to make at least a moderate living. Pictured here is the B. D. and T. L. Awbrey Store, specializing in dry goods and millinery. It was a partnership between two brothers, Ben and Tom Awbrey. Ben Awbrey is standing to the left, and Tom Awbrey is standing in the aisle with arms folded. The older gentleman in the center is their father, J. T. B. Awbrey. (Courtesy of Pat Awbrey.)

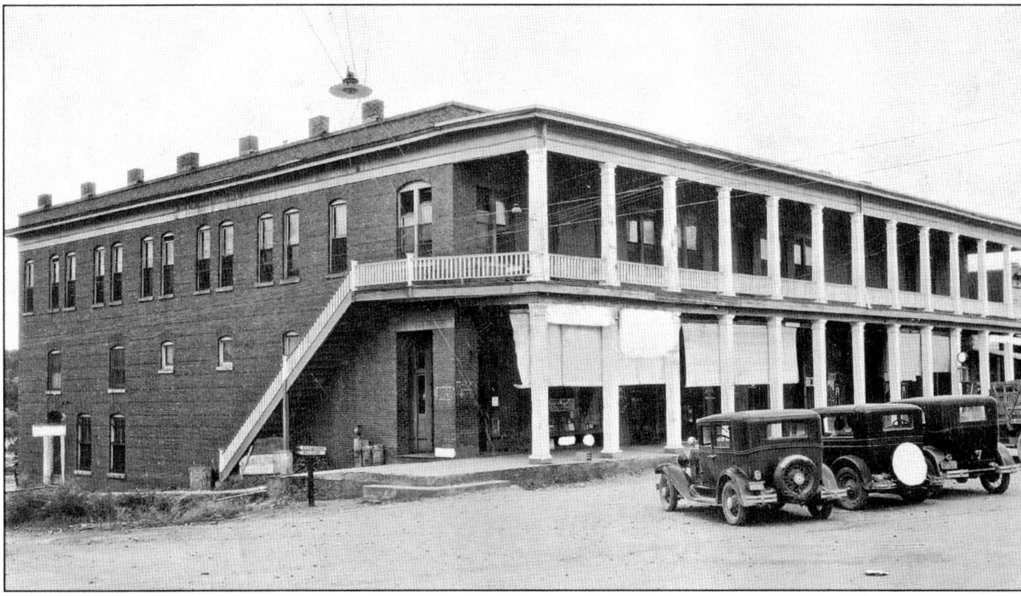

Stewart's Hotel, Wadley's largest building, was housed on the second floor. Carter's Drug Store occupied the corner of the first floor, and the Wadly Post Office was in the rear with its entrance being the white door casing and sign. (Courtesy of Marian Edge.)

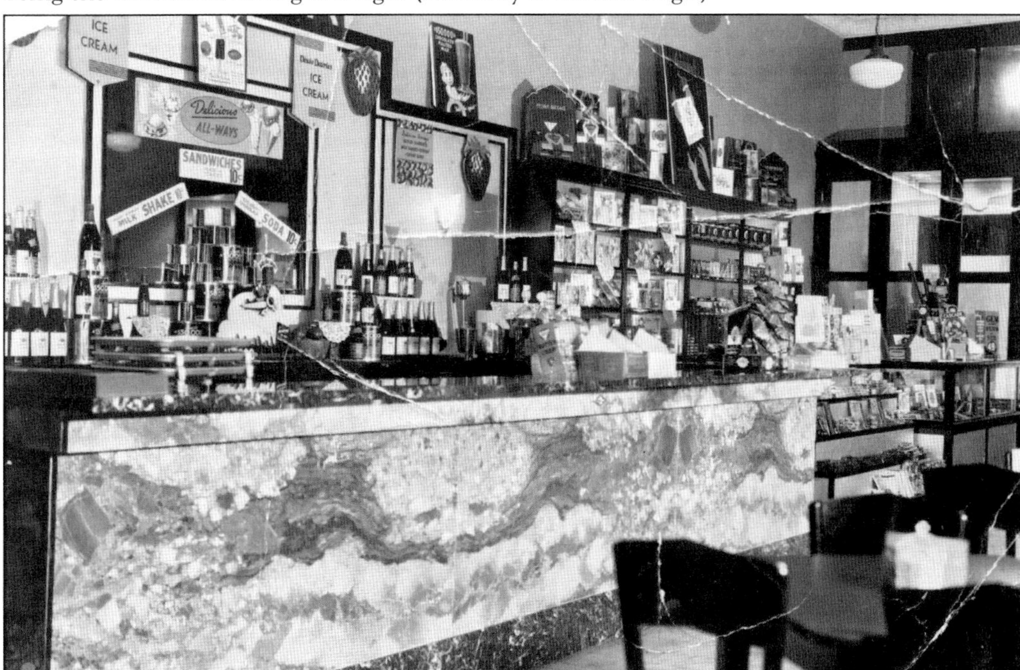

At Roanoke's City Pharmacy, prescriptions were filled by Loyce Harris or Charles Neighbors while patrons ate a lunch consisting of a sandwich and milkshake for 20¢ served by Maybelline Henderson. Children spent their 10¢ allowance on a Cherry Coke from the fountain, and the taste was indescribable. Dr. J. R. Manley had his medical office in the back room. All this was years before the phrase "one-stop shopping center" was considered. (Courtesy of the Randolph County Museum.)

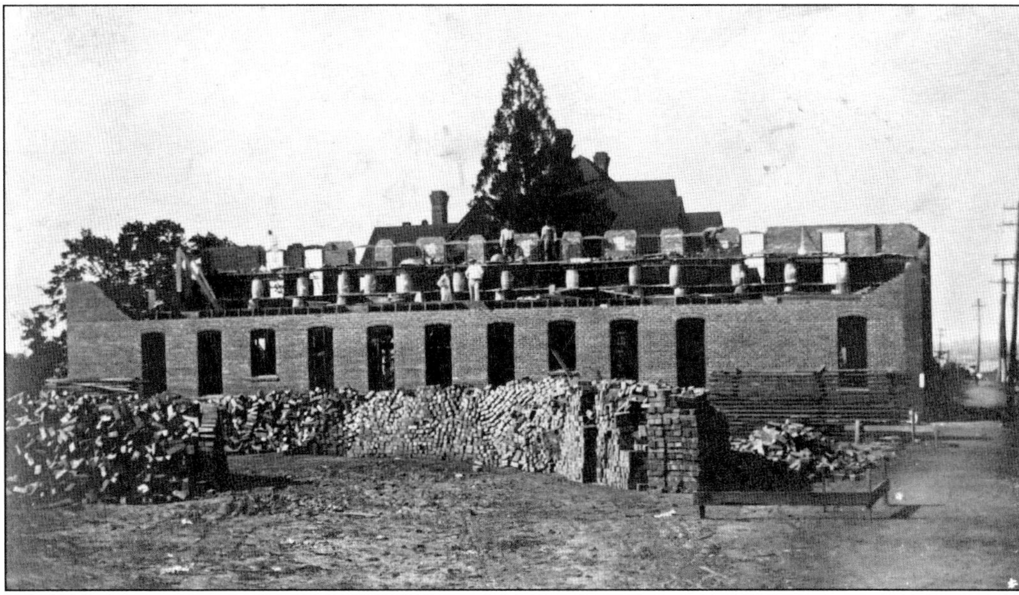

Roanoke's largest and most elaborate hotel was the Bonner Hotel, built for Bob Bonner in 1917. The three-story building was located just a block from the AB&A Depot for easy access for traveling salesmen riding the train to Roanoke. Emil Zobel, a well-known Roanoke architect and builder, designed the building, and Mitchum and Collier were the contractors. Two generations of Bonners operated the hotel. (Courtesy of Jean Windsor.)

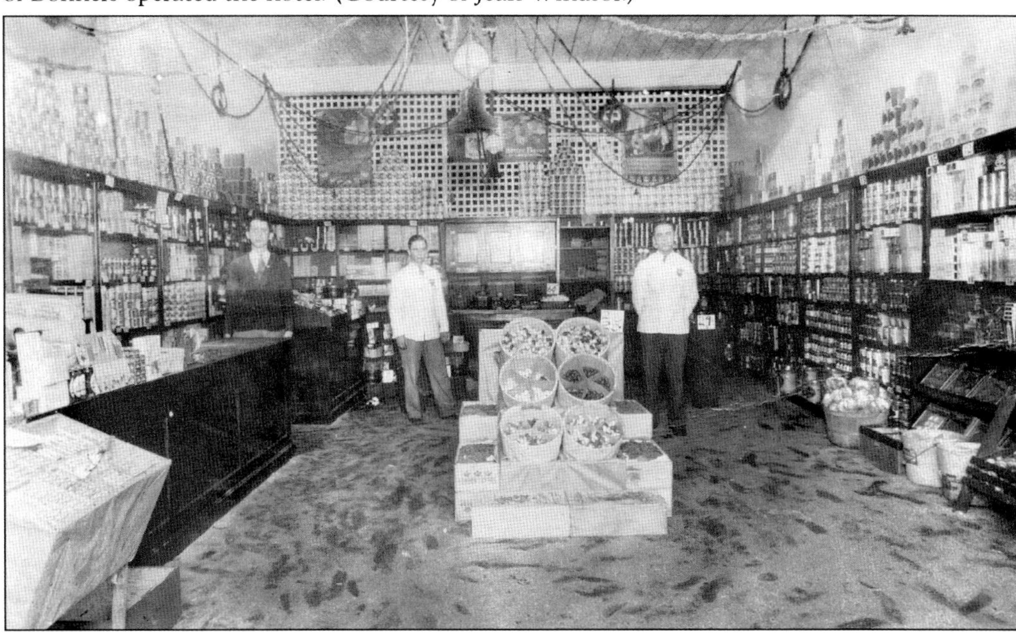

The Great Atlantic and Pacific Tea Company, otherwise known in Roanoke as the A&P Grocery Store, was one of the earliest chain stores to locate a store in Randolph County. This photograph, c. 1935, existed in a day of wood floors when granules of Birdisco Compound, a dust control product, was spread over the floor to keep layers of dust from settling on the produce. Brown Kitchens (right) was manager. Pictured with him are Ezra Williamson and Olin Arnett. (Courtesy of Brown Kilchens Jr.)

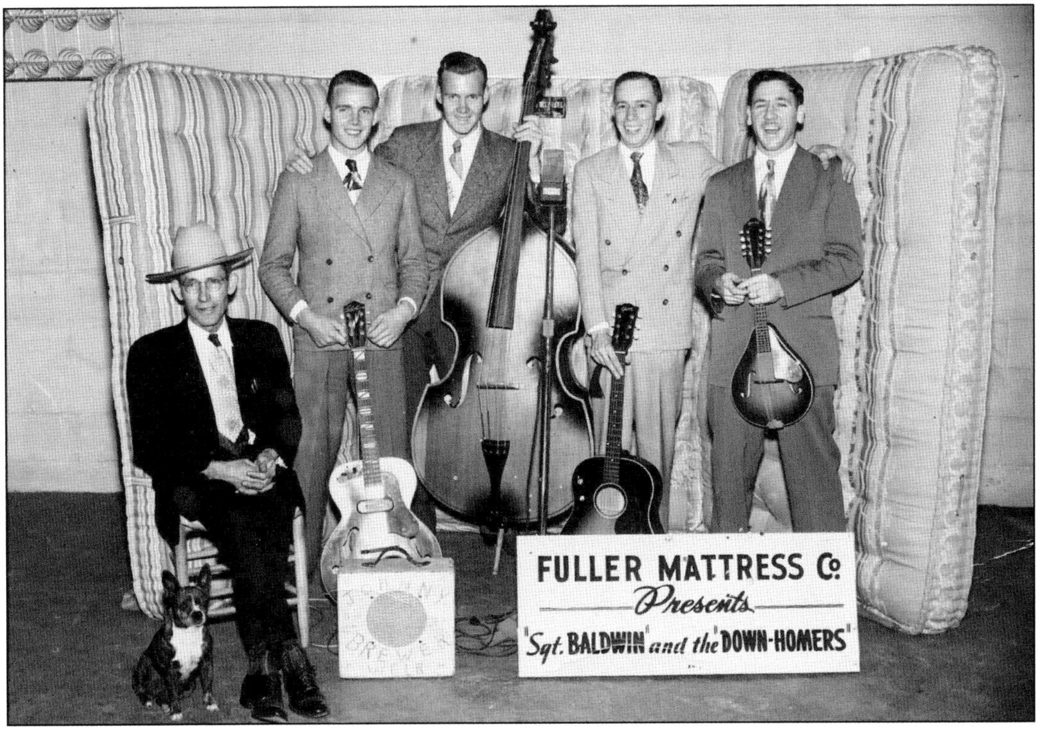

C. D. Fuller, seated, sponsored "Sgt. Baldwin and the Down-Homers" on radio station WELR as advertising for his Fuller Mattress Company in the early 1950s. The band members from left to right are Johnny Brewer, guitar; Gay Brewer, bass; Sergeant Baldwin, guitar; and Chess Robinson, mandolin. (Courtesy of the Brewer family.)

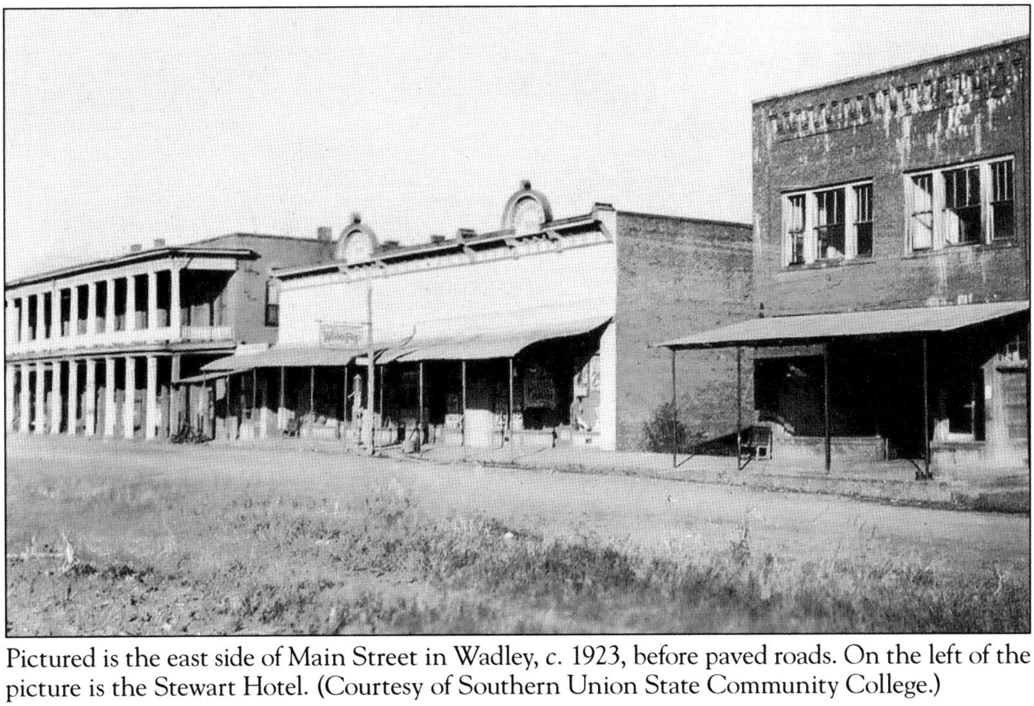

Pictured is the east side of Main Street in Wadley, c. 1923, before paved roads. On the left of the picture is the Stewart Hotel. (Courtesy of Southern Union State Community College.)

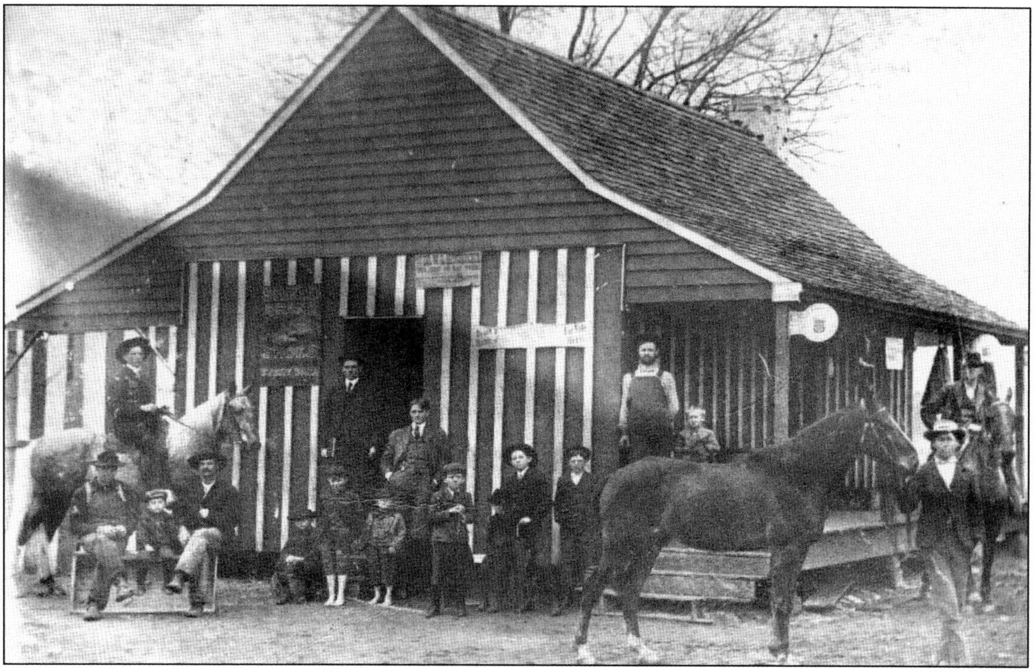

The blacksmith shop was a very important business in the early days. Most farmers had one, and every town had one. This is a picture of the blacksmith shop in Rock Mills in the 19th century. Listed in the business directory of 1887 is the name J. C. Turner, blacksmith. (Courtesy of Harold Breed and Jeff Towler.)

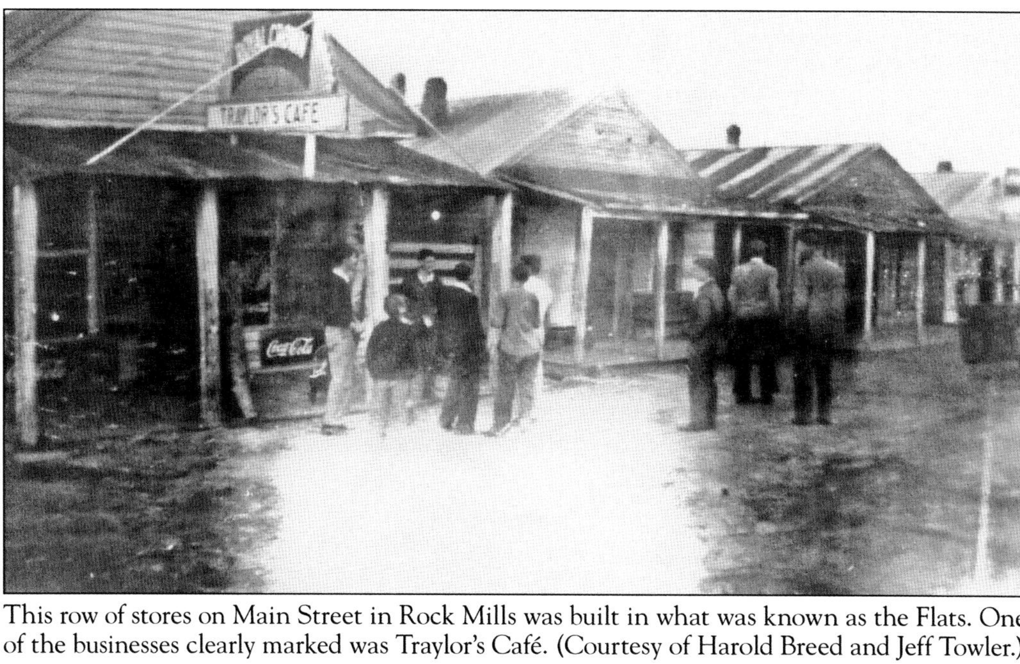

This row of stores on Main Street in Rock Mills was built in what was known as the Flats. One of the businesses clearly marked was Traylor's Café. (Courtesy of Harold Breed and Jeff Towler.)

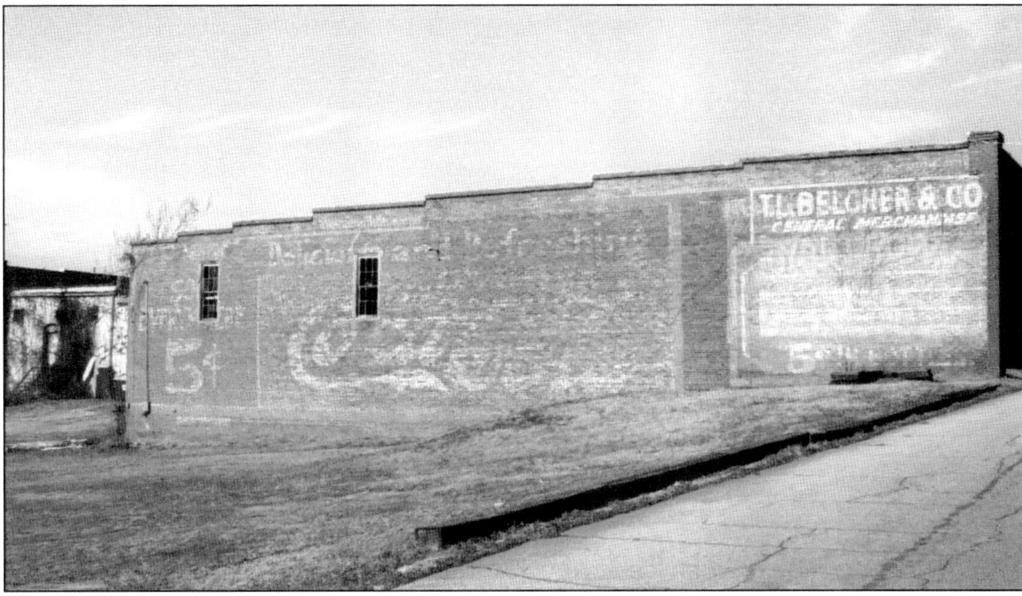

The first Coca-Cola Bottling Company was located in this building facing Church Street at the beginning of the 20th century. Coca-Cola moved to Three Points, and T. L. Belcher operated out of the building, initially retailing primarily farm equipment and supplies. He later moved his business across Main Street, and in January 1901, the City of Roanoke closed all bars and went into the business of selling alcoholic beverages. This building became the dispensary, and J. M. Belcher became the dispenser. Receiving constant criticism from preachers, the dispensary closed in 1907. (Courtesy of Wyner Phillips.)

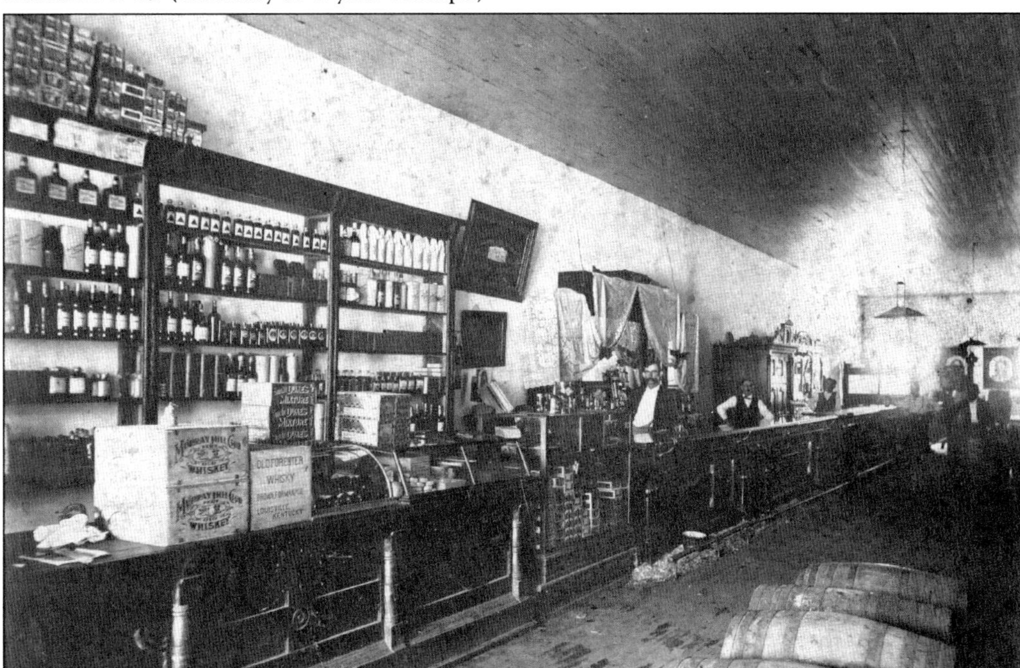

Pictured is the inside of the Roanoke Dispensary operated by Belcher *c.* 1901–1907. (Courtesy of W. T. [Bill] Belcher III.)

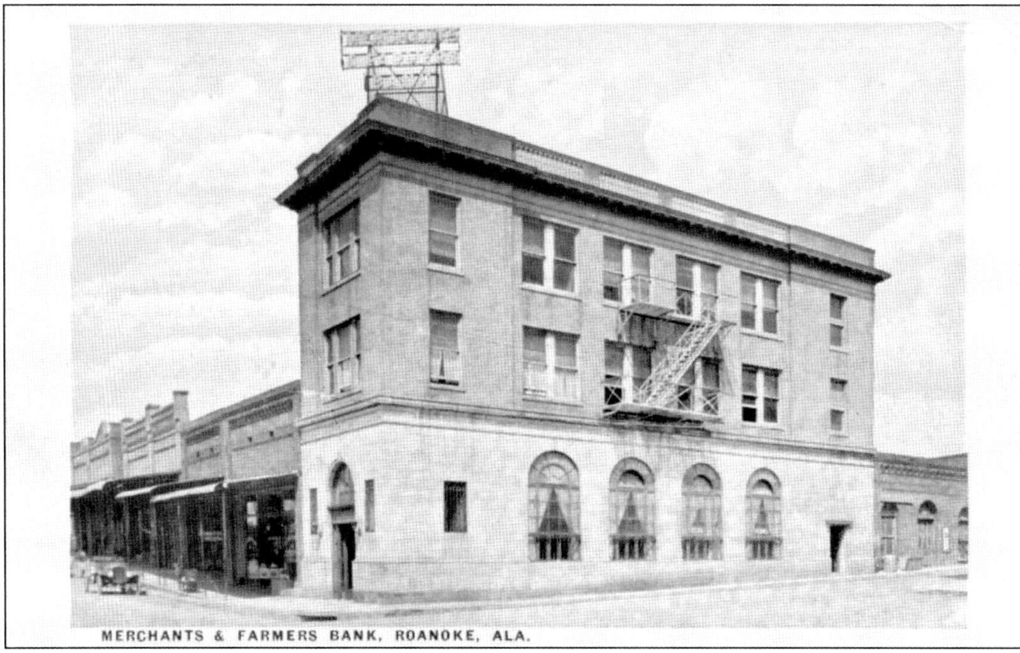

The tallest and most dominant building in downtown Roanoke was the Merchants and Farmers Bank, built *c.* 1920 by R. J. Hooton and organized by R. J. Hooton and Henry Knight. The bank failed during the Great Depression but was reopened as City Bank and Trust Company by Joe Owens, Iverson Wright, and P. J. Hooton and continued operations until it was sold and moved to the new building on East Main Street. It is now known as Wachovia Bank. (Courtesy of Meredith Sears.)

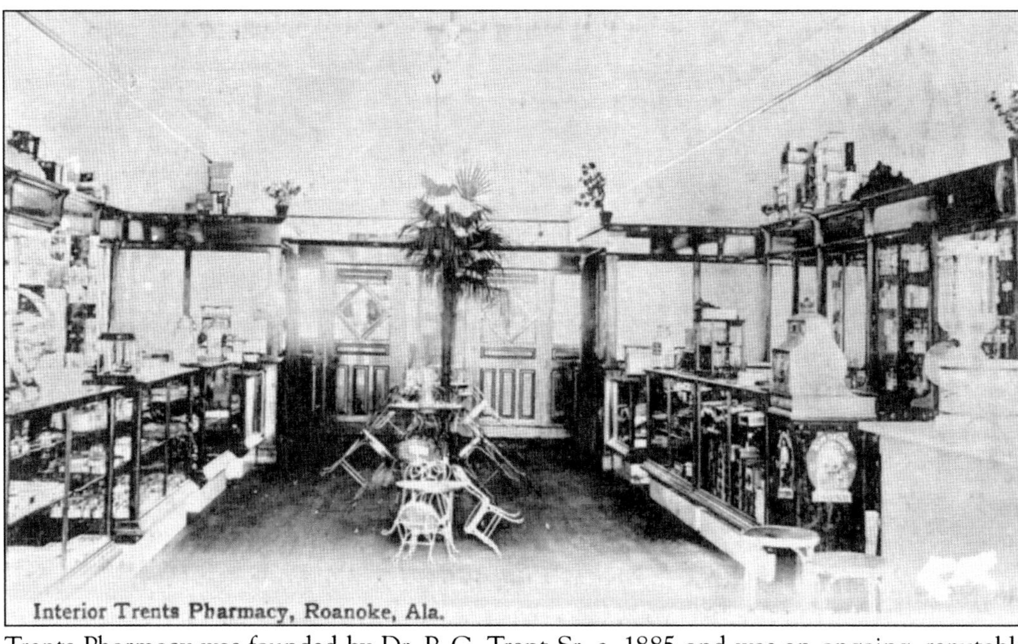

Trents Pharmacy was founded by Dr. P. G. Trent Sr. *c.* 1885 and was an ongoing, reputable Roanoke business for two generations. Many of the photographs were printed in Germany for Trents Pharmacy. (Courtesy of the Randolph County Museum.)

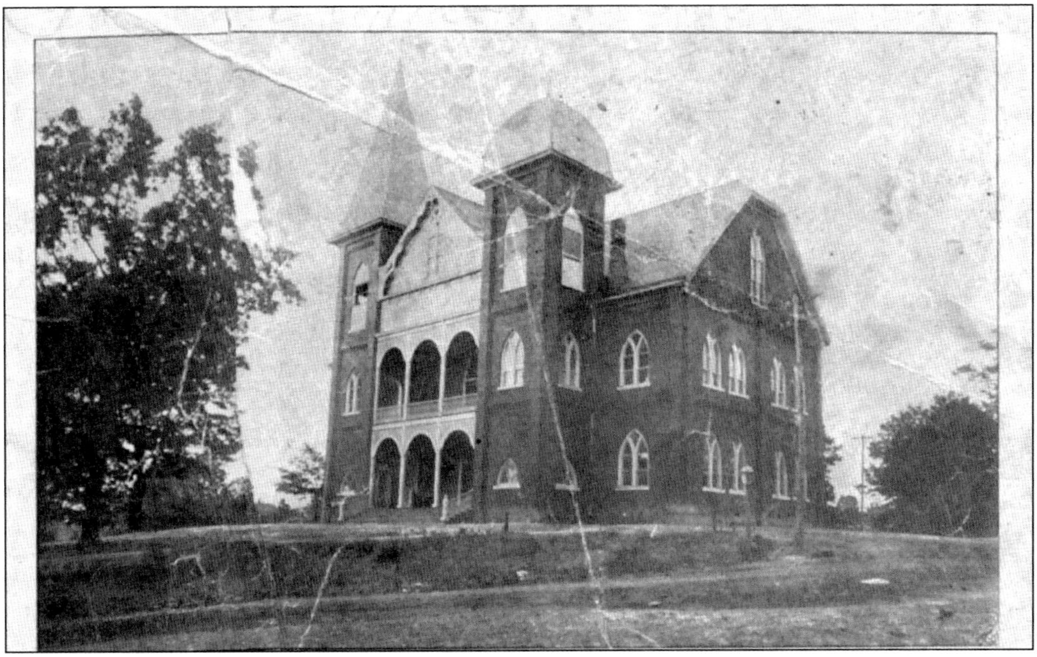

Roanoke's first school of significance was built in 1873–1874 and was named Roanoke Institute. W. A. Handley donated the land, and the building cost $6,500 but was destroyed by fire in 1891. The stockholders of the school rebuilt on the same location and the new building became Roanoke Normal College. It burned in 1923. (Courtesy of the Randolph County Museum.)

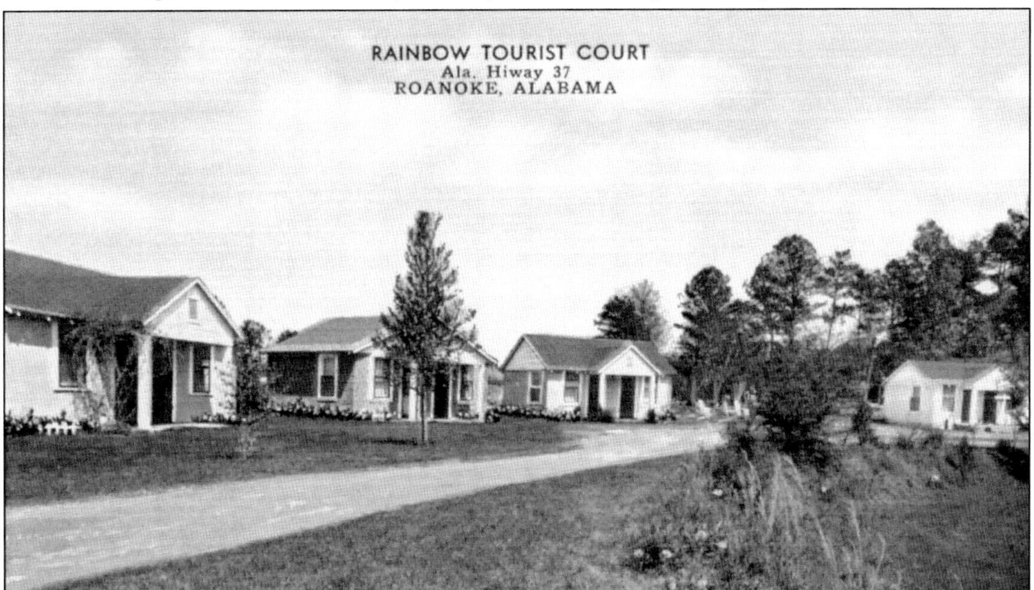

In early the 1950s, Alabama Highway 37 became U.S. Highway 431 and was known as the North–South Fast Route. People from northern states traveling to Florida came through Randolph County, and travelers reaching Roanoke at dusk needed a room to spend the night. New businesses known as tourist courts or motor courts, later combining the words motor and hotel into "motel," sprang up to meet those needs. (Courtesy of Joy Harris.)

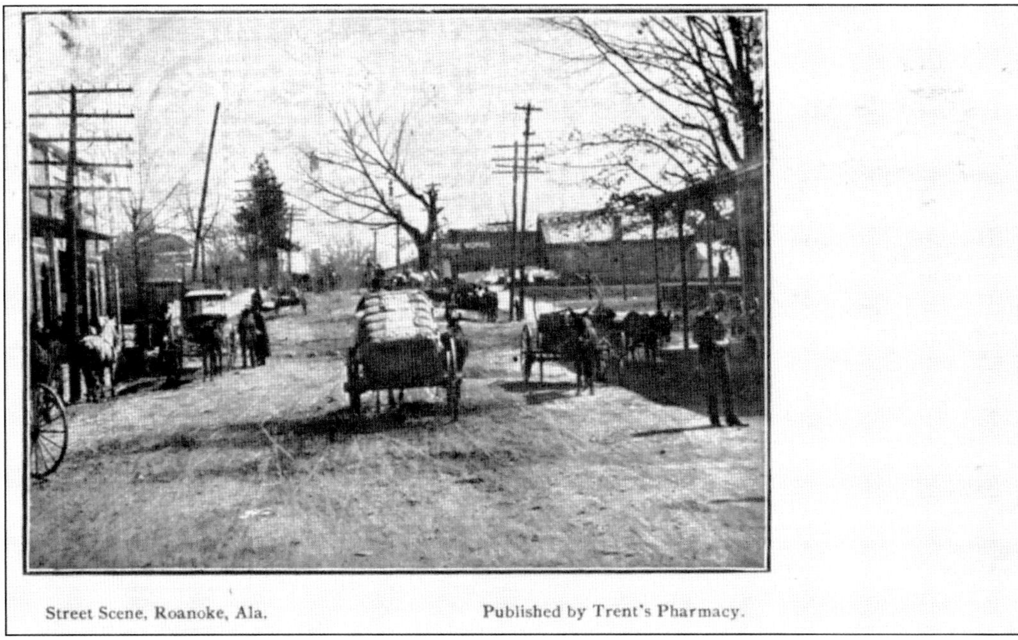

Looking east on Main Street in Roanoke on an autumn day *c.* 1906, the cotton crop is being harvested, ginned, and sent on the way to the Schuessler Warehouse one bale at a time. The street on the right, just past the T. C. Goodwin store building, is Church Street. The next building with the white monuments in front was the Marble Works, and the building on the left was a buggy and harness store. (Courtesy of Jean Windsor.)

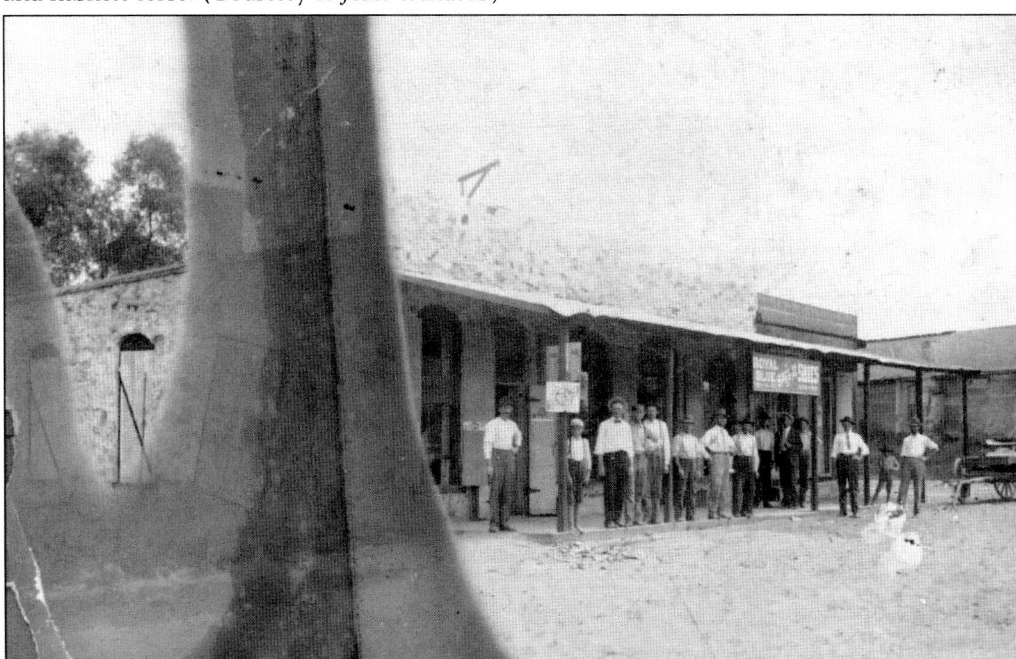

Pictured here is one of the many stores located in what was called the Flats, located in Rock Mills before 1900. The flats were on the left side of the road headed east before the bridge. (Courtesy of Harold Breed and Jeff Towler.)

Employees of Harper's Café on Chestnut Street, Roanoke, c. 1915 are John Rice (left) and Paul Bailey. The Coca-Cola sign indicates that the label on the bottle is paper. Paper labels were discontinued in 1915. Harper's Café closed in 1931. (Courtesy of Nannie Butler.)

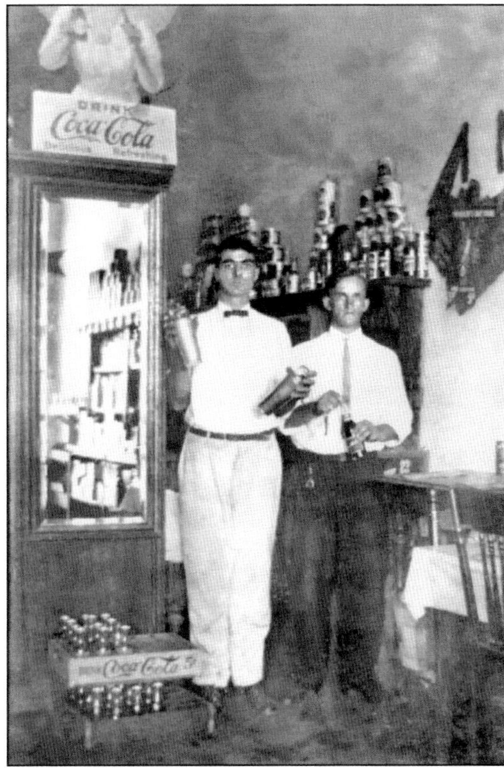

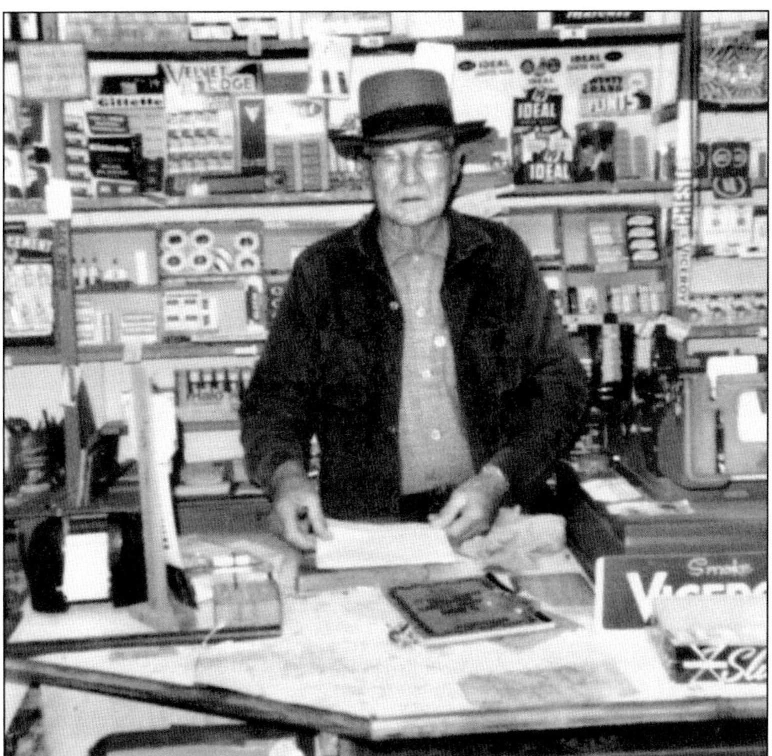

Rice's store on Highway 431 between Roanoke and Rock Stand was established by John Rice after Harper's Café closed in 1931. This photograph gives clear indication that Rice, at 80 years of age, still maintained a neat country store. (Courtesy of Diane Carson.)

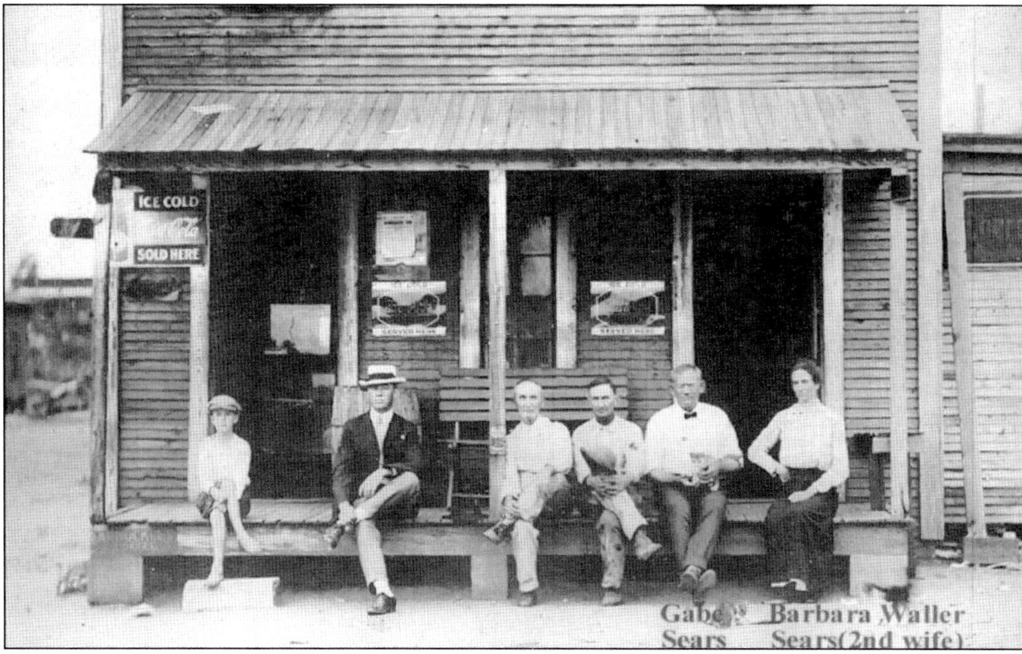

Shown is the Louina Store that was located in the Louina community. Operators of the store were Gabe Sears and his wife, Barbara (sitting on the right of the front porch). (Courtesy of Glover Prescott.)

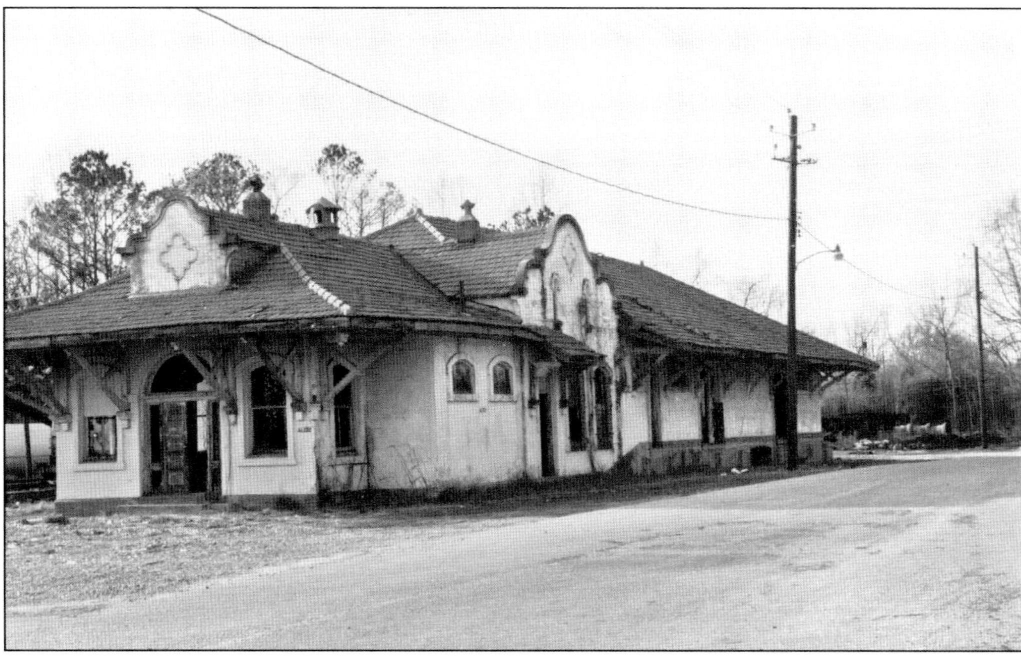

Built in 1907 by the AB&A Railroad, the Roanoke Depot was the destination point for most of Roanoke's incoming merchandise for about 60 years. Passengers boarded here for out-of-town trips for about 40 years. It stands vacant in this 2004 photograph, but the grandiose architecture is reminiscent of the prosperity of former times. The depot was destroyed by fire of unknown origin in July 2006. (Courtesy of Wyner Phillips.)

Five

Groups and People

In the course of history, there have always been individuals who were inspiring, respected, and, in the eyes of constituents, natural-born leaders. Randolph County has had many of those, but one person alone cannot accomplish great things. It is the people who are attracted to this leader, who are initially enthusiastic followers of the leader, who group together to make the ideas of the leader a reality. These people, who often go unnoticed to the historian, we wish to include in our reminiscences.

Recognized leaders deserve special recognition, and many are included in this chapter. It was through their ingenuity and innate abilities that people were led to join together to form organized groups, often to accomplish specific goals, and sometimes to provide services to their fellowman. Group efforts are noteworthy and demand respect for the good things that happen as a result of those efforts.

Individuals make up all kinds of groups: business, social, fraternal, service, educational, or religious. These individuals can never be overlooked because they are the originators of the far-reaching thought. The individual shared that thought and made it grow. He organized the group, and then individuals together worked to accomplish the goals of the initial thought. Such individuals and groups are what made Randolph County the ideal place to spend a lifetime.

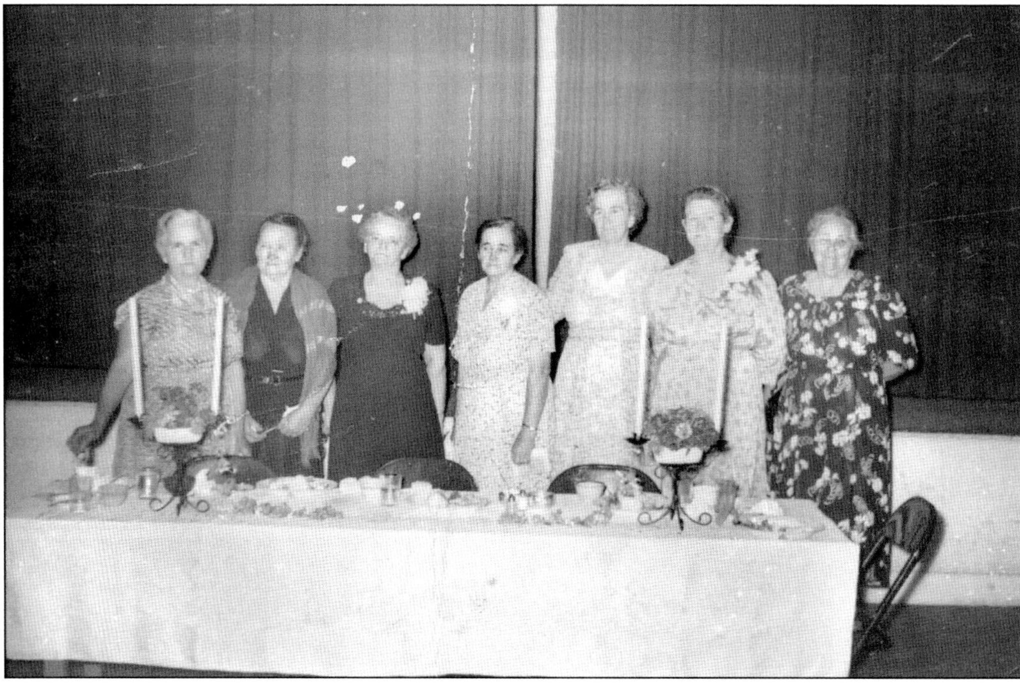

Shown is the Swagg Extension Homemakers' Club in the 1950s. From left to right are Della White, Lemma White, Ida Williamson, Mamie Williamson, Reta Rice, Julia Yarbrough, and Lizzie Bean. (Courtesy of Deborah Gabriel.)

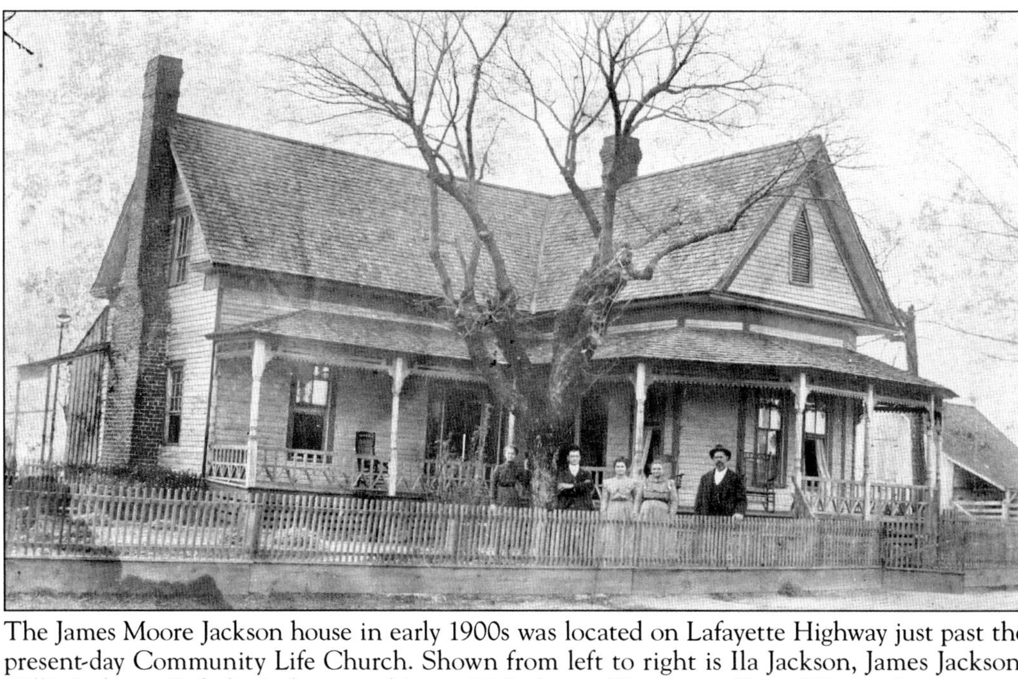

The James Moore Jackson house in early 1900s was located on Lafayette Highway just past the present-day Community Life Church. Shown from left to right is Ila Jackson, James Jackson, Gillie Jackson, Ophelia Jackson, and James M. Jackson. (Courtesy of Jean Windsor.)

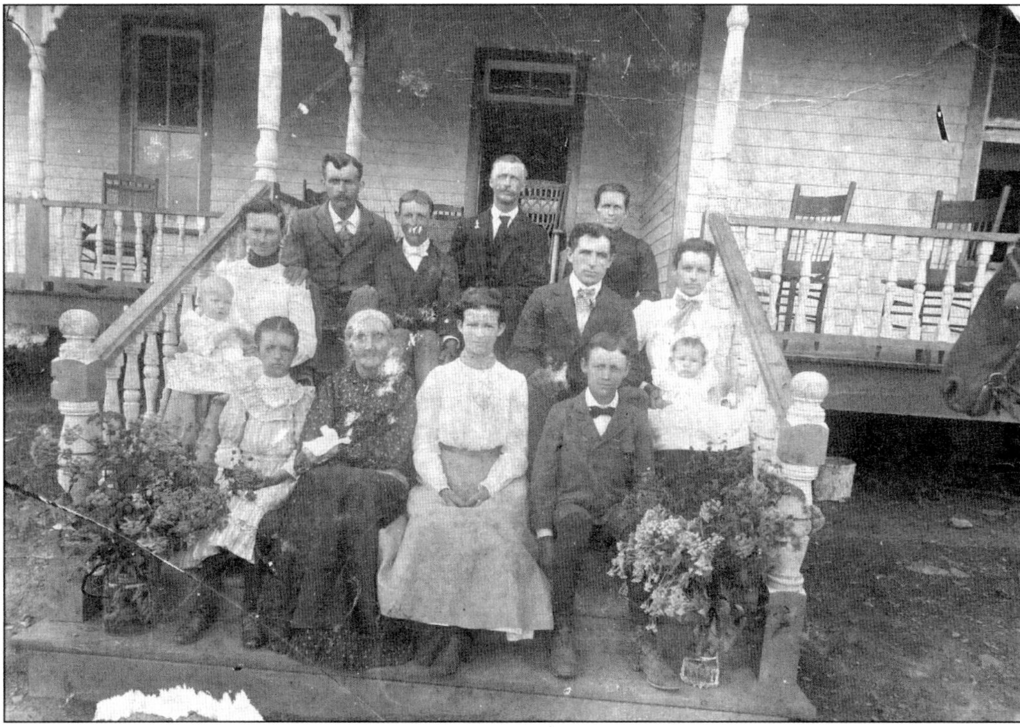

Sitting on the front steps of the B. J. Mitchum home are Doc Caldwell, Carrie Bell, Homer Mitchum, Will Mitchum, Ben Mitchum, Katie Mitchum, George Heard, Frank H. Heard, Allyne H. Traylor, Suzanna Jenkins Meacham, Katie M. Harris, and John Mitchum. (Courtesy of Jean Windsor.)

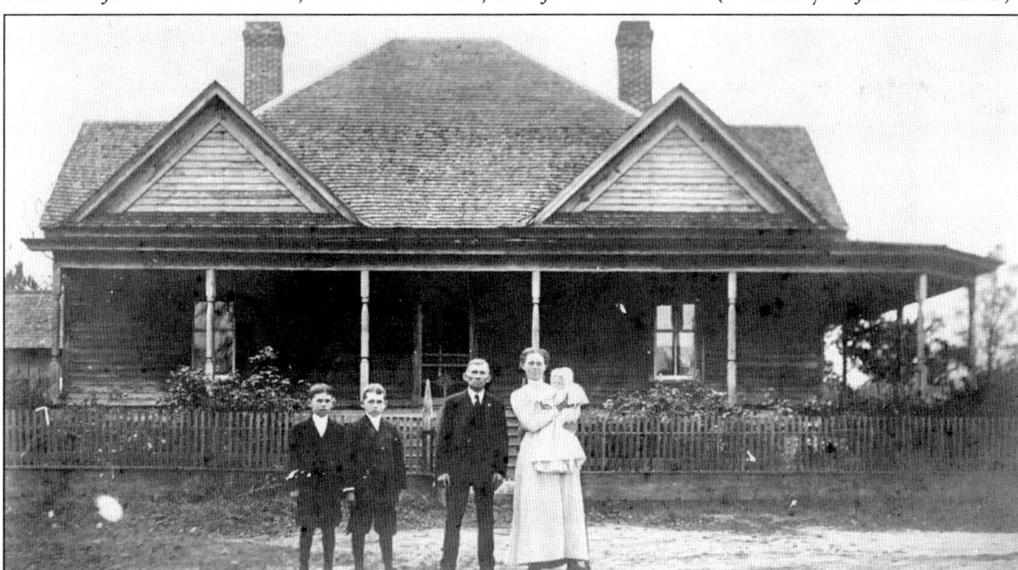

The home of John and Lula Redmond Sledge is located on Country Club Road, Roanoke. John Sledge was the first rural mail carrier from the Roanoke Post Office. From left to right are sons Ernest and Laurene Sledge, John Sledge, and Lula Sledge holding daughter Addie Belle (later Mrs. Mervin Harper). Pictured in 1913, this house has been the home of five generations of the Sledge family. (Courtesy of Thelma Sledge.)

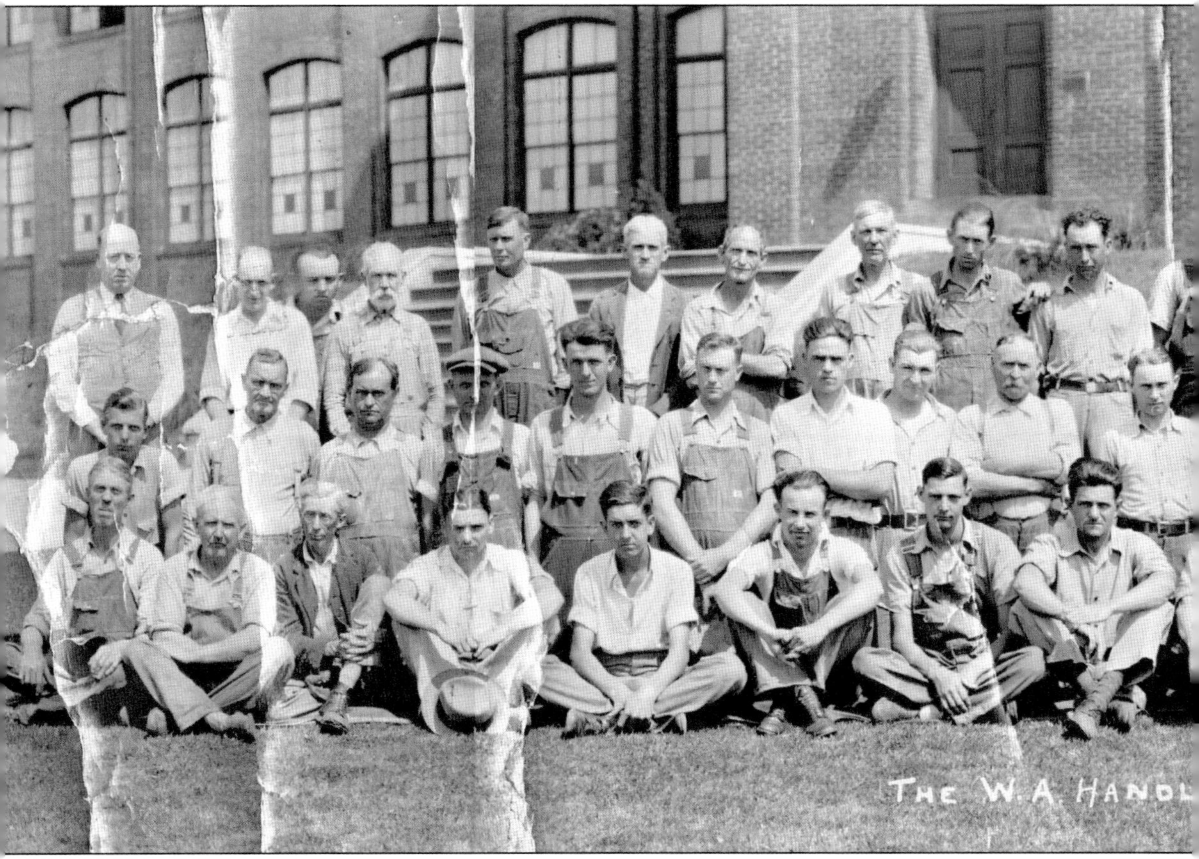

Shown are W. A. Handley Manufacturing Company card room workers in 1933. Pictured are, from left to right, (first row) R. J. Breed, unidentified, Ed Shelnutt, unidentified, Roy Fetner, Denson Sharman, Charles Saith, unidentified, Aaron Whitley, Manse Gray, Wilson Breed, Junior Cook, Hiram Sadler, L. A. McKinnon, Charlie Fetner, unidentified, Joe White, and Garfield Gann; (second row) Elton Breed, Tommy Pollard, unidentified, Burl Ridings, Curtis Fetner, Elton Smith, Hubert Stevens, unidentified, Frank Cole, Charlie Williams, two unidentified,

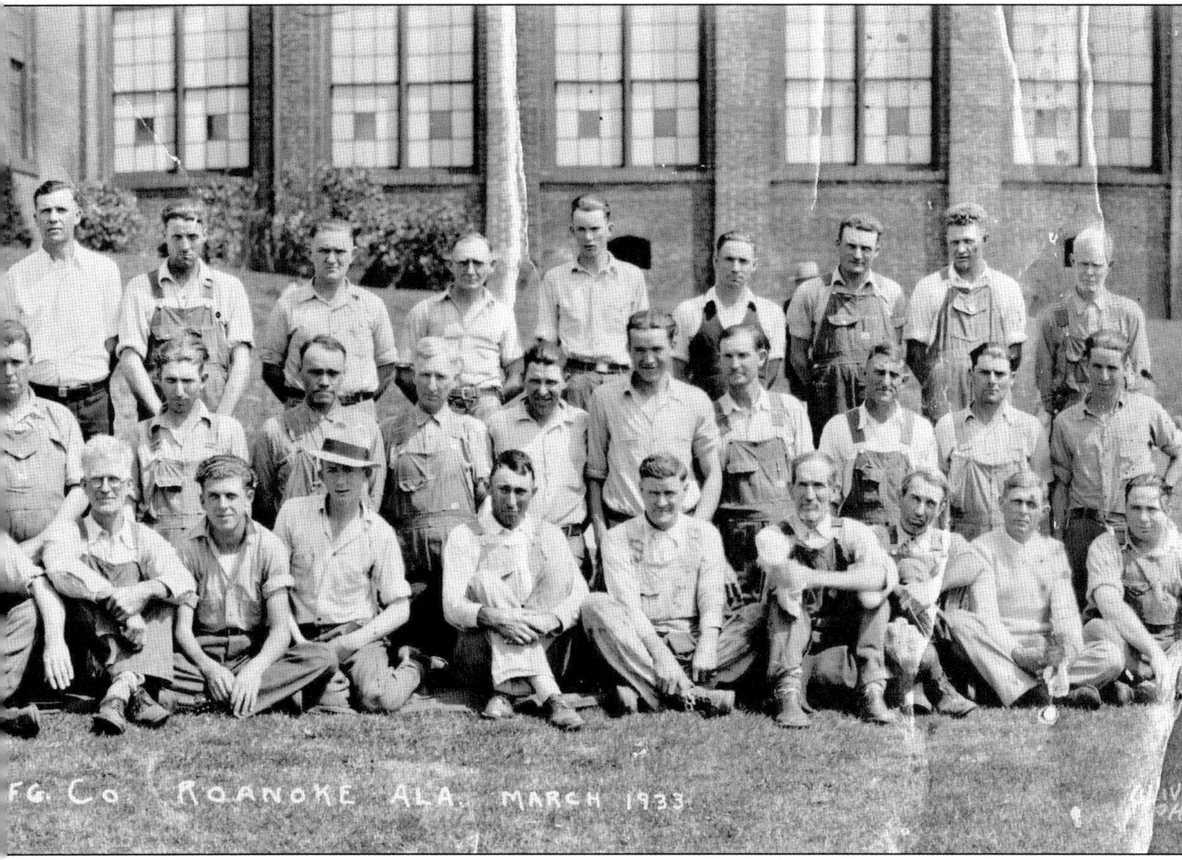

Waymon Adams, Noah Brown, Louis Burgess, Lavert Fetner, Shellie Nolen, W. S. Pike, Joe Sudduth, and Plemer Fetner; (third row) C. G. Bramlett, H. M. Spivey, Bill Garner, unidentified, David McCullough, Johnny Breed, Wyatt Jackson, John White, Reuben Nolen, Lee Garner, Grady George, Harmon Benefield, ? Stillwell, unidentified, Will Bennett, ? Dudley, and four unidentified. (Courtesy of Joseph Gilliland.)

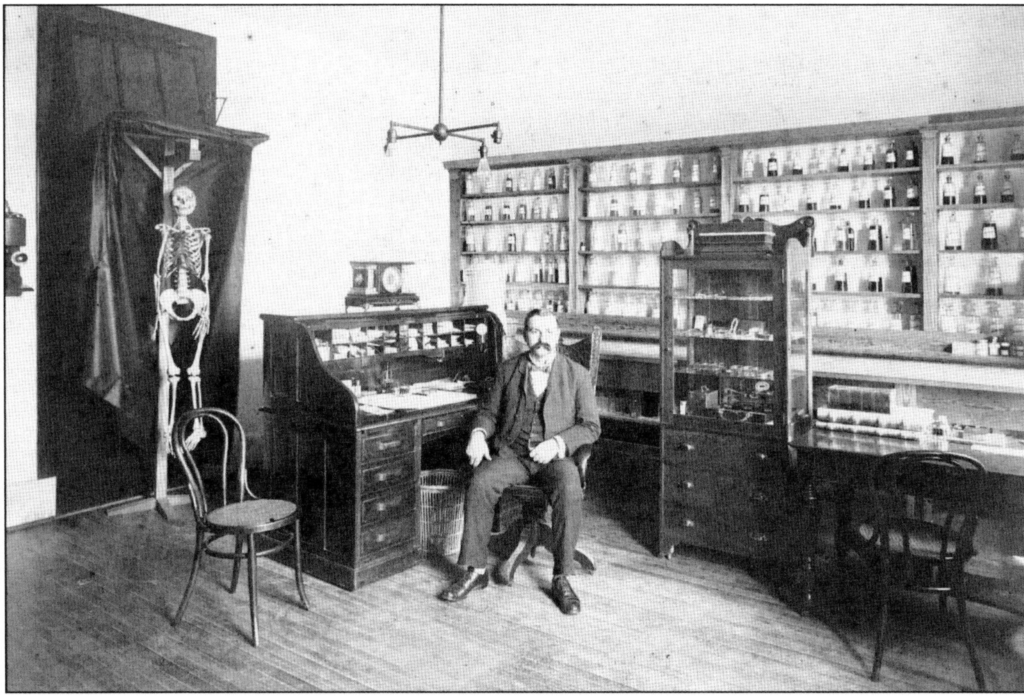

Pictured is Dr. J. C. Swann, M.D., founder of the Bank of Wedowee, in his medical office around 1900. (Courtesy of Glenda Hale.)

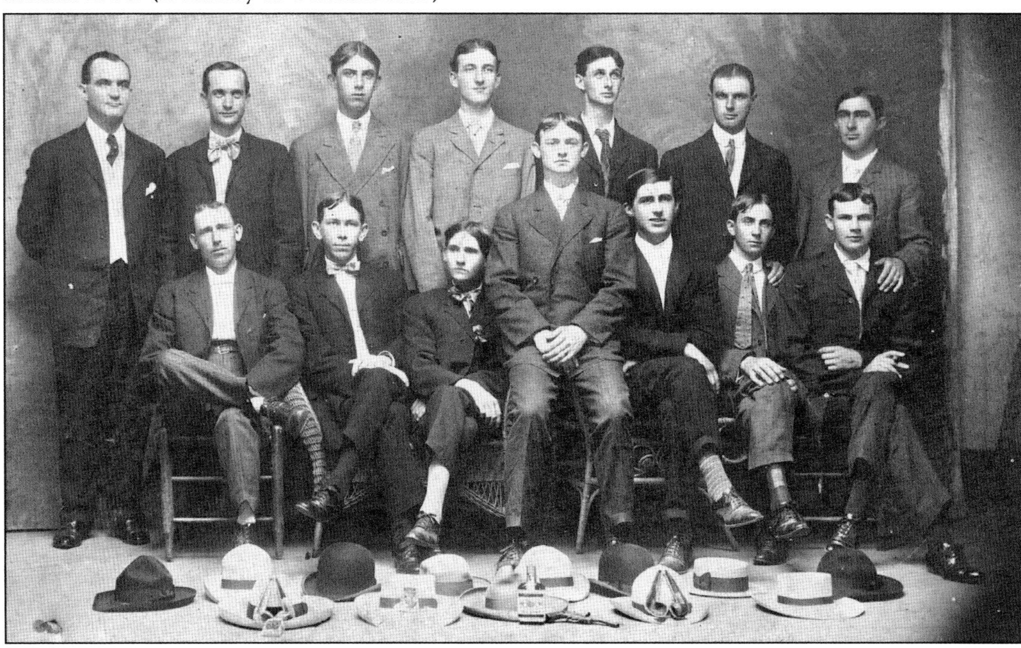

The Roanoke Athletic Club, *c.* 1910, was composed of Roanoke businessmen. They had a gymnasium upstairs in the Awbrey building, generally known as Steinback's. A varied array of hats and personal items are neatly placed on the floor. Among those pictured are, from left to right in the first row, W. E. Corley, unidentified, W. E. McIntosh, B. C. Jones Jr., Frank Manley, and Dr. J. R. Manley. Standing third from left is Ben Handley. (Courtesy of Raymond Hodges.)

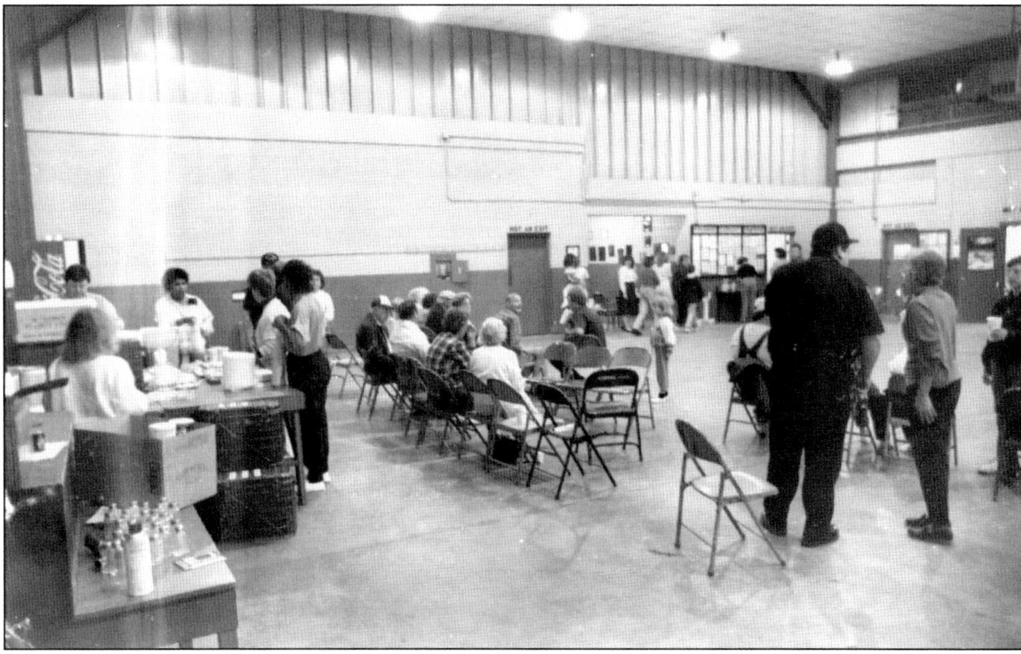

The Randolph County Chapter of American Red Cross was chartered in 1918. For 45 years, from 1958 to her retirement in 2003, Dovie Tobin was chapter manager. She is pictured talking with police officer Wendell Ford on October 16, 1991, providing emergency services at the Roanoke National Guard Armory during a storm when many citizens were forced to evacuate their homes overnight. (Courtesy of the *Randolph Leader*.)

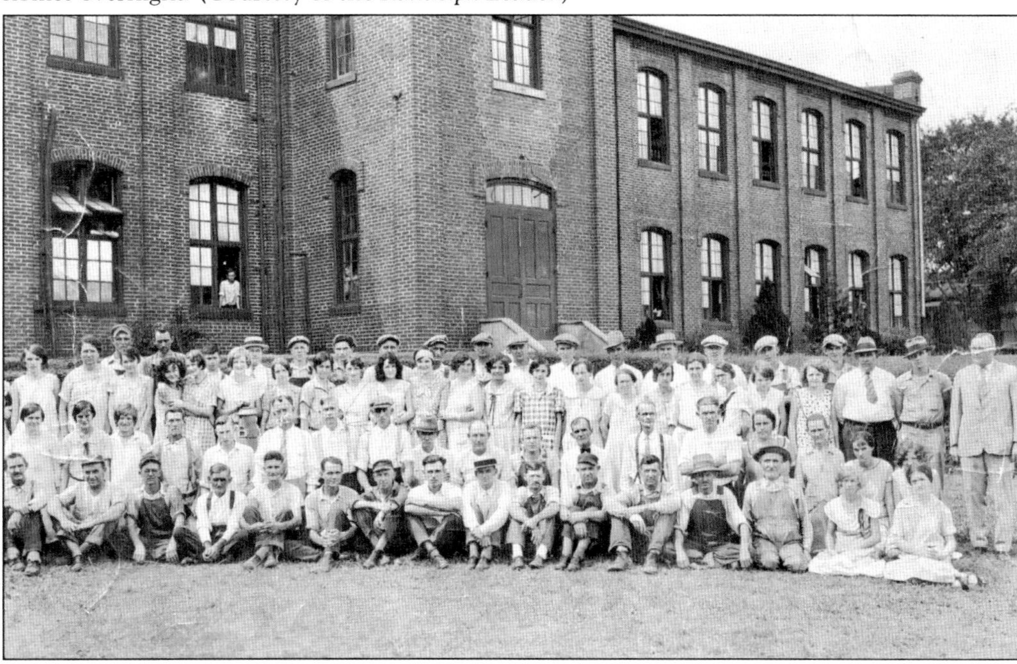

Workers of W. A. Handley Manufacturing Company took a break from their labors and posed for this picture, *c.* 1925. They are on the backside of the mill before the expansion of 1929 covered this spot of ground. (Courtesy of Patricia Cole.)

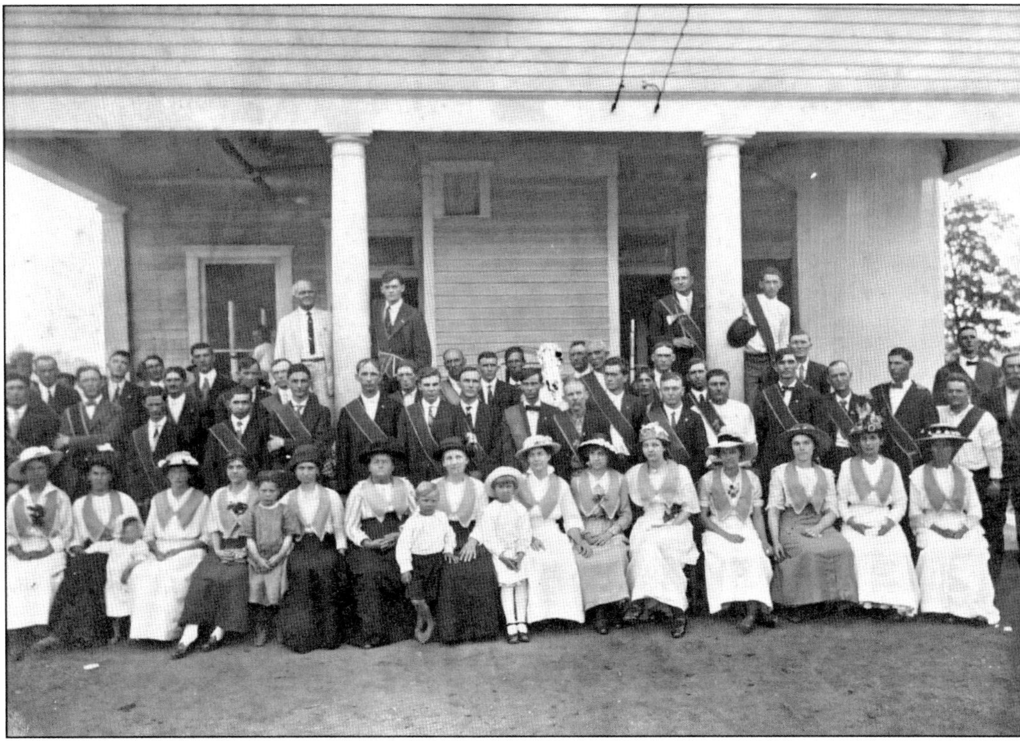

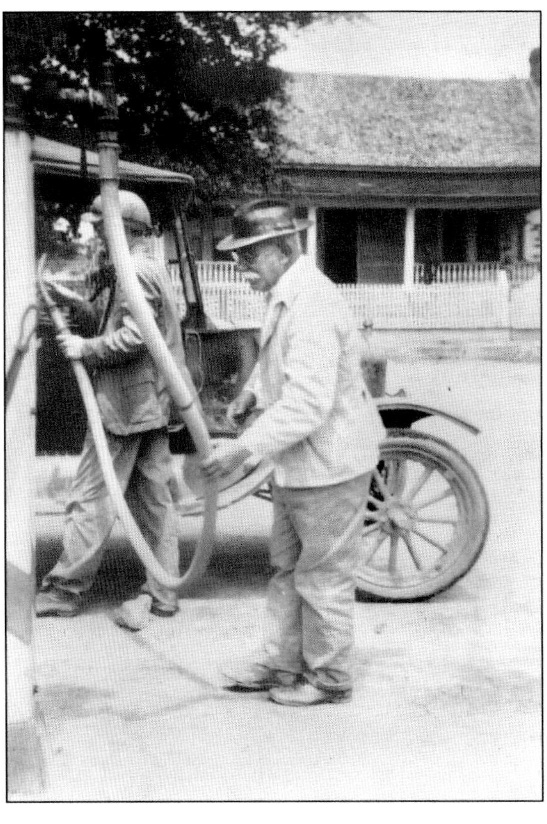

A fraternal organization, the Improved Order of Red Men, was organized in Roanoke January 27, 1905, with 20 original members. Members are pictured here in 1915 at the Lowell community Center on Handley Avenue. The ladies auxiliary was the Degree of Pocahontas. Among the ladies pictured are Annie Mae Philpott, Kathaleen Heard, Hattie Lane Heard, ? Baker, Maggie ?, Mrs. Cliff (Jimmie) Walker, Lola McCarley, Mrs. Carless (Arrie Heard) Griffin, Mrs. Osley (Nora) Cook, Dora Barfield, and Mrs. John L. (Willie) Rice. Among the men pictured are Willie Wilkes, Cliff Walker, Lucius Chase, Robert Riley, Brice Nolen, Patillo Cook, Claudell Riley, Alec A. Cook, John Riley McClendon, Carless Griffin, Ernest Riley, John L. Rice, Nathan Hornsby, Will Yarbrough, Robert Lee Nolen, and Estelle McClendon. (Courtesy of Idus Heard.)

Robert Lee Bradshaw of Bacon Level community is having some gas put into his motorized vehicle, *c.* 1925. (Courtesy of Bob Bradshaw.)

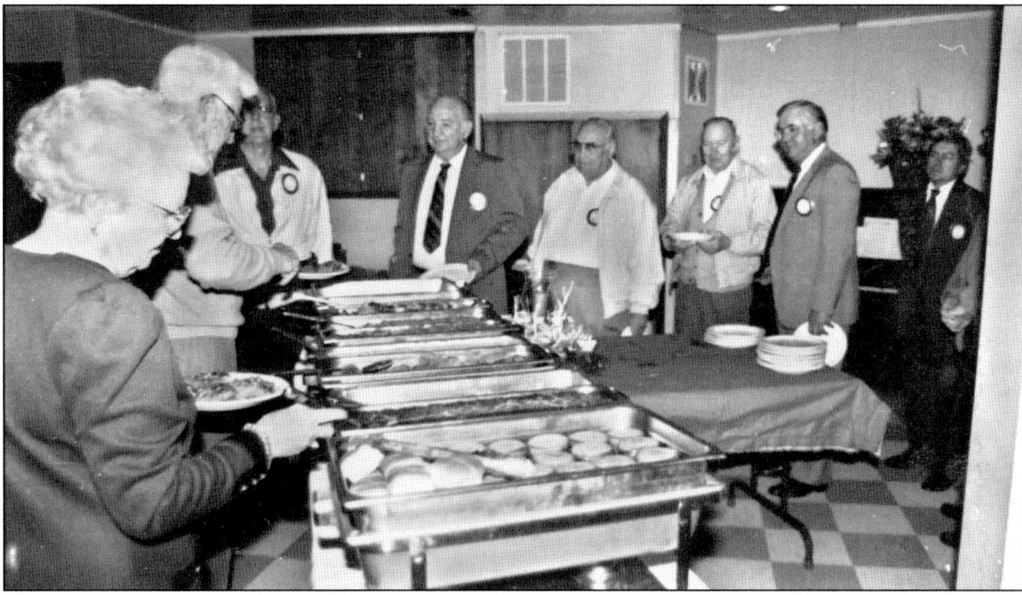

Roanoke has had an active Rotary Club for approximately 65 years. The club has always met Thursday at noon initially at the Bonner Hotel, until its restaurant closed, then the City Café, until it closed, and now at the Galley. This photograph of December 26, 1990, shows, from left to right, members John Effie Tate, Dr. John Tate, Bill Davis, unidentified out-of-town guest, J. Thomas Landers, J. P. Phillips, Ralph Watkins, and Harold Heard at the City Café. (Courtesy of the *Randolph Leader*.)

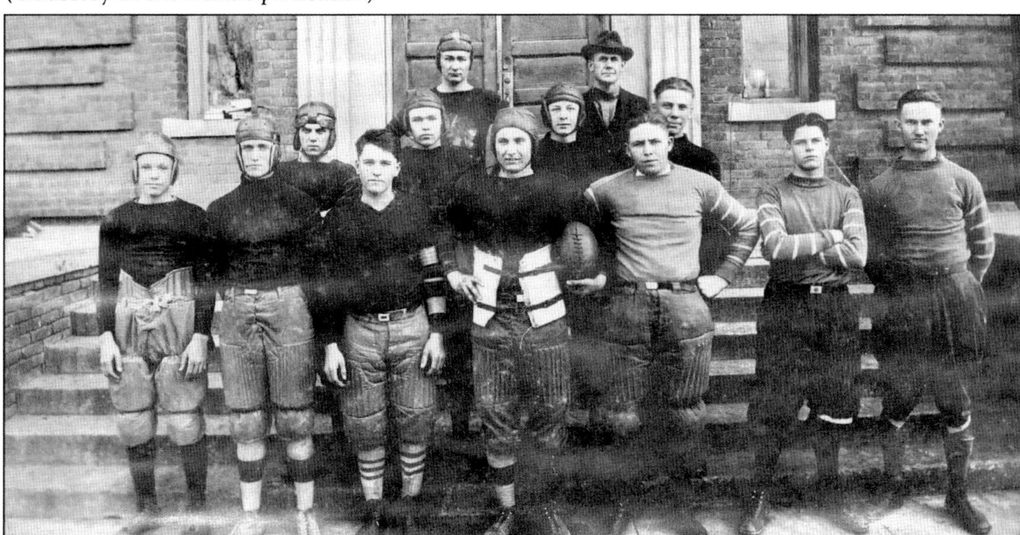

Handley High's first football team, 1921–1922, was undefeated, winning both games under the leadership of Coach George Yarbrough. The roster was Floyd Brown (left end), Charles White (right guard), Walter Culp (left guard), J. C. Fincher (left tackle), Roby Buckalew (quarterback), Heyman Enloe (center), Lewis Yates (full back and captain), Ward Mooty (half back), Cofield Widner (right-guard), Sam Enloe (half back), Henry Hudson (right tackle), and Iverson Wright (right end). That is 11 on the field and one on the bench waiting his turn to substitute. (Courtesy of the Randolph County Museum.)

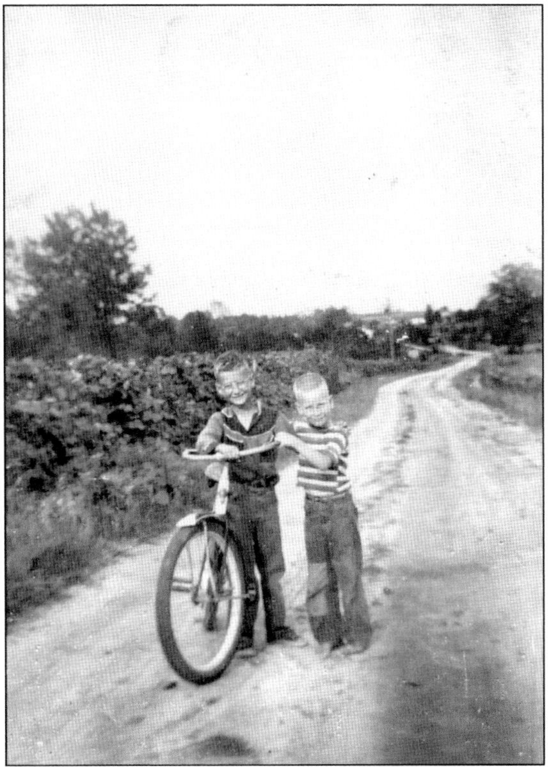

Two brothers, one bicycle! The mid-1950s was a time when siblings shared, whether that was their choice or not, sometime because one bicycle was all there was. Holding the bike is Ralph Wilder and wanting to hold the bike is younger brother, Warren Wilder, sons of Reuben E. Wilder and Vera Carson Wilder. (Courtesy of Warren Wilder.)

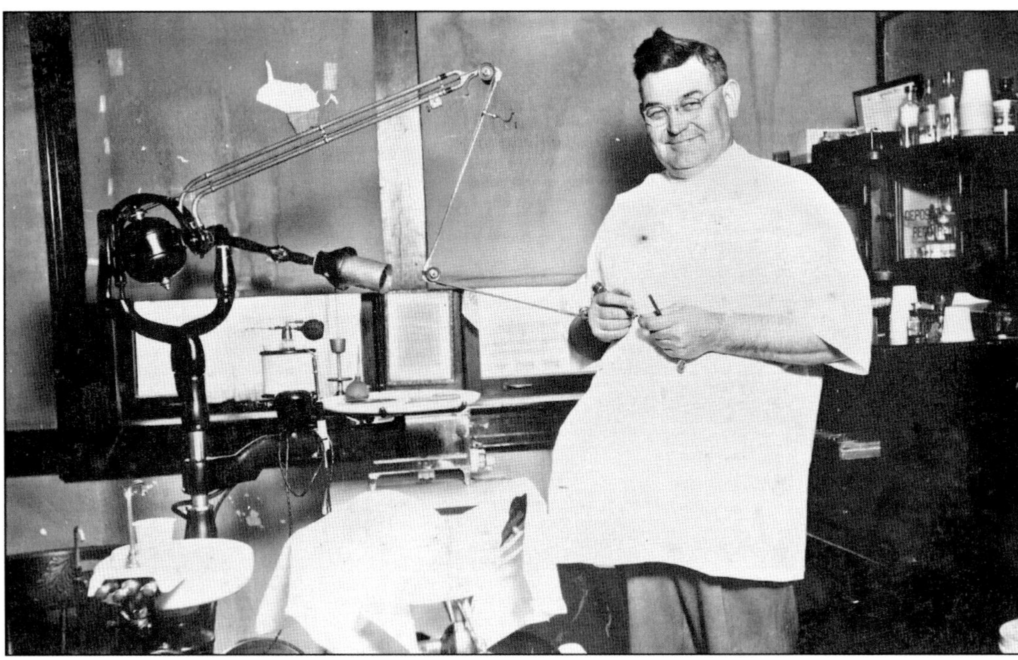

Dr. W. B. Ford, dentist, is pictured in his office on the second floor of City Bank and Trust Company building, *c.* 1945. Around 1950, he moved his office to the Ella Smith house on the corner of East Main and Vaughn Street. Dr. Ford was Roanoke's mayor for two terms during the 1940s. (Courtesy of Robert Ford.)

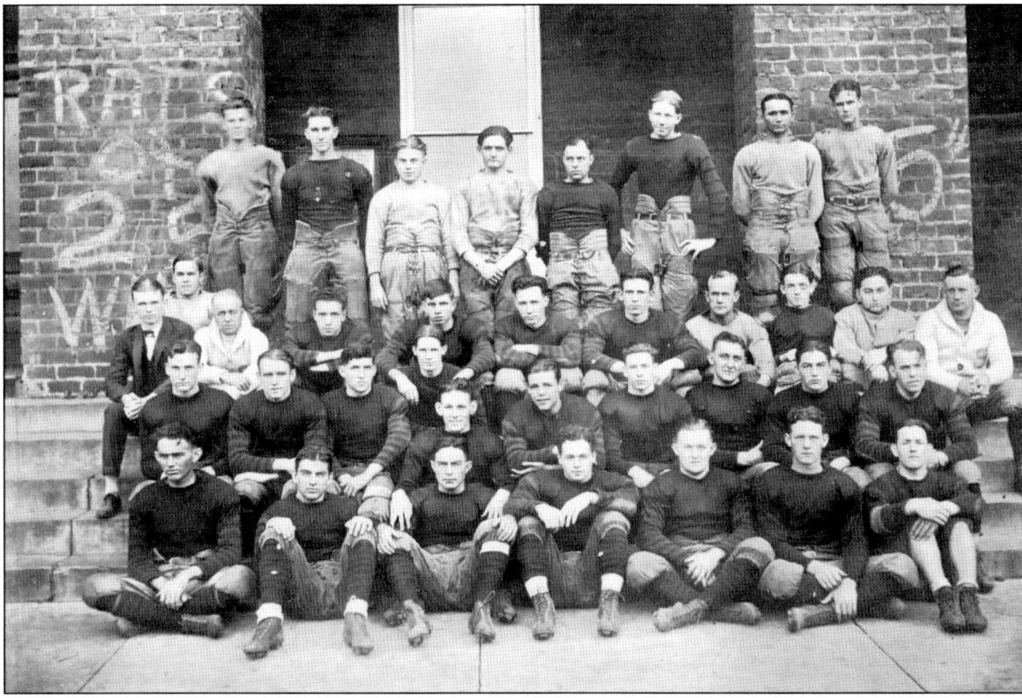

Shown is the football team of Randolph County High School in Wedowee, c. 1925. (Courtesy of Dwayne Pate.)

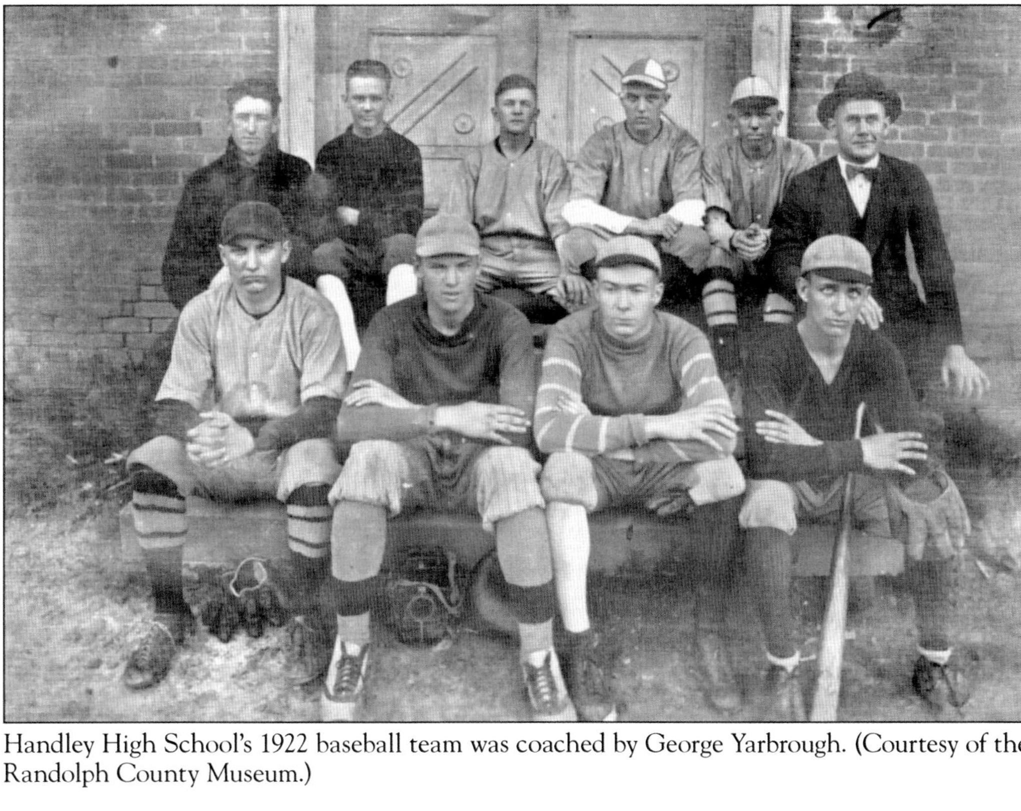

Handley High School's 1922 baseball team was coached by George Yarbrough. (Courtesy of the Randolph County Museum.)

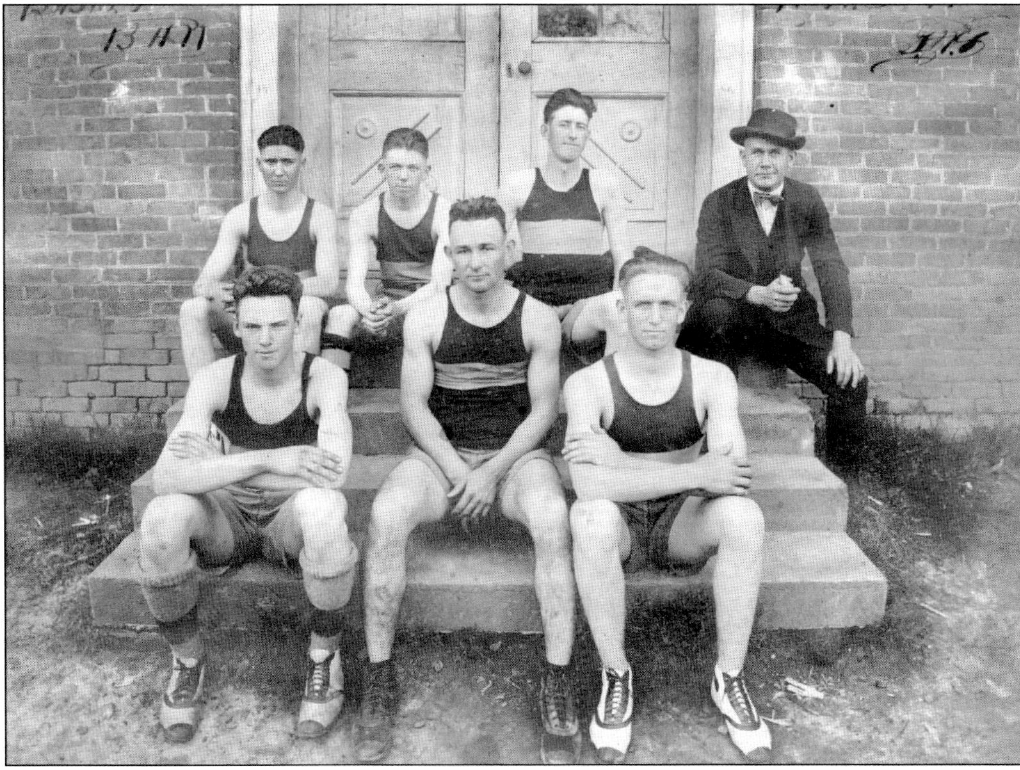

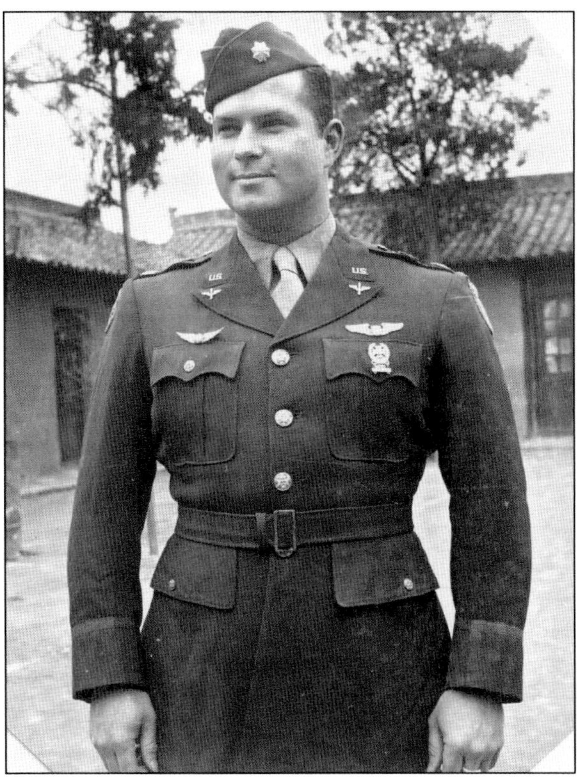

Handley High's basketball team of 1921–1922 was coached by George Yarbrough, and had one substitute. The only identified player is Hugh Stevenson, middle of back row, who later became Handley's coach and coached an undefeated football team that won the state championship. (Courtesy of the Randolph County Museum.)

Maj. Raymond Hodges, commanding officer of the 1st Bomb Squadron, Chinese American Composite Wing, and test pilot, Air Force Proving Ground, Eglin Field, Florida, flew 61 combat missions in China and Burma during World War II. He was awarded the Chinese Silver Star, three Distinguished Flying Crosses, two Air Medals, and the Chiang Kai-Shek Medal. (Courtesy of Raymond Hodges.)

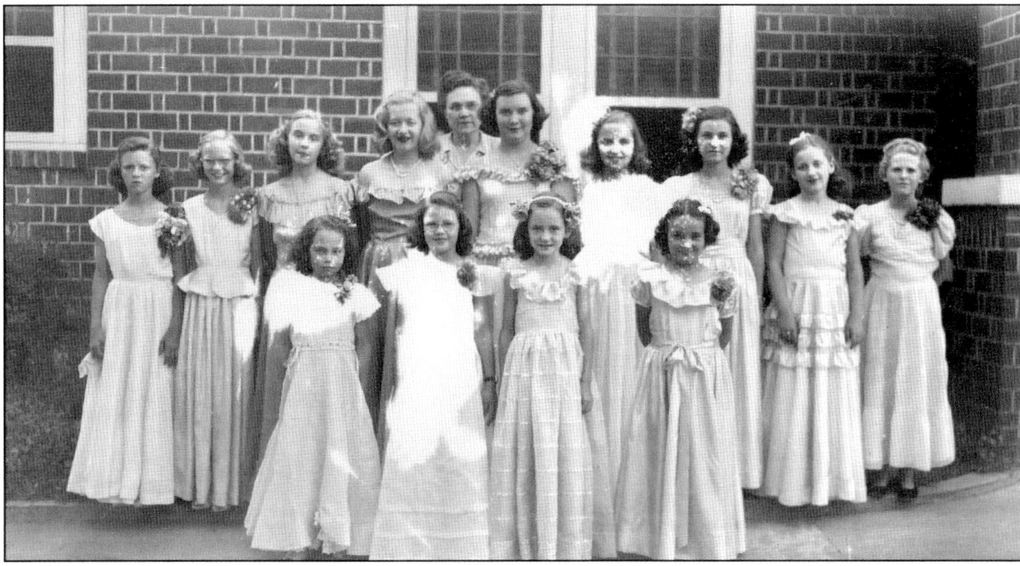

Mrs. Homer Howell's piano students are dressed for recital, *c.* 1948. Among those pictured are Lou Ellen Hearn, Jane Huey, Glenda Griffin, Janie Jordan, Eddie Brown, Ann Moon, Cornelia Wright, Harriett Huey, Mrs. Howell, Gwen Cook, Nancy Huey, and Carolyn Knight. (Courtesy of Gerald Knight.)

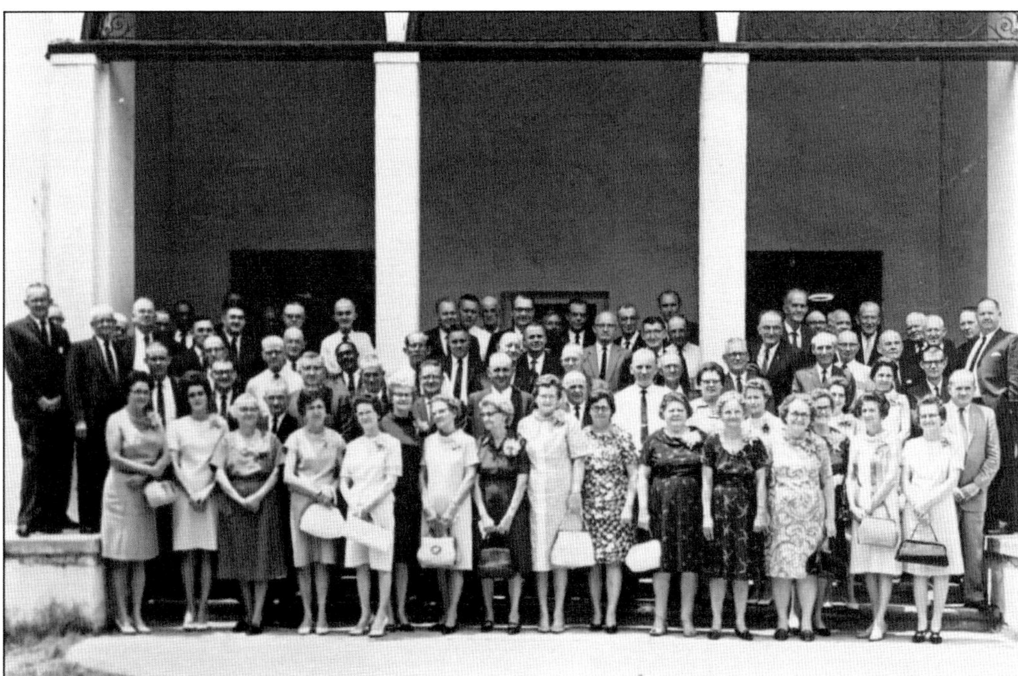

W. A. Handley Manufacturing Company employees with at least 25 years of employment are pictured on the steps of the Lowell auditorium, *c.* 1960. (Courtesy of Gerald Knight.)

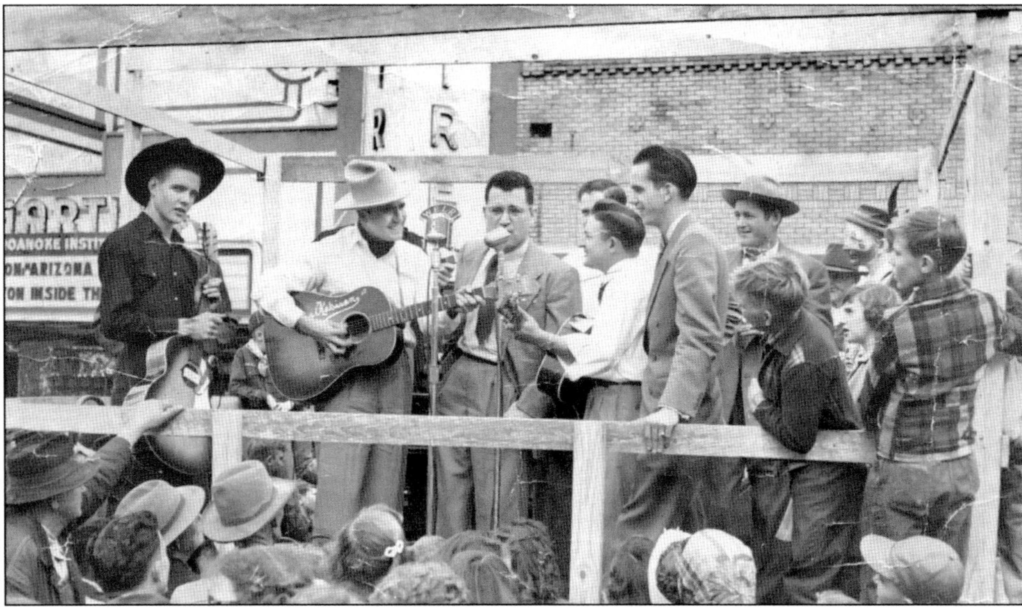

WELR radio moved to downtown Roanoke on a Saturday afternoon, *c.* 1952. Providing the entertainment from the back of a truck were, from left to right, Johnny Brewer; Danny Pate; Dick Killebrew, radio announcer and singer; Johnny Hodges, radio announcer and guitar player; Lucky Joe Almon, leaning on rail; clown Pappy Lee Farmer; and the boy holding onto the post is James Watson many years before his Banjo Players Hall of Fame induction. (Courtesy of the Brewer family.)

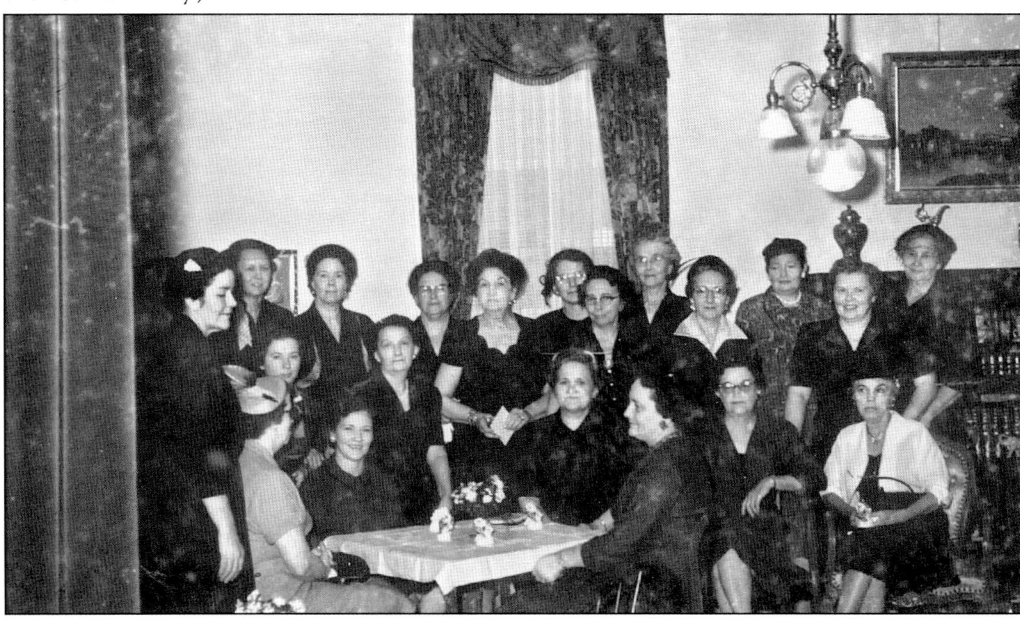

The Crepe Myrtle Garden Club held a regular meeting at the home of Mrs. Burns Parker, pictured in the center with paper in hand. Among the other ladies shown are Evie Hodges, Louise Huey, Evelyn Cooper, Mary Will Phillips, Hallie Staples, Mrs. Blake Wood, Sarah Burkhalter, Marie Ginn, Sara Cotney, Pat Baird, Mrs. Parker, Bessie Dunn, Alma Baird, Irene Lane, Mrs. Don Long, Frances Dunn, and Mrs. Byrd Blake, *c.* 1955. (Courtesy of Wyner Phillips.)

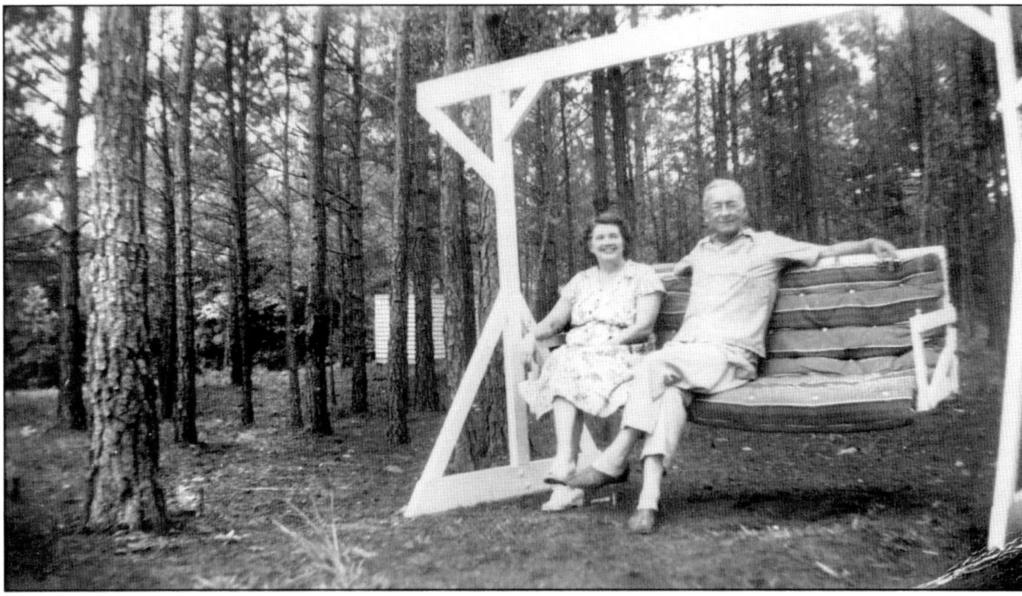

Samuel Mark Wylie (1894–1957) with his wife, Laura Lee Willis, moved to Wadley in 1929 and set up his first sawmill on the present site of Plantation Patterns. In 1938, he moved his planer and sawmills to Dickert, where he employed around 100 people. After his death, his sons and son-in-law took over the business. In 1974, the business was sold to Kimberly-Clark. (Courtesy of Ellen [Wylie] Sims.)

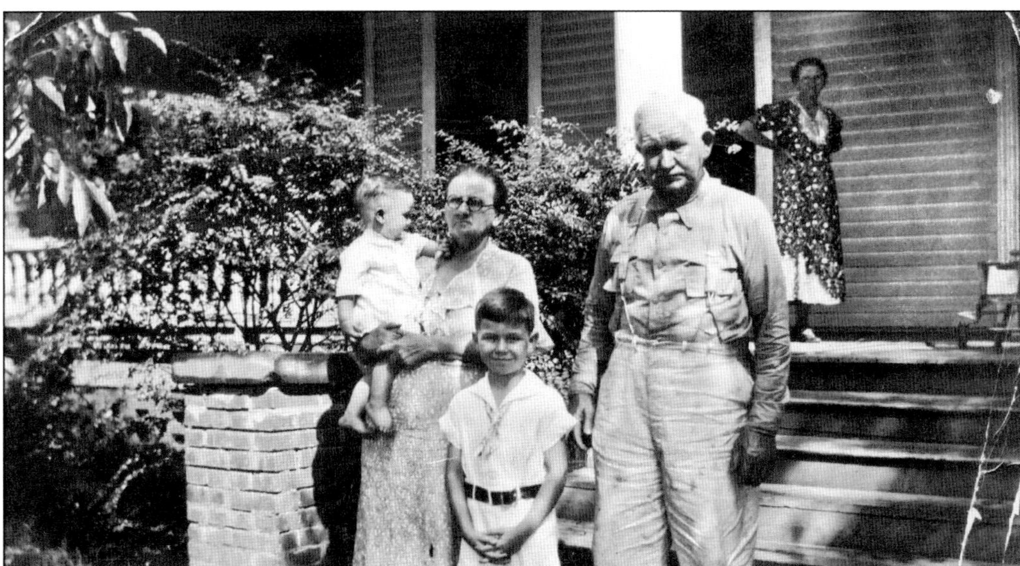

Pictured is Bob Bonner, owner/operator of the Bonner Hotel, in front of his home, which was adjacent to the hotel. Standing with him is his wife, Lucille Vinson Bonner, holding grandson Henry V. "Spec" Bonner (present mayor of Roanoke), and another grandson, Hubert Bonner Jr., is standing between them. On the porch is Spec's maternal grandmother, Ida Cox. The Roanoke Fire Station No. 1 now occupies the site where the elegant home stood for so many years. (Courtesy of Henry V. "Spec" Bonner.)

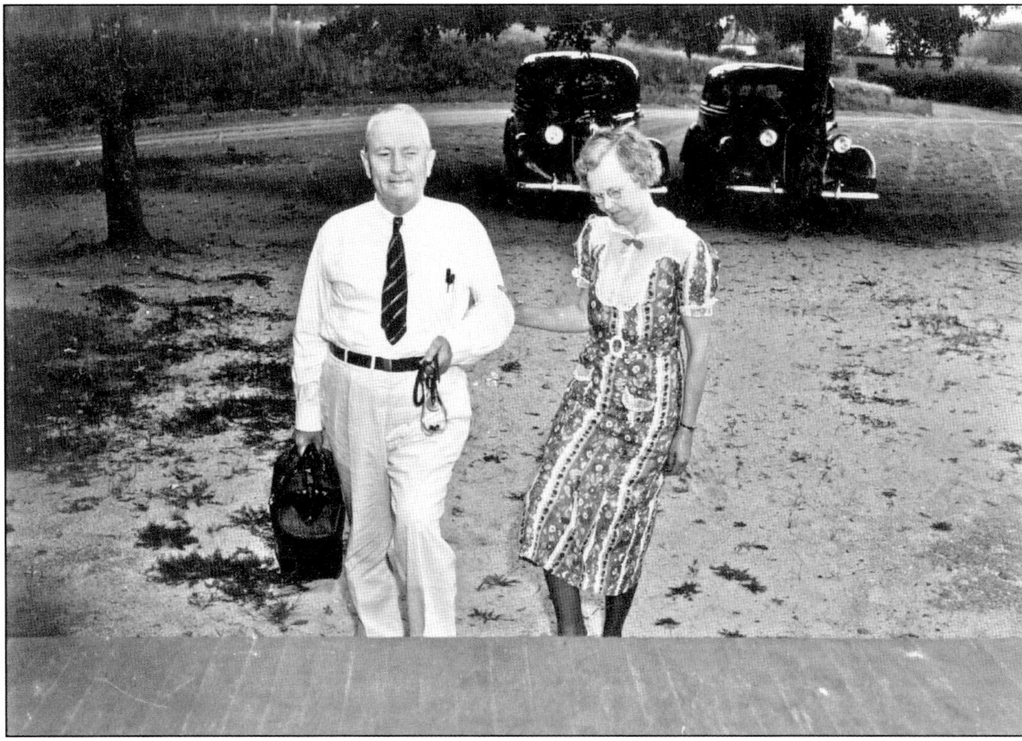

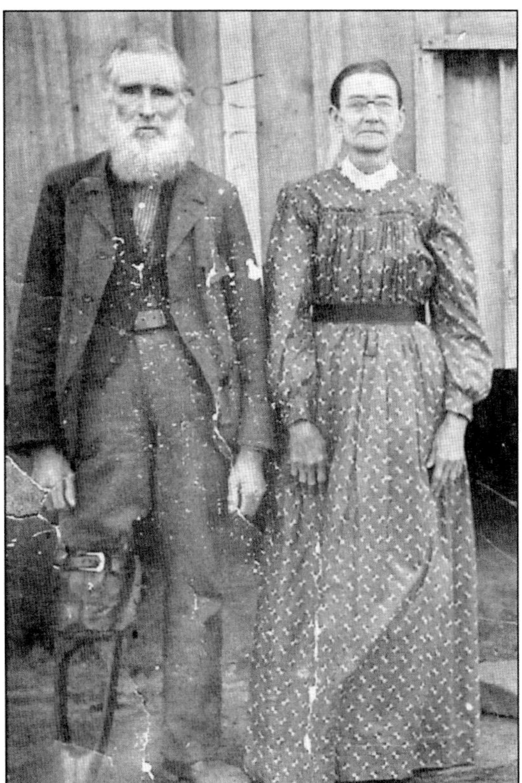

Dr. and Mrs. James Thomas Clack are coming home from making house calls to Wadley patients in 1938. Tom Clack and Resa Floyd attended Roanoke Normal College during the 1890s. Tom became a physician, and he and Resa teamed up for the journey of life. At age 38, a tragedy occurred when blindness struck Tom, but Resa's eyes took the place of the her husband's and, perhaps for the first time in American history, a totally blind physician continued his practice for 38 more years. On September 13, 1940, Dr. and Mrs. Clack traveled to New York and appeared on *Ripley's Believe it or Not* radio show, which was broadcast nationwide and featured him as the only blind practicing doctor in the United States. Dr. Clack died in 1956 at the age of 80. (Courtesy of Joyce Pool.)

Calvin Chase and Elander Taylor Chase were married in 1865, approximately 30 years before they posed for this photograph. Calvin was a veteran of the Confederate army and was wounded at the Battle of Chickamauga. The homemade right leg is a result of that wound. (Courtesy of Lynn Chase.)

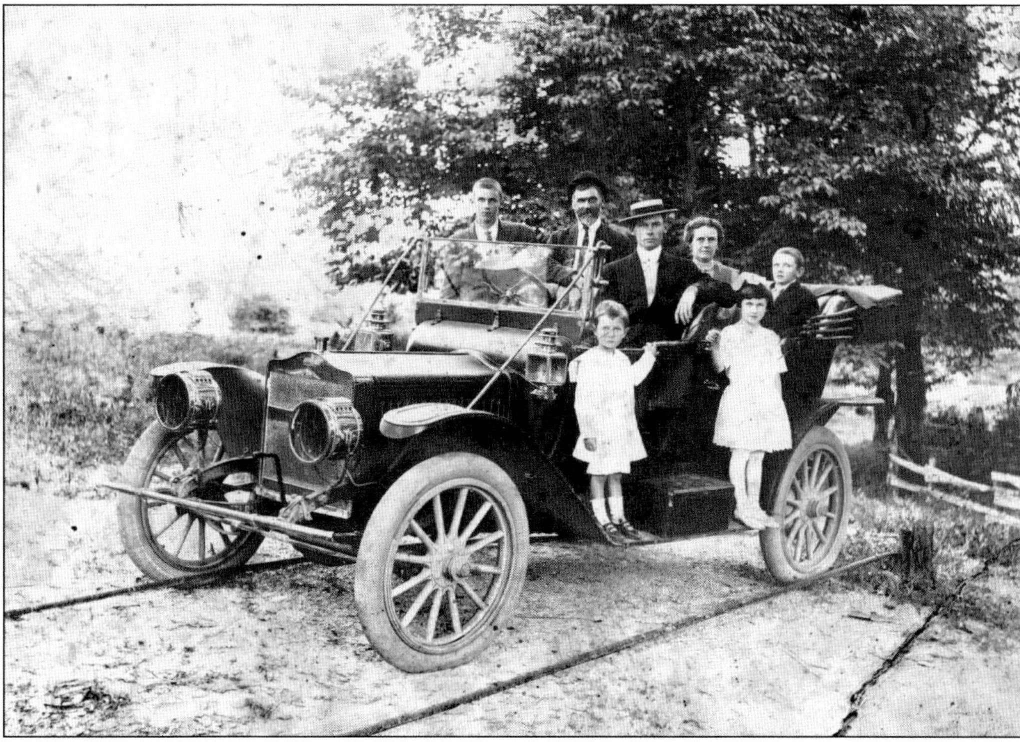

Nixon Lucas was one of the leading men in the development of Malone, a prosperous Randolph County community in the early years of the 20th century. Having moved there in 1908, he established a turpentine distillery that operated for about 10 years and employed more than 200 people. He accumulated more than 6,000 acres of woodland to furnish the raw materials for turpentine. The Nixon family is pictured in 1913 in their new Willis-Knight automobile (in the day when there were hardly any cars in Randolph County). Pictured are Nixon Lucas, with beard; Mrs. Nixon Lucas in back seat; Charlie Lucas in front seat; Jesse Lucas on left; Birch Lucas on back seat; and Bob Lucas and Alye Lucas on running board. (Courtesy of Laura [Lucas] Pittman.)

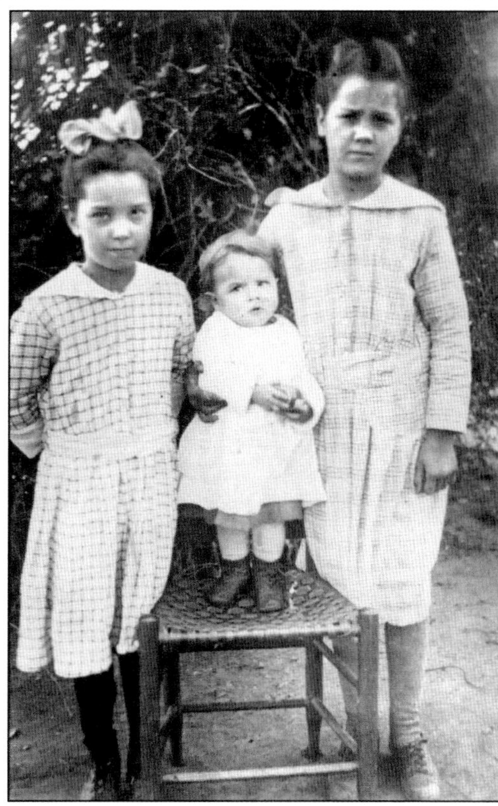

Often the death of a parent left older children to raise the younger ones. Such was the case in the family of James Cody Burson. In this picture are two sisters, Lena (left) and Leila, primary caretakers of their baby brother, Hubert, following the death of their mother, Lois Robinson Burson, on February 12, 1918. (Courtesy of Lois [Walls] George.)

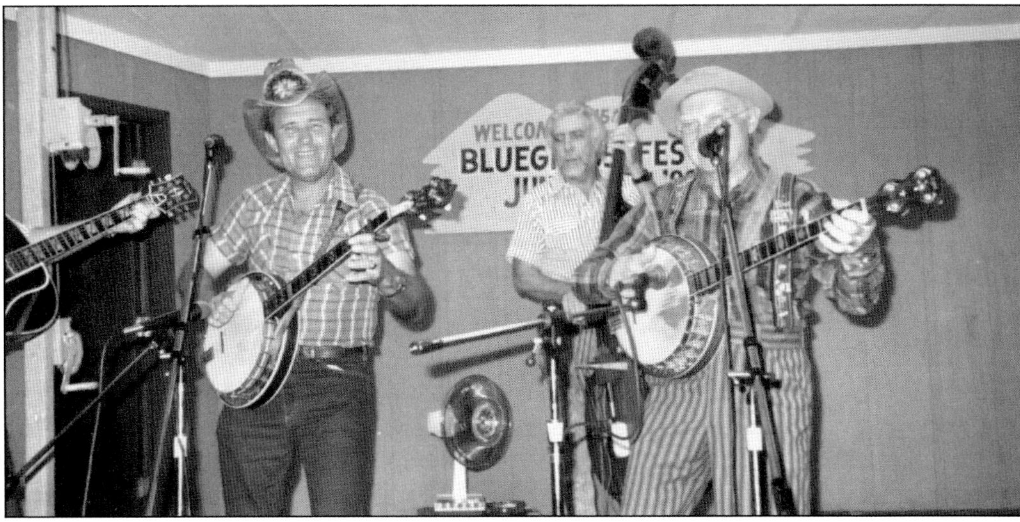

One of Randolph County's most famous citizens is James Watson, shown playing banjo with his good friend of many years, Grandpa Jones, who is perhaps best remembered for his years on the *Hee Haw* television show. James grew up near the once-thriving community of Malone. His primary profession is painting contractor, an occupation that he initiated at a young age and built such a distinguished reputation that time for playing the banjo has been primarily limited to weekends. James and Grandpa Jones developed a similar style of banjo picking known as frailing or clawhammer style, and his unique ability has kept him in high demand. He has played with many different bands, outlived many of his contemporaries, performed nationwide and on national television, did 26 shows at the 1982 World's Fair in Knoxville, Tennessee, was with Lester Flatt at Lester's last performance, and is the only Randolph County citizen ever to be inducted into the Banjo Players Hall of Fame. (Courtesy of James Watson.)

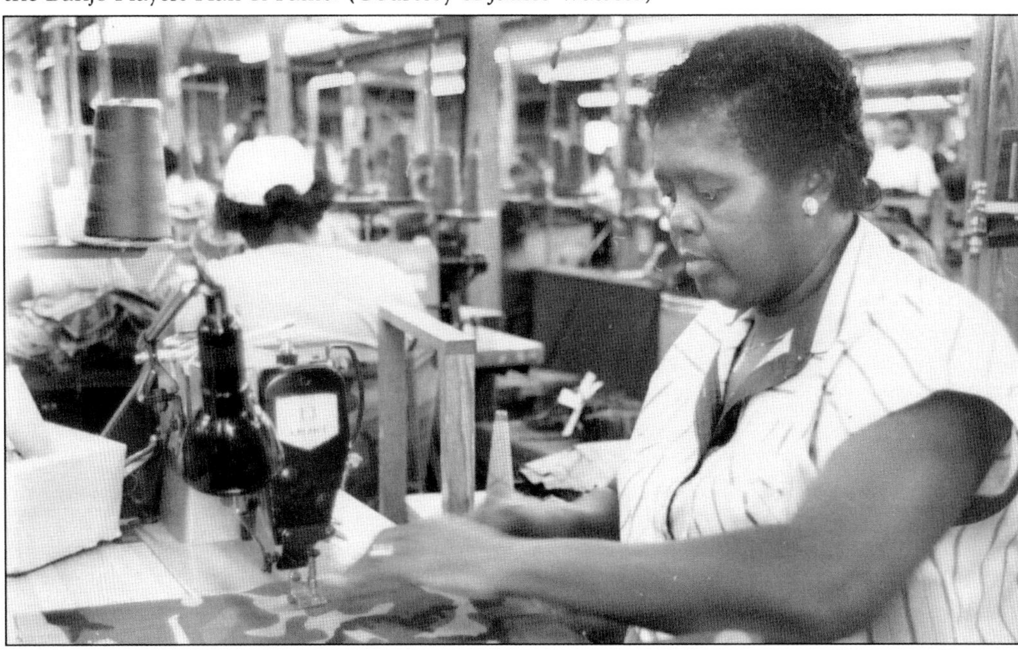

Machine operator Peggy Beasley shows expertise in making a camouflage uniform on August 22, 1990, at Terry Manufacturing Company. (Courtesy of the *Randolph Leader*.)

Nan Enloe lifts the drape revealing the monument erected to the memory of Winfred Page Enloe Sr. Page Enloe was manager of the W. A. Handley Manufacturing Company for 19 years, having succeeded his father, Harvey Enloe, whose similar monument stands just to the left. The building in the background is the mill's community center, which contained a movie theater for mill employees and their families. The monuments are directly in front of the W. A. Handley Manufacturing Company. (Courtesy of the Randolph County Museum.)

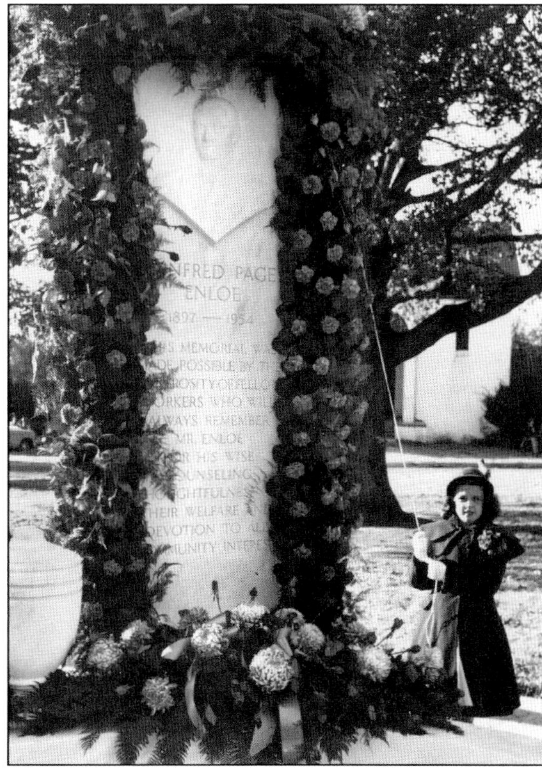

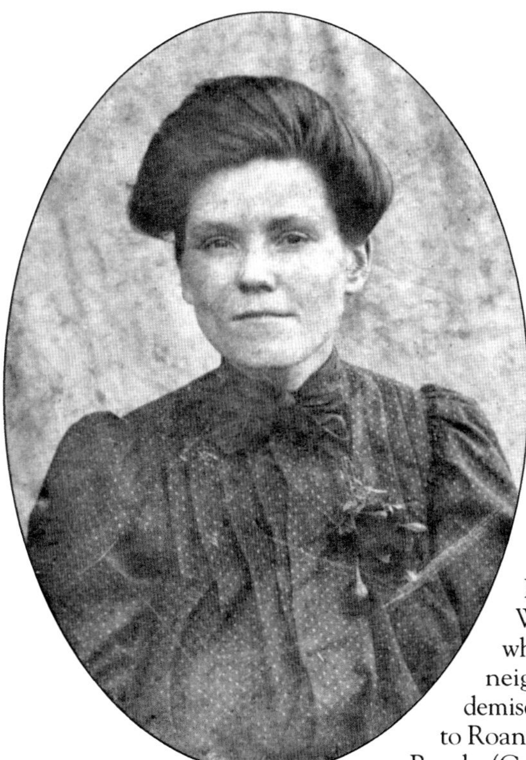

Pictured is Marta Lavena Elizabeth Adamson Windsor, born September 21, 1884, near Malone, where she lived most of her life, with the nearest neighbor about a mile away. After her husband's demise, she and her one daughter, Ann Windsor, moved to Roanoke, where Ann worked as a seamstress at Palm Beach. (Courtesy of Ann Windsor.)

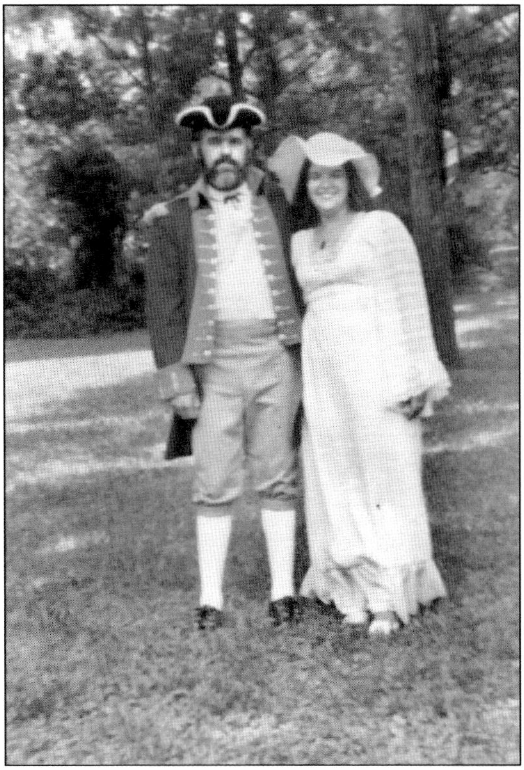

Joe and Paula Lambert are dressed appropriately to depict and honor the 200th birthday of our nation. The celebration started with a promenade in downtown Roanoke, while hundreds came from surrounding counties to join in the celebration. Bicentennial week was recognized throughout the nation and celebrated from June 27, 1976, to July 4, 1976. (Courtesy of Paula [Burson] Lambert.)

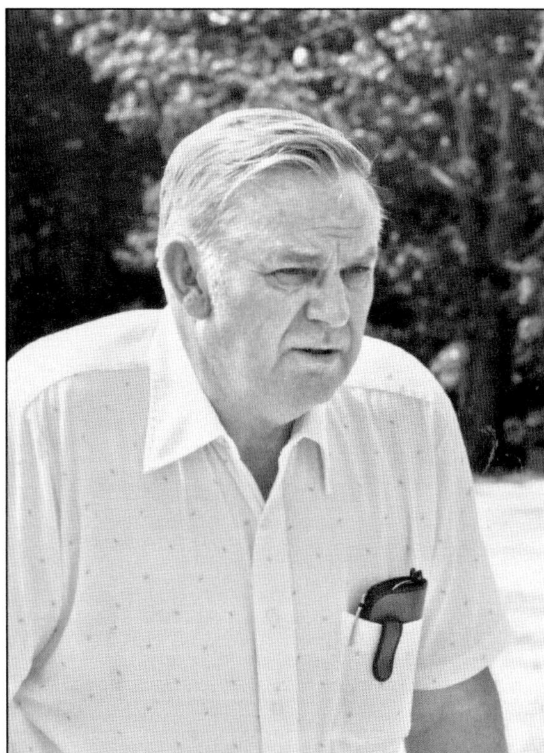

Gus W. Young (1918–1999) received a degree in education in 1941, as well as a degree in agricultural education in 1942 from Auburn University. Although childhood polio disqualified him for military service during World War II, he served his country and state for two terms in the House of Representatives. He later started and taught in the first Agricultural Department at Woodland High School; moreover, Young pastored several churches in the area. (Courtesy of Murrah Wilson.)

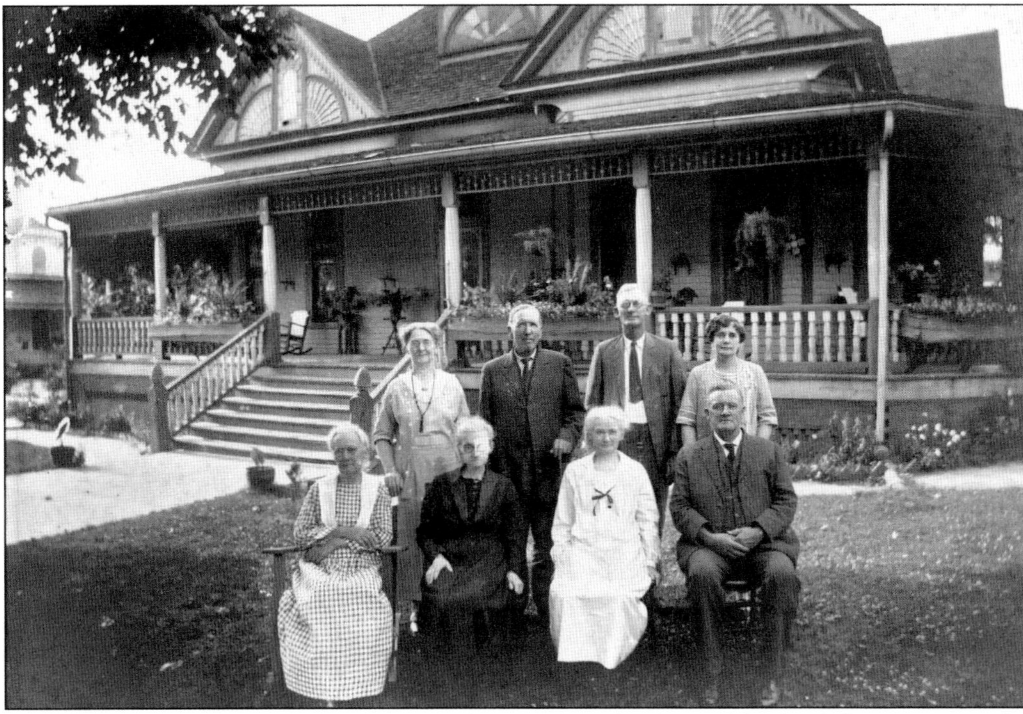

Several generations of the W. T. Belcher family are gathered in front of the family home in Roanoke. This house is now the home of Cheaha Mental Health. (Courtesy of W. T. [Bill] Belcher III.)

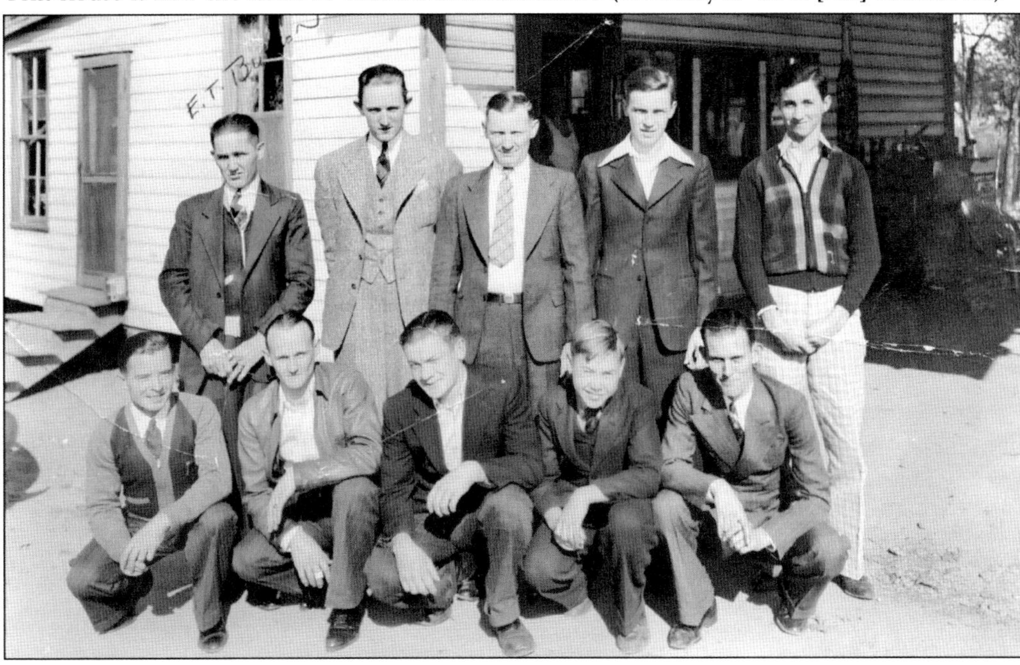

A group of young men in their Sunday best are gathered in front of Berry Green's store in Omaha in the early 1920s. This store was truly the center of the community in the early 1900s. Upstairs was the Masonic Lodge, and downstairs, for a time, was a place for the telephone operator for the area. (Courtesy of Paula [Burson] Lambert.)

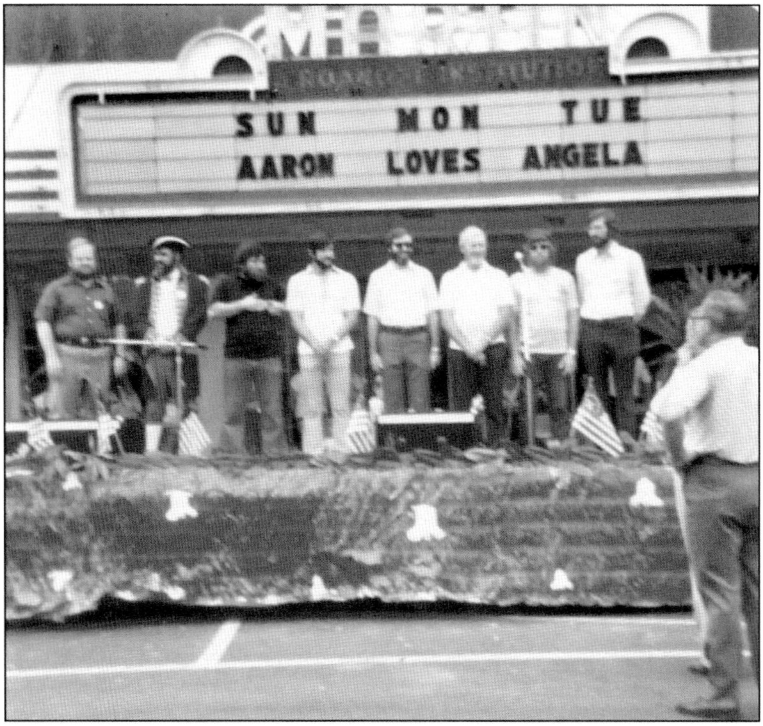

The personal interest highlights of Roanoke's old-fashioned promenade were aimed at judging beards, mustaches, and Vandykes. The gentlemen shown are contestants who were unafraid of seeing how their guise fairs with those of our forefathers. From left to right are Clarence Hodges, Joe Lambert (first place), Jerrell Hodges, Mike Adcock (second place), Ray French (third place), Jack Irvin, Larry Norred, and David Stevenson. (Courtesy of Paula [Burson] Lambert.)

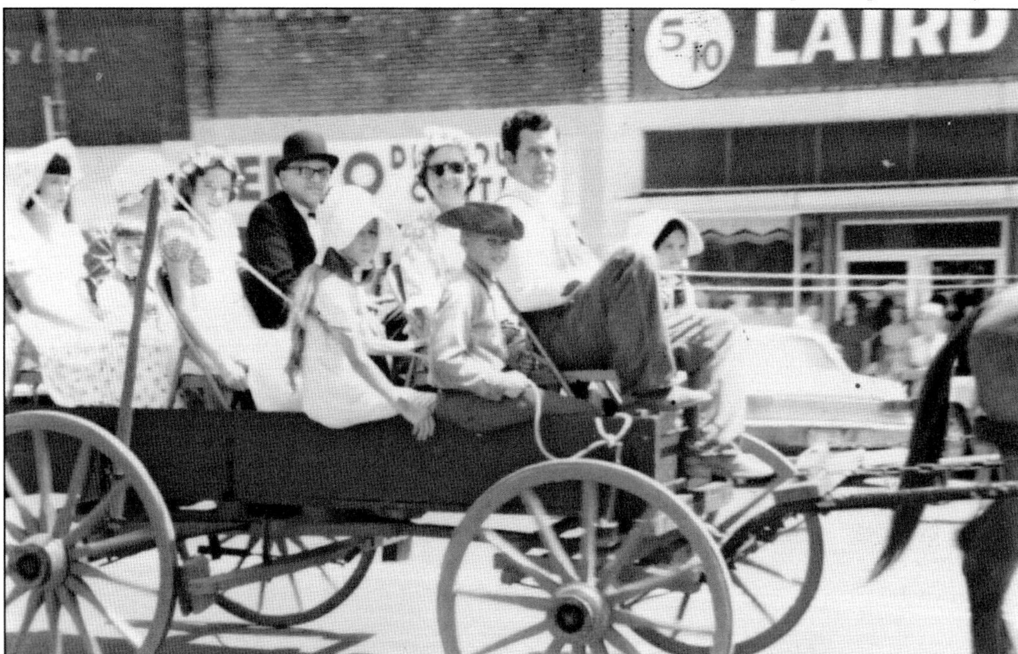

People came from all over the county to join the many costumed wagons, old cars, floats, and horses. Riders were the Odie Gregg family of Rock Mills, members of the Randolph County Historical Society, and the John Randolph Chapter of the Daughters of the American Revolution. The Daughters of the American Revolution were the honored participants in the parade. (Courtesy of Paula [Burson] Lambert.)

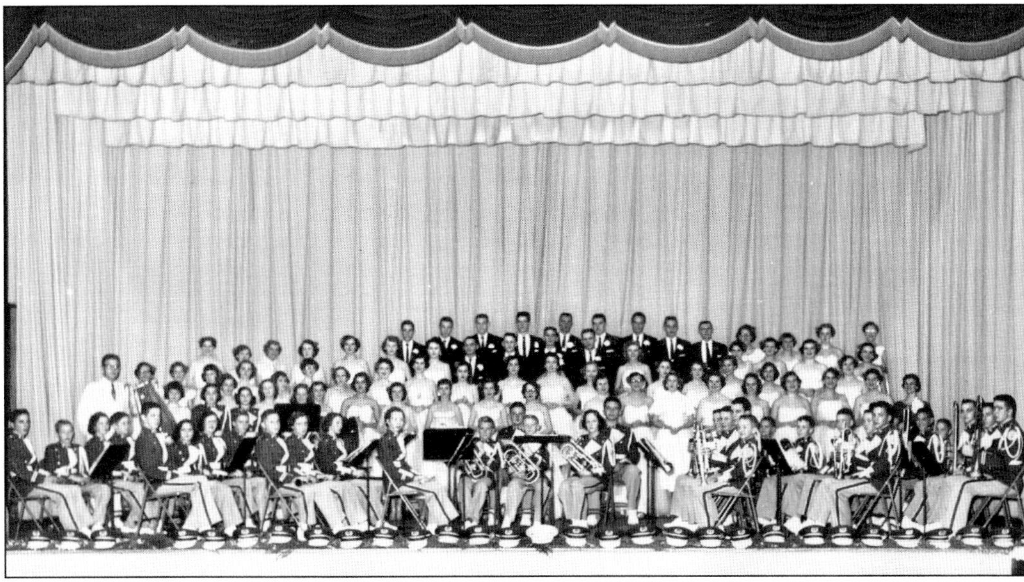

The first joint concert of Handley High School Band and Glee Club was the Christmas concert of 1953. The Glee Club director was Marin Hamer, the lady standing on the extreme right with the dark dress and corsage. John Thomas, the band director, is standing on the extreme left in the white suit. The concert was held in the city auditorium when the seats were made of solid wood and were contoured for audience comfort but were not cushioned. (Courtesy of Betty Bradshaw.)

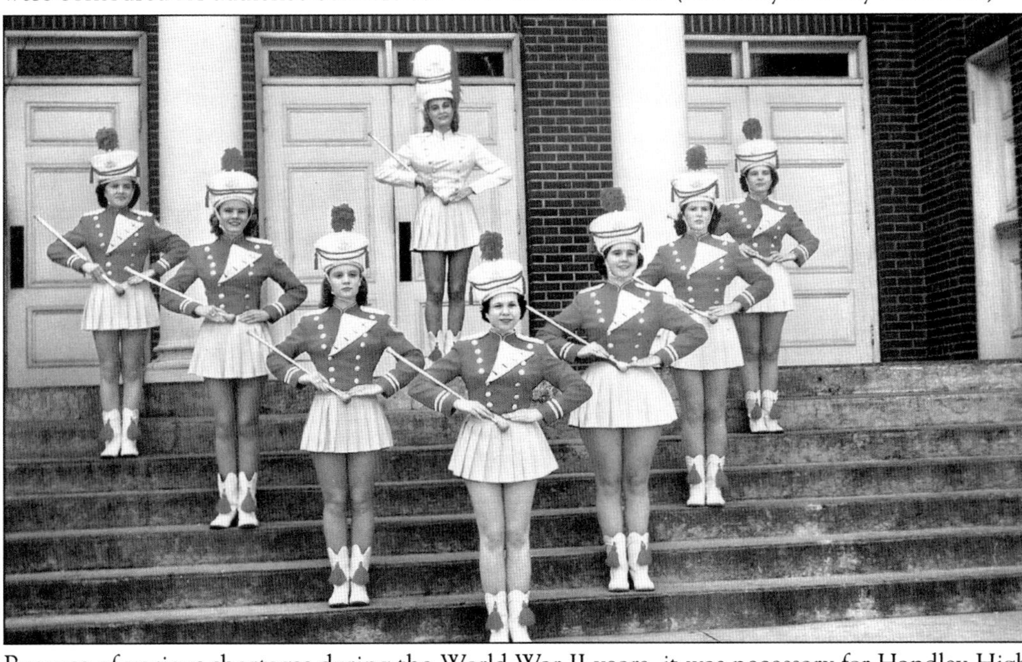

Because of various shortages during the World War II years, it was necessary for Handley High School to eliminate some programs, and one of the cut backs was the band. It was not until 1952 that a new band was organized, and the first majorettes are pictured on the front steps of the city auditorium. The head majorette, dressed in an all-white uniform, was Nan Enloe. From left to right are Jeanette Beverly, Jennie Cotney, Elizabeth Belcher, Lillian Howell, Sherry Cauthen, Betty Beverly, and Patsy Hodges. (Courtesy of Betty Bradshaw.)

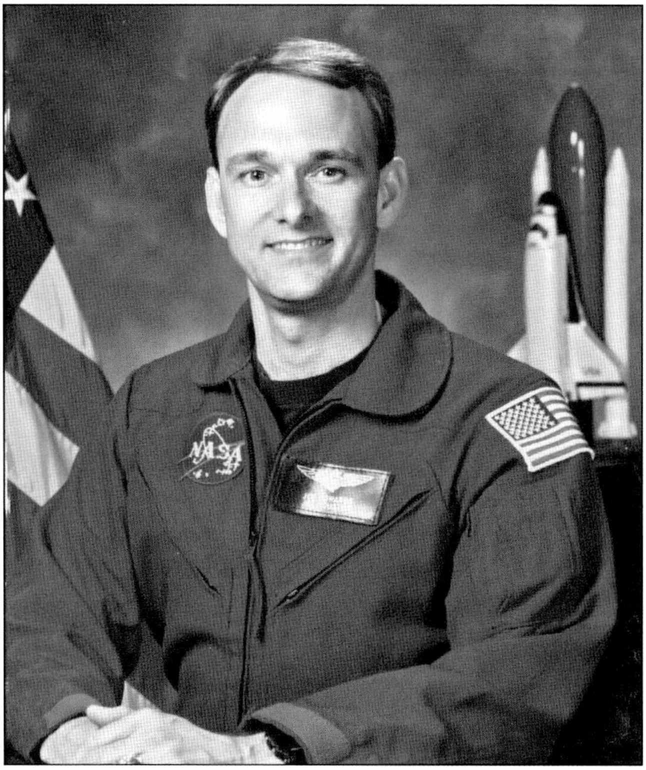

Joe Edwards, son of Joe Frank and Jane McMurray Edwards, possesses an exhaustive list of education, honors, experience, and credentials. He has flown 4,000 hours in over 25 different aircraft and logged over 650 carrier-arrested landings. In 1994, he was selected as an astronaut and piloted STS-89 in 1998. He orbited the Earth 138 times for a total of 3.6 million miles. He retired from the navy and NASA in 2000. (Courtesy of Joe and Jane Edwards.)

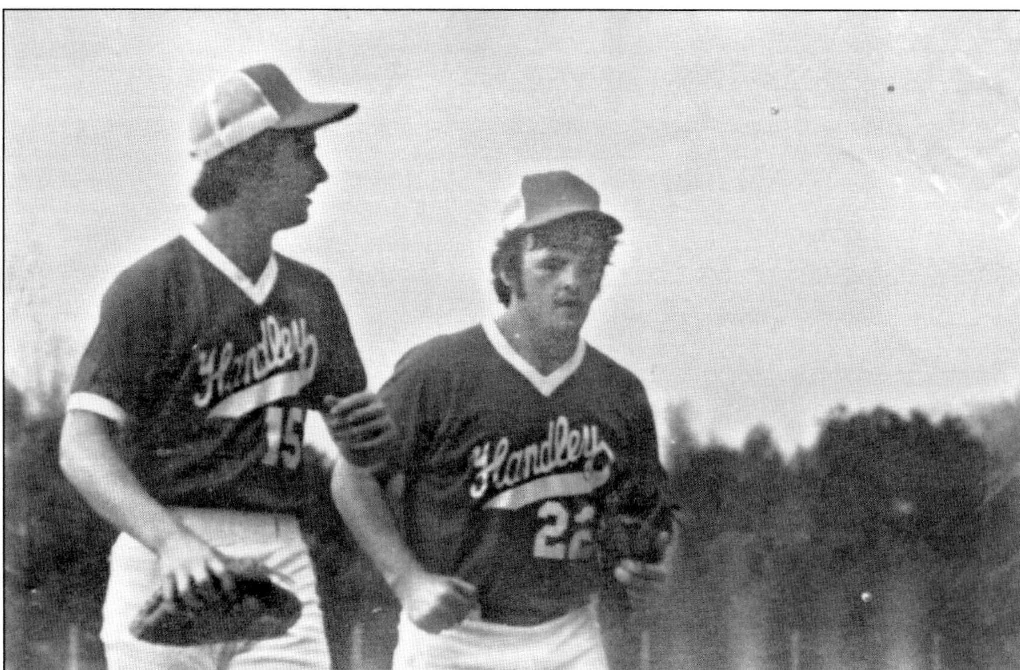

Pictured are two Handley Tigers, Rex Shelnutt (No. 15) and Mark Johnson (No. 22), talking about the great play they just made in the 1978 baseball state playoffs. (Courtesy of Pam [Burson] Johnson.)

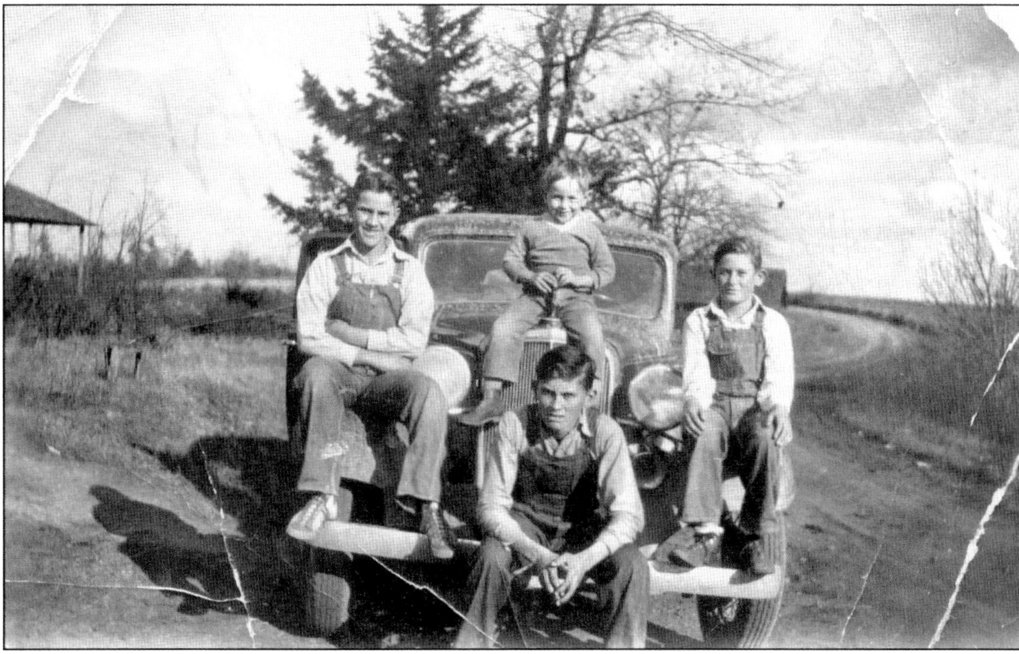

This band practice was important to the children of the band members, giving them an opportunity to visit with friends. Children often accompanied their parents wherever they went. In this *c.* 1933 picture are Paul Burson (on the left fender) and Kenneth Burson (straddling the hood ornament). (Courtesy of Kenneth Burson.)

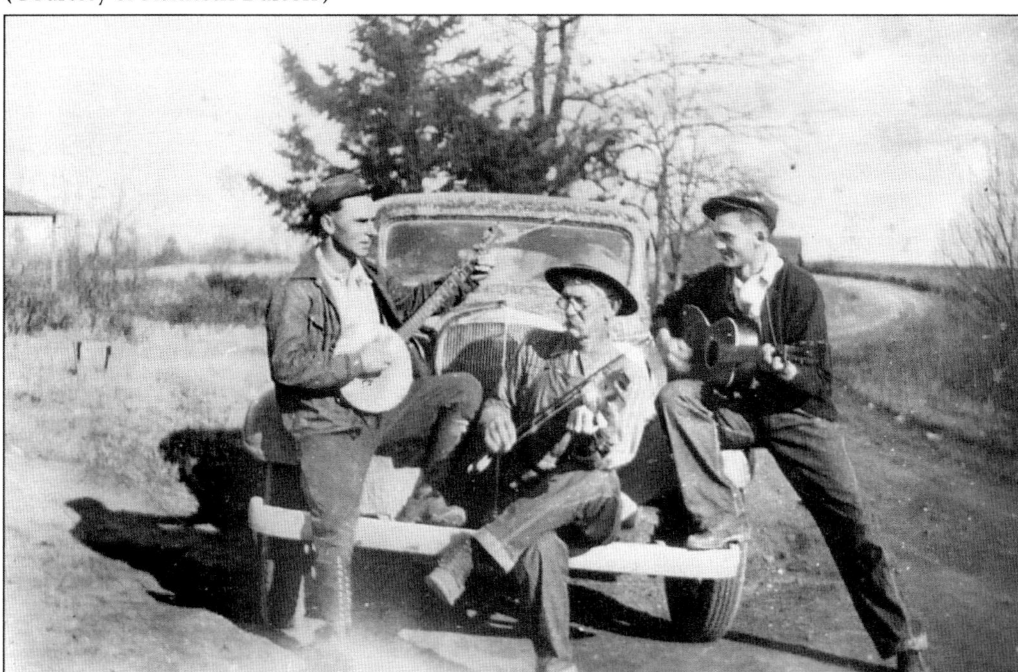

Local band members met occasionally for practice. From left to right in this *c.* 1933 picture are Woodrow Camp, James Cody Burson, and Looney Bledsoe. These men were very important to the square dances in the community. (Courtesy of Kenneth Burson.)

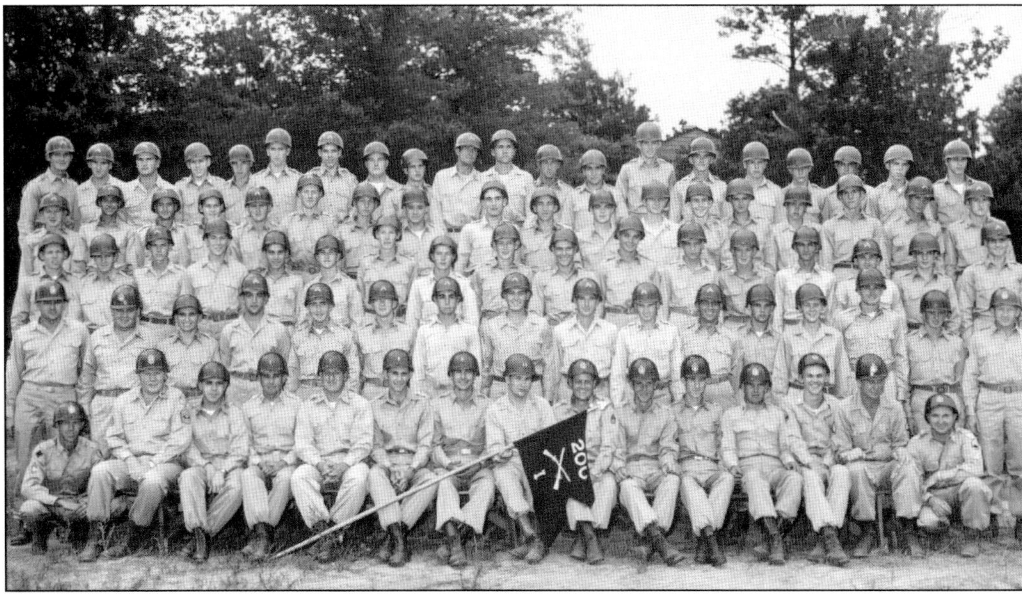

Pictured is the Roanoke National Guard in 1950 before the call-up to Korea. This large number signifies the patriotism of Randolph County citizens. Some were deferred, but most of these men answered the call to the Korean War. Some came back with a Purple Heart. Some did not come back at all. (Courtesy of Joe Gilliland.)

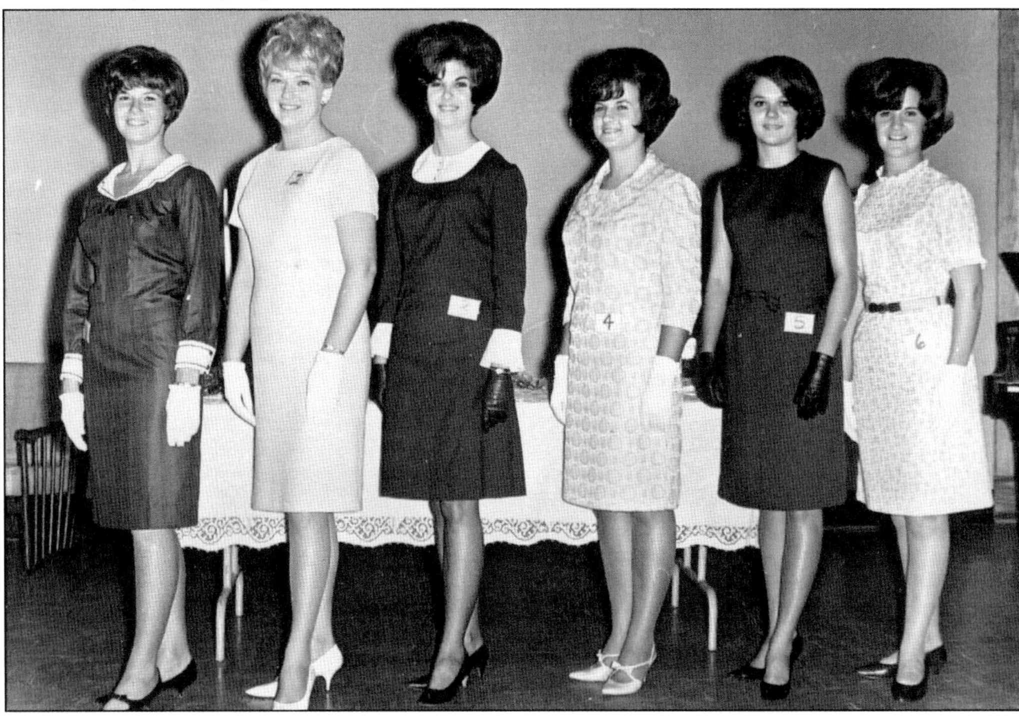

Pictured are the Farm Bureau Cotton Maid contestants of 1966. From left to right are Judy Burke of Wadley, Janie Ward of Roanoke, Kate Dobson of Wedowee, Nancy Head of Rock Mills, Trudy Collier of Roanoke (1966 Maid), and Jan Hall of Wadley. (Courtesy of Eulette Ward and Janie [Ward] Cobb.)

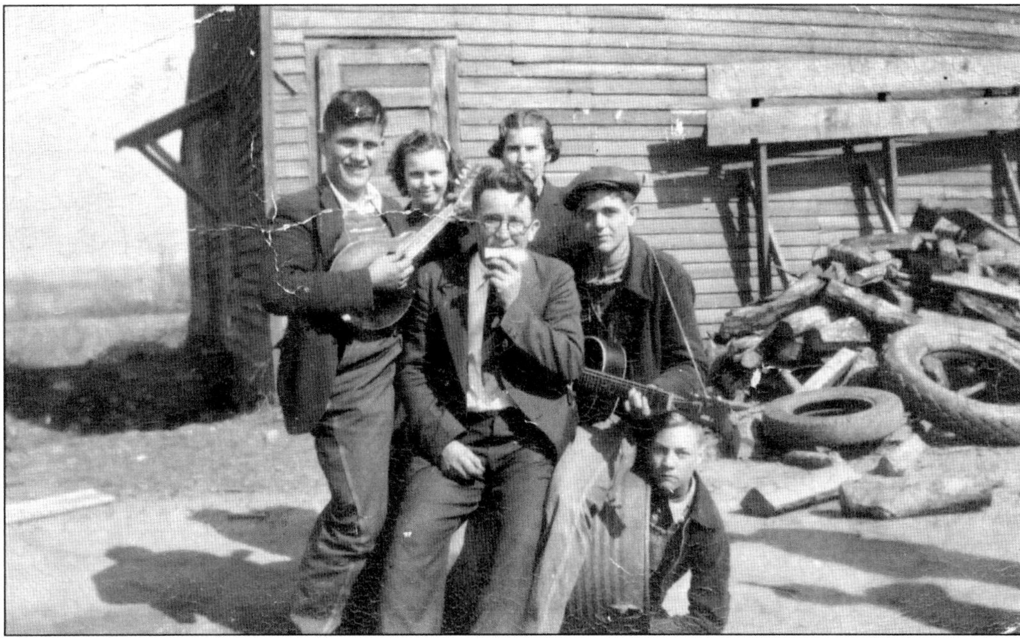

The band trained its own replacements and they began their training at a young age, as seen in this *c.* 1934 picture. Practicing together was important. They met usually at the same time as the older members. The band in training used this time as a rare moment to just enjoy the company of other children. (Courtesy of Bernice [Wilson] Burson.)

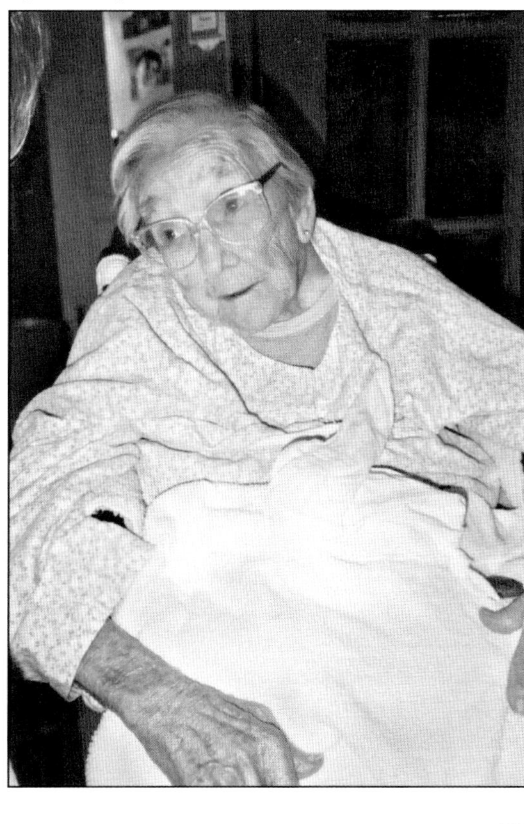

Lucy Noles Green is thought to be the oldest person in Randolph County. She was born on December 31, 1900, as one of 11 children. She has lived her entire life within a radius of 10 miles of where she was born and attended the same church, Providence, all of her life, until recent failing health prevented her attendance. Though she traveled, Randolph County remains her home for 106 years and counting. (Courtesy of Lois [Walls} and Paula [Burson] Lambert.)

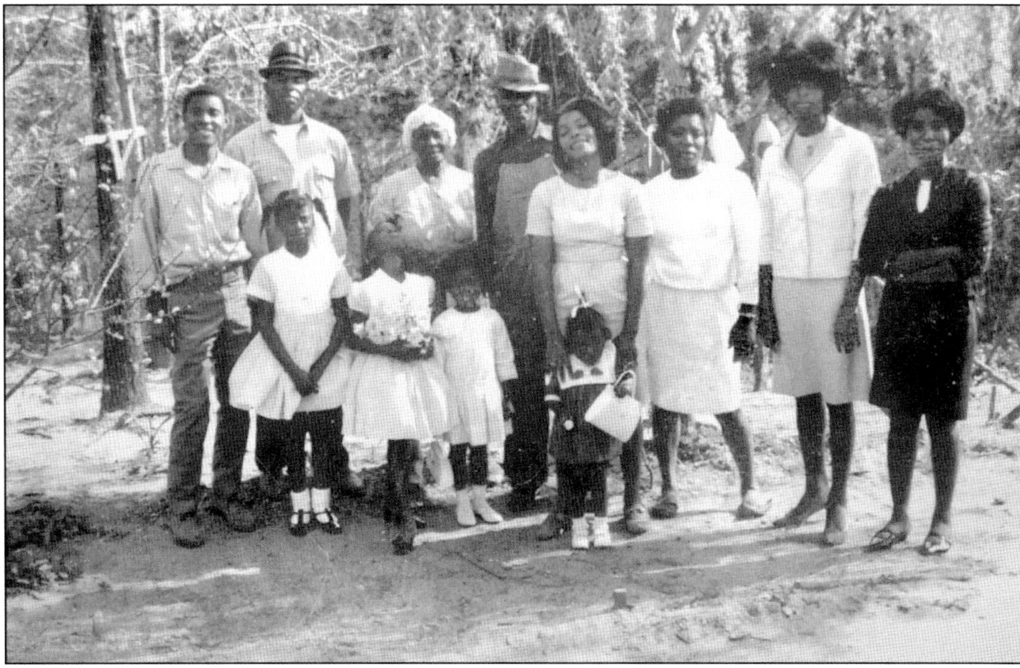

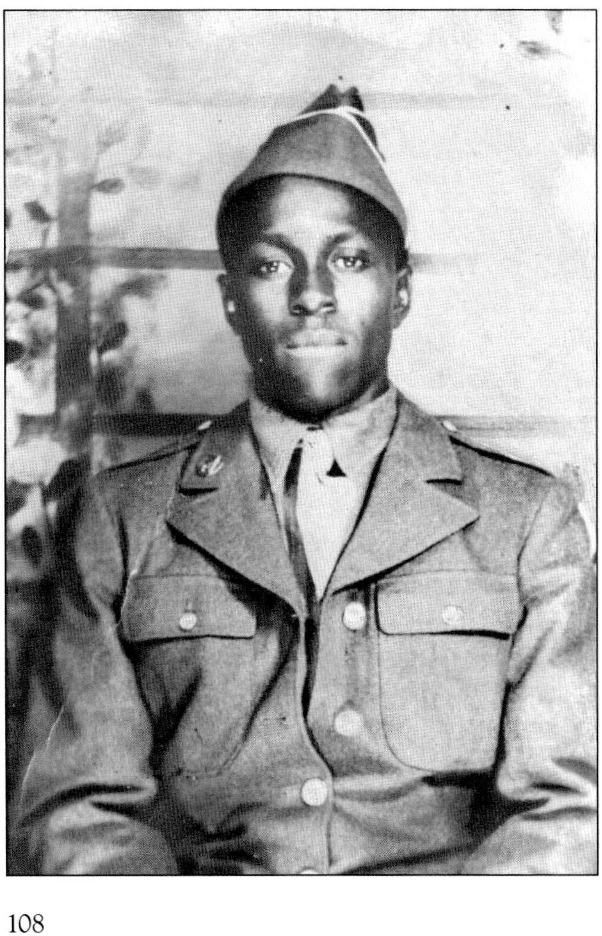

This photograph was taken at the home of Rig and Maggie Thornton in the Springield Community on Easter Sunday 1965. Pictured from left to right are (first row) Denise Thornton, Tracy Thornton, Anita Rowland, and Michelle Rowland; (second row) Gene Thornton, King George Thornton, Maggie Edwards Thornton, Rigland Thornton, Maggie Thornton Rowland, Lillie Mae Baker Thornton, Earnestine Thornton, Doris Mae, and Thornton Mbonzo. (Courtesy of Gene Thornton.)

Sanders "Sandy" Thornton, brother of King George Thornton, was in the Army Air Corps during World War II and served in the Solomon Islands during the war. After the war, he worked at the same job with Goodyear Tire Company for 35 years. (Courtesy of Gene Thornton.)

Lizzie Turner Baker was the wife of Eddie Benjamin Baker, and they had 12 children. Lizzie worked as a midwife for many years, delivering hundreds of babies, including all of her daughter-in-law's (Susie Baker) 19 children. The 19 children included 6 sets of twins and all were healthy. Lizzie died February 6, 1949, at the age of 83. (Courtesy of Gene Thornton.)

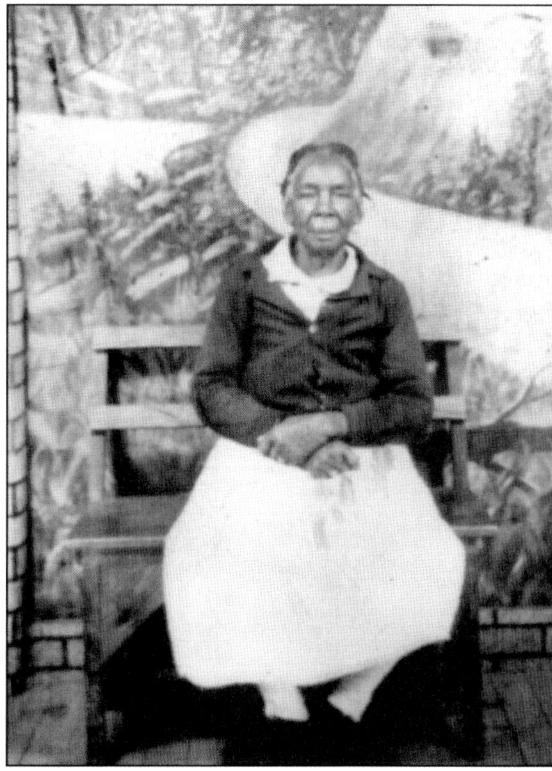

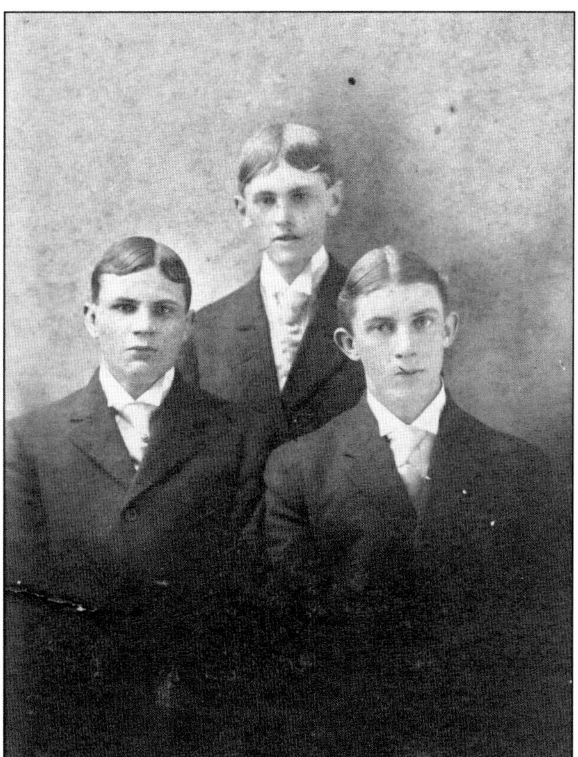

Pictured are Dr. J. R. Manley (left), Ben Handley (center), and W. E. McIntosh (right). Dr. Manley was a practicing physician in Roanoke for many years. Ben Handley was grandson of W. A. Handley. W. E. McIntosh had been to New York to promote the Ella Smith Doll. On the way home, he was killed in a train wreck. The closing of the doll factory was attributed to his death. (Courtesy of Raymond Hodges.)

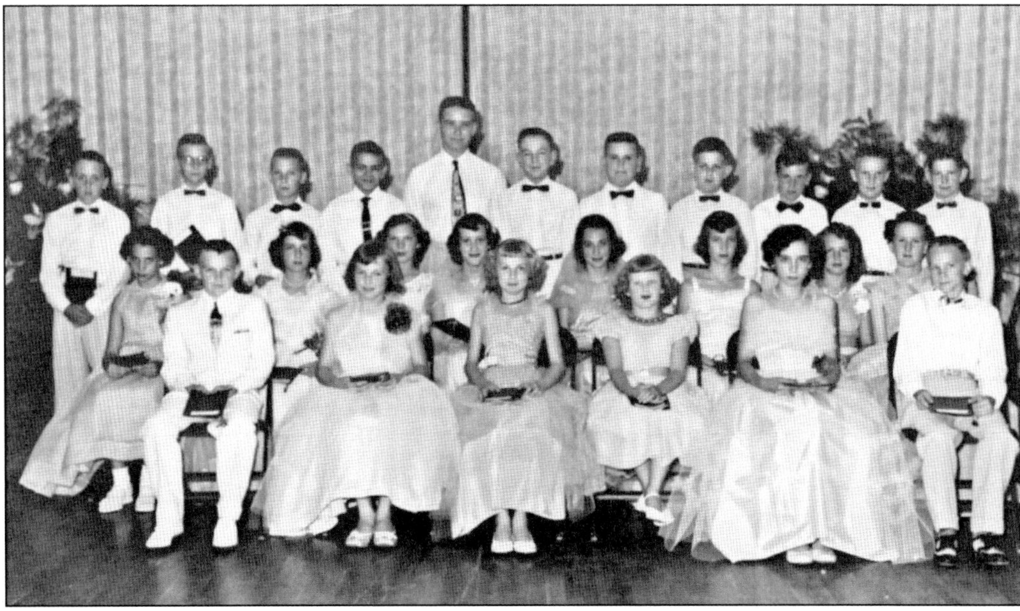

Pictured is Knight Enloe's 1955 sixth-grade graduating class. From left to right are (first row) Jason Roberts, Reba Wilder, Charlotte Daughtry, Mary Ann Lane, Margaret Stallings, and Larry Brady; (second row) Fay Roberts, Carolyn Wade, Sandra Wilson, Patricia Young, Martha Barnes, Roy Ann Anthony, Alice Knight, and Katherine Dalrymple; (third row) Thurmon Noles, Michael Dobson, Jimmy Cottle, Richard Thrower, Manuel Daniel, Harold Cunningham, Joe Brooks, Jerry Nolen, Frank Cranford, Jimmy Huddleston, and John Wilson. Graduation exercises were held in the Lowell Auditorium. (Courtesy of the Randolph County Museum.)

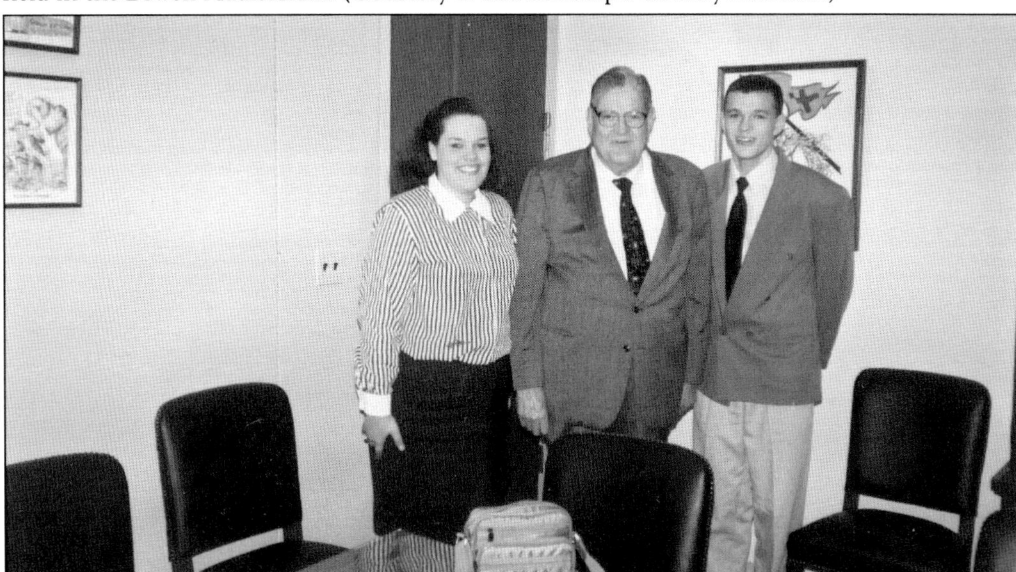

Inspired by the history lessons of Wayne Cato, who taught at Handley High School for many years, De Lambert and Neil Fetner traveled to Washington, D.C., as part of the Washington Work Shops Federation. While in Washington, De and Neil were able to meet Howell Heflin, who served as an Alabama state senator from 1979 to 1997. Senator Heflin has been called the "Spokesman for Southern Agriculture." He is also from Randolph County. (Courtesy of De Lambert.)

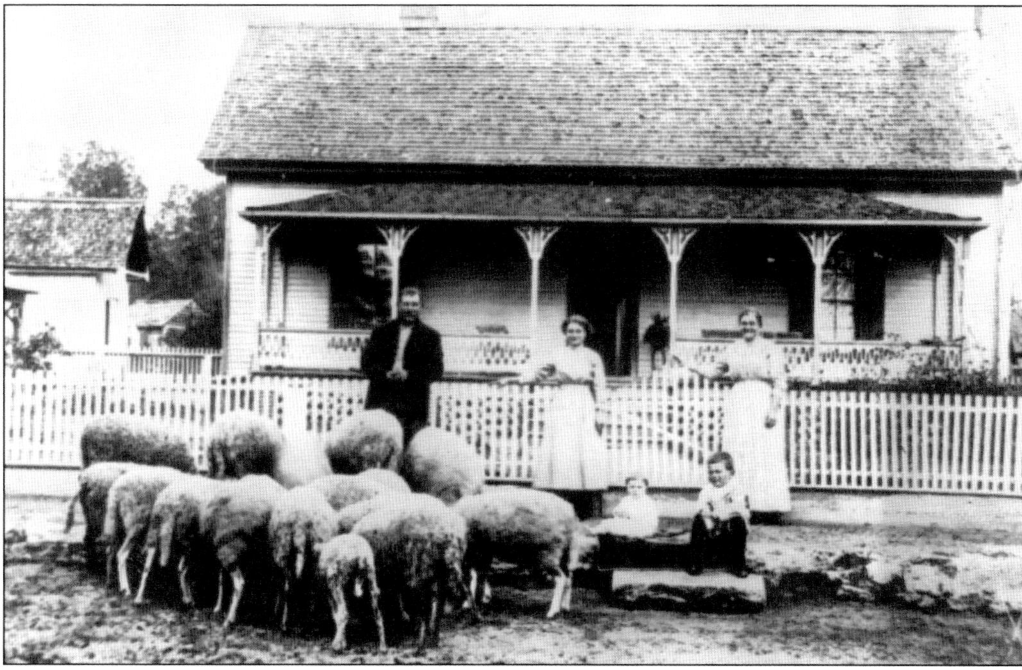

Pictured is the Robert Lee Bradshaw family, *c.* 1911, near Bacon Level. From left to right are (sitting) Ruby Carolyn Bradshaw (daughter) and Robert Gibson Bradshaw (son); (standing) "Bob" Bradshaw, Merla Ray Bradshaw (daughter), and Emma Vistula Gamble Bradshaw (wife). Bob operated a country store with gas pump, blacksmith shop, and small mill and also farmed 200 acres. In 1903, he was postmaster of Thurman Post Office. (Courtesy of Raymond Hodges.)

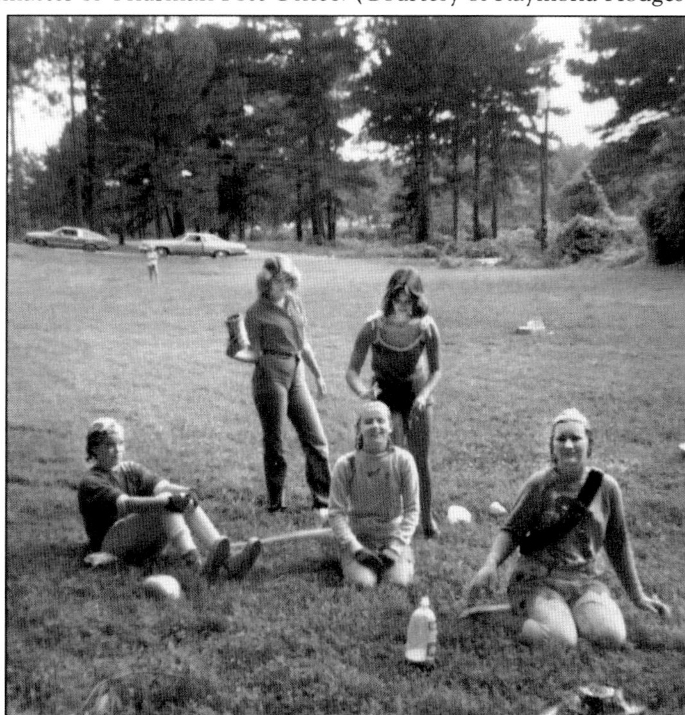

This photograph signifies what some are willing to go through for acceptance into the high elements of society. In the process of initiation into the Handley High JUG Club (Just Us Girls) are Beth Morrison, left; Rene Easterwood, center; and Benita Bryant. The standing initiators are Donna McKinney, left, and Pam Burson. (Courtesy of Pam [Burson] Johnson.)

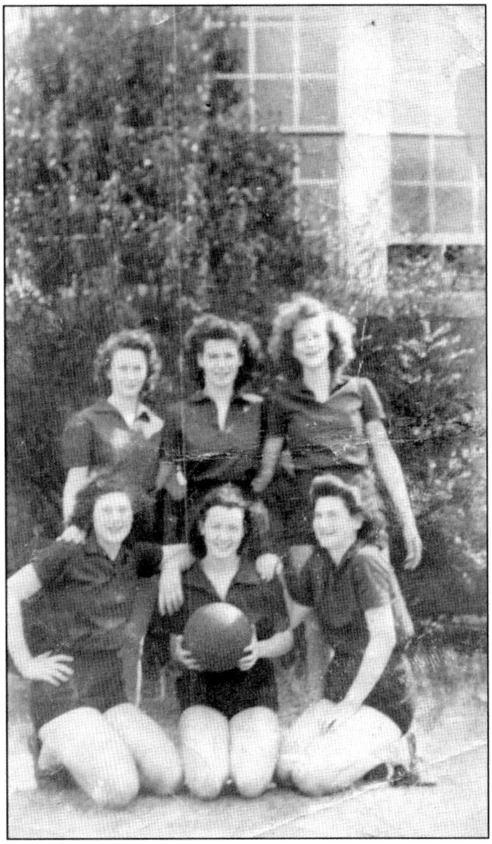

In 1946, the Woodland High School basketball team won the county tournament. Shown here from left to right are the team members: (first row, forwards) Martha Burson, Linda Haynes, and Bertie Mae Burson; (second row, guards) Irene Benefield, Janette Parker, and Carolyn Traylor. (Courtesy of Bertie Waldrep.)

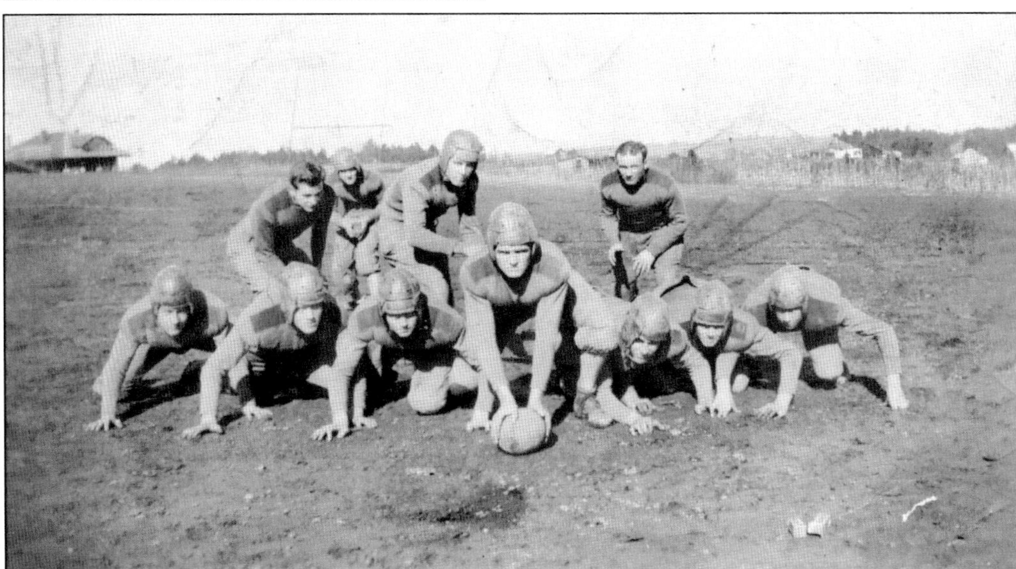

School activities played a big part in community entertainment in the early years just as they do today. These Woodland football players are practicing for their next game around the year 1930. The second player on the right in the front row is Tuerman Wilson. (Courtesy of Bernice [Wilson] Burson.)

Six

AROUND THE COUNTY

The first settlers in the county loved what they saw and stayed to make it their home. The present citizens recognize the wonders of their county today and enjoy living here. Ideally situated near the center of three of the largest cities in the southeast, approximately 90 miles from Atlanta, Montgomery, and Birmingham, Randolph offers country charm with easy access to the benefits of the large cities.

Randolph is a large county. From north to south, its length is 25.5 miles, and the width averages 21.375 miles. Located in central Alabama, it shares the state line on the east with the state of Georgia and the Chattahoochee River.

The county is noted for its gently rolling hills and the abundance of what the historian Henry McCalley called the "purest and coldest freestone water in the world," and the springs and branches, not to mention the rivers and the resulting lake. The schools here are outstanding and the variety of churches makes any visitor feel at home.

Many people of historical significance came to Randolph County because of the aforementioned attributes and were instrumental in business and industrial developments. They developed the resources of the county, which provided jobs that attracted residents, enticed them to stay, and caused others to move in. They helped to build the great legacy that has been handed down to the present generation.

The county owes its reputation not only to its physical attributes but also to its citizens, young and old, who have contributed their talents toward the rendition of the great song that is Randolph County.

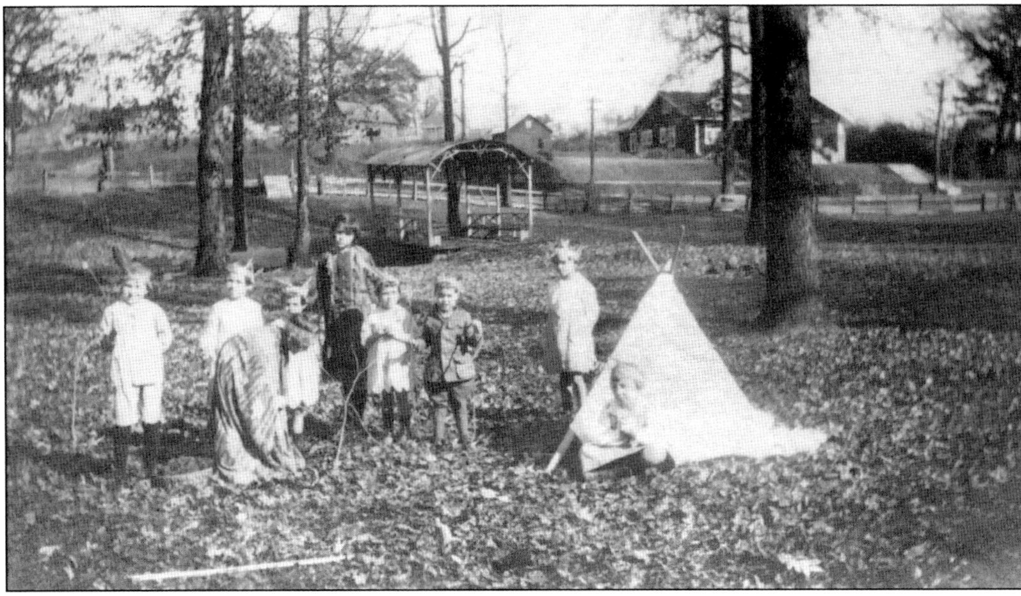

These children are playing Cowboys and Indians on the front lawn of the Roland Griffin home. (Courtesy of Glenda Hale.)

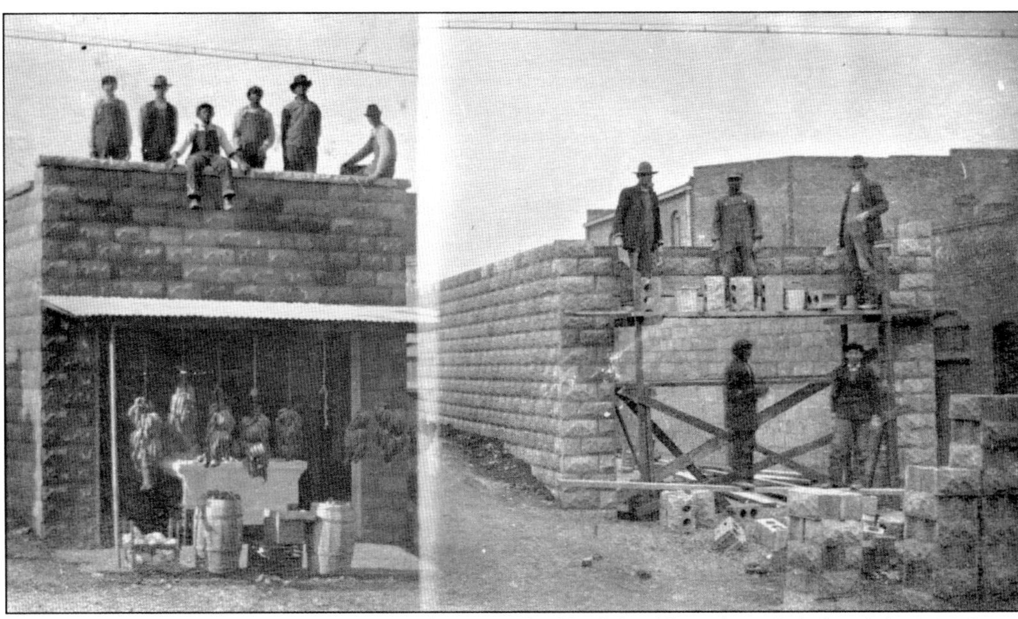

Under construction by B. J. Mitchum and crew is the block building directly behind the McMurray building. It became the law office of Burns "Red" Parker, then Stevenson Insurance Agency, and presently Bill Montgomery Insurance Agency. (Courtesy of Jean Windsor.)

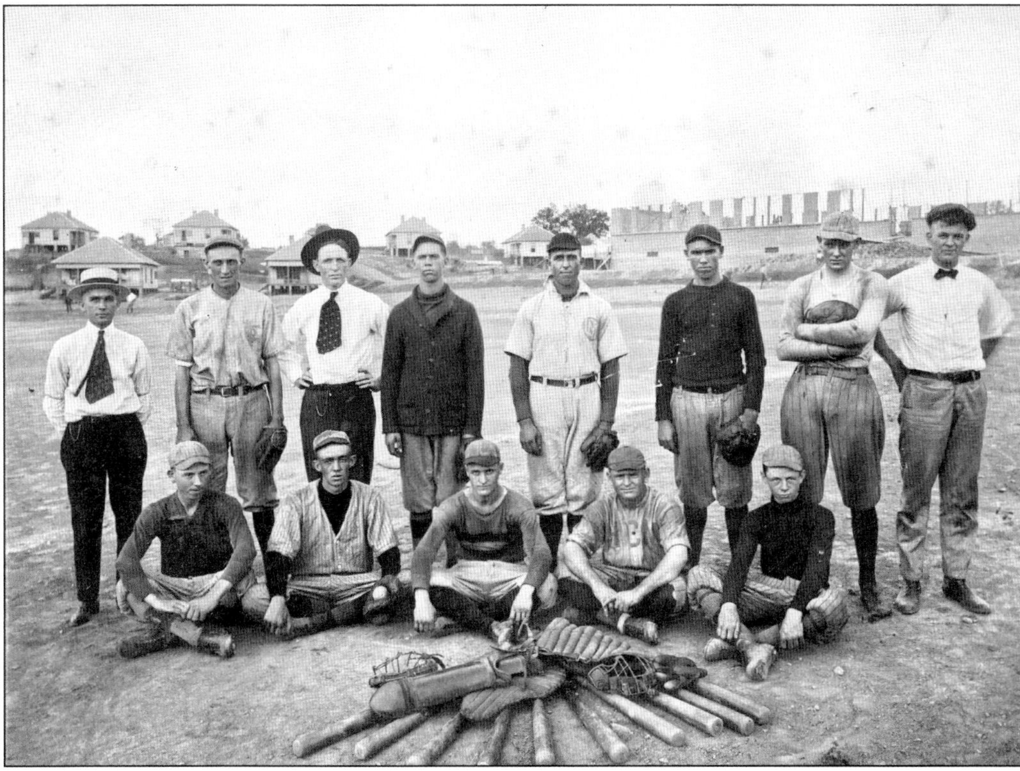

Pictured is the W. A. Handley Manufacturing Company baseball team in 1921. From left to right are (seated) Speedy Bramlett, Monk Patterson, Lefty Spears, Will Yarbrough, and ? Griffin; (standing) Lewis Dudley, Steve Young, Willie Wilks, George Daniel, Earn Riley, Al Daniel, Alf Chittman, and ? Eddins. In the background, the Knight-Enloe School is under construction for the children of mill employees. Also shown are 6 of the 240 houses that the mill built for employees. (Courtesy of Squat Yarbrough.)

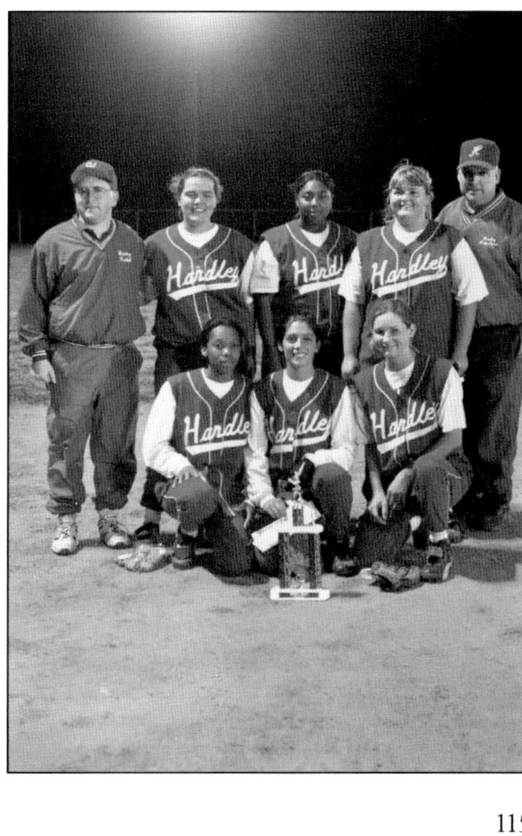

The Senior Lady Tigers class of 2000 are pictured here after winning the County Softball Tournament; from left to right are (first row) Kristi Cofield, Amanda White, and Crystal Blackmon; (second row) coach Chuck Marcum, Natalie Lambert, Sanethia Trammel, April Cummings, and coach Randy Hall. (Courtesy of Natalie Lambert.)

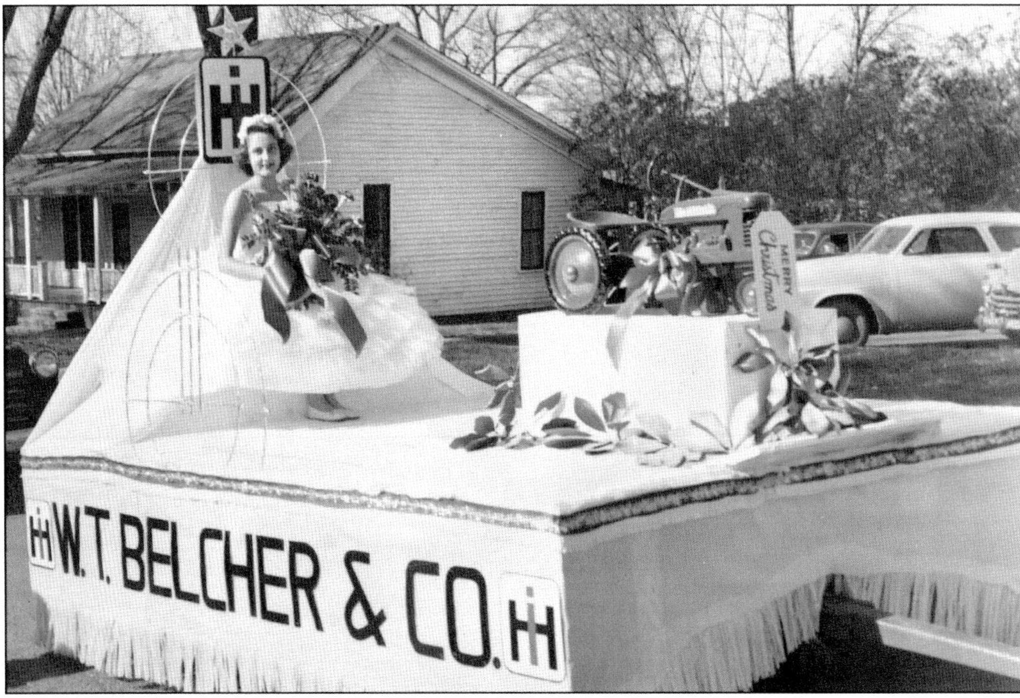

Shown is Nan Enloe representing W. T. Belcher and Company, the local dealer in tractors. The tractor displayed here was later sold in a yard sale. (Courtesy of W. T. [Bill] Belcher III.)

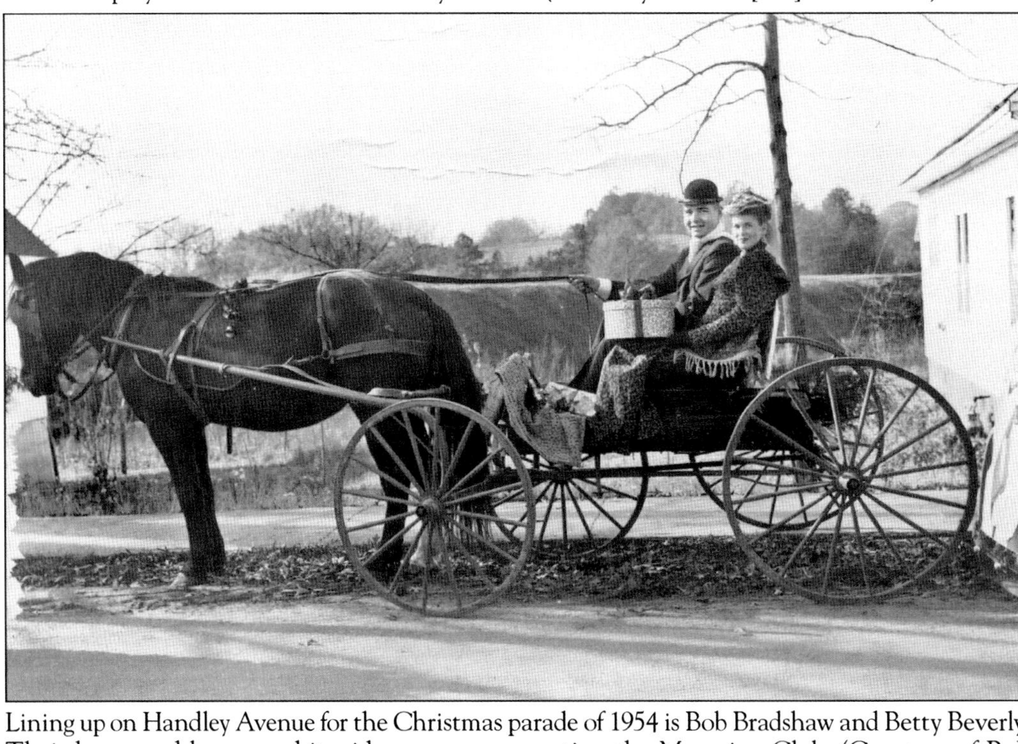

Lining up on Handley Avenue for the Christmas parade of 1954 is Bob Bradshaw and Betty Beverly. Their horse and buggy and its riders were representing the Magazine Club. (Courtesy of Bob and Betty Bradshaw.)

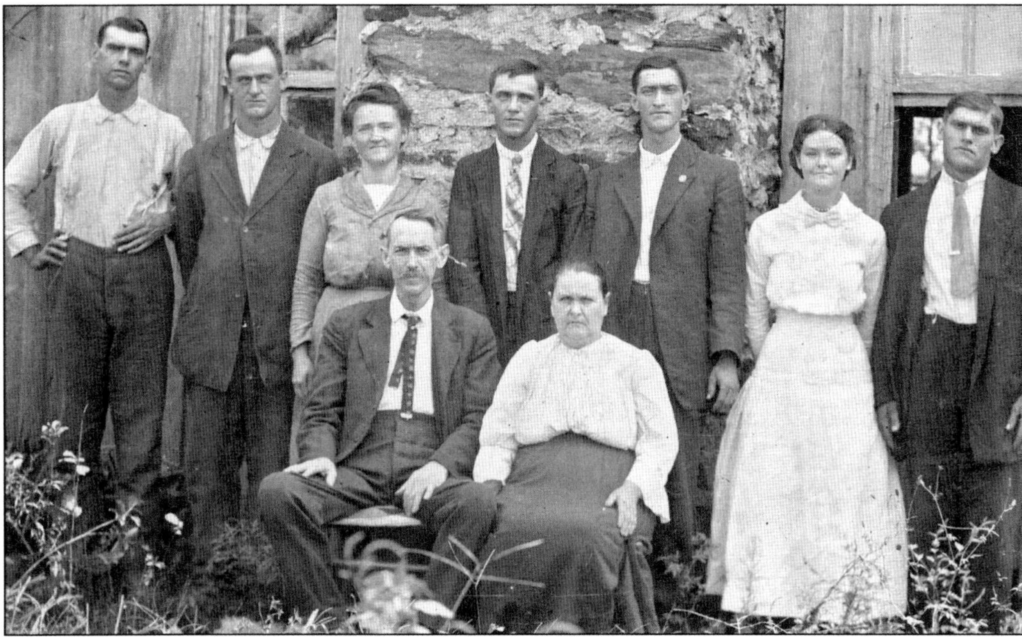

James Daniel Burson, wife Alma Juhan, and their children are shown here outside their home located in the Omaha community. James and Alma are seated. Standing from left to right are Edwin Nathaniel, John William Jackson, Elizabeth, Henry Woodruff Grady, Julian Juhan, Beulah, and Bulan Son. After he married, Bulan Son owned and operated the local syrup mill, where all the neighbors brought their cane to be made into syrup every fall. (Courtesy of Bertie Waldrep.)

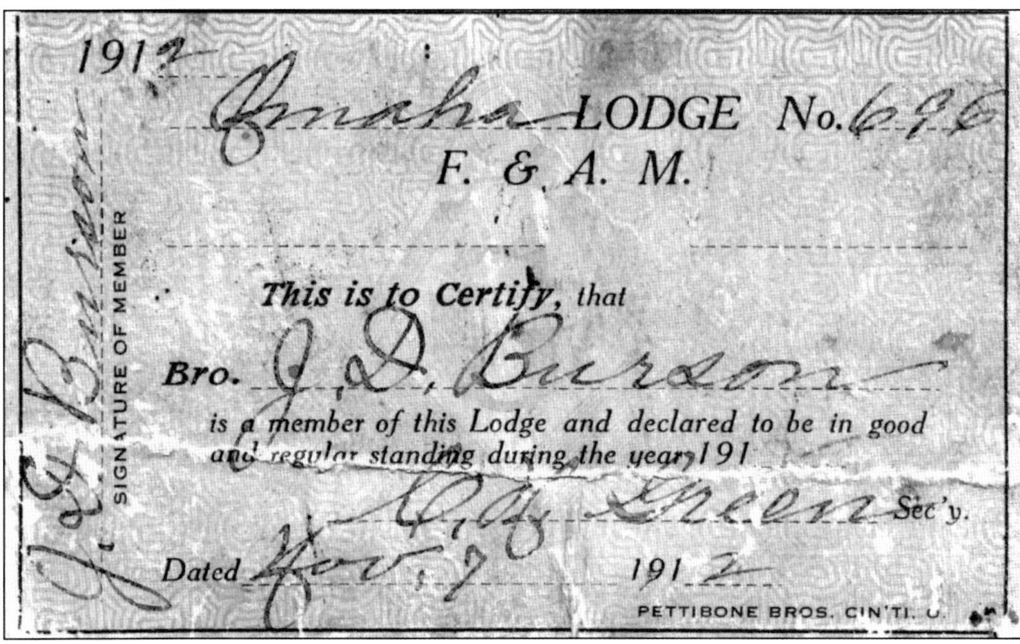

1912

Omaha LODGE No.

F. & A. M.

This is to Certify, that

Bro. J. D. Burson

is a member of this Lodge and declared to be in good and regular standing during the year 191

Sec'y.

Dated Nov. 7 1912

PETTIBONE BROS. CIN'TI. O.

SIGNATURE OF MEMBER J. D. Burson

Freemasonry in Randolph County goes back over 100 years. Currently there are three lodges: Wedowee, Graham, and Roanoke. In early times, there were between 8 and 10 lodges throughout the county with membership in the several hundreds. Today, as in years past, Freemasonry founds itself on making good men better. (Courtesy of Bertie Waldrep.)

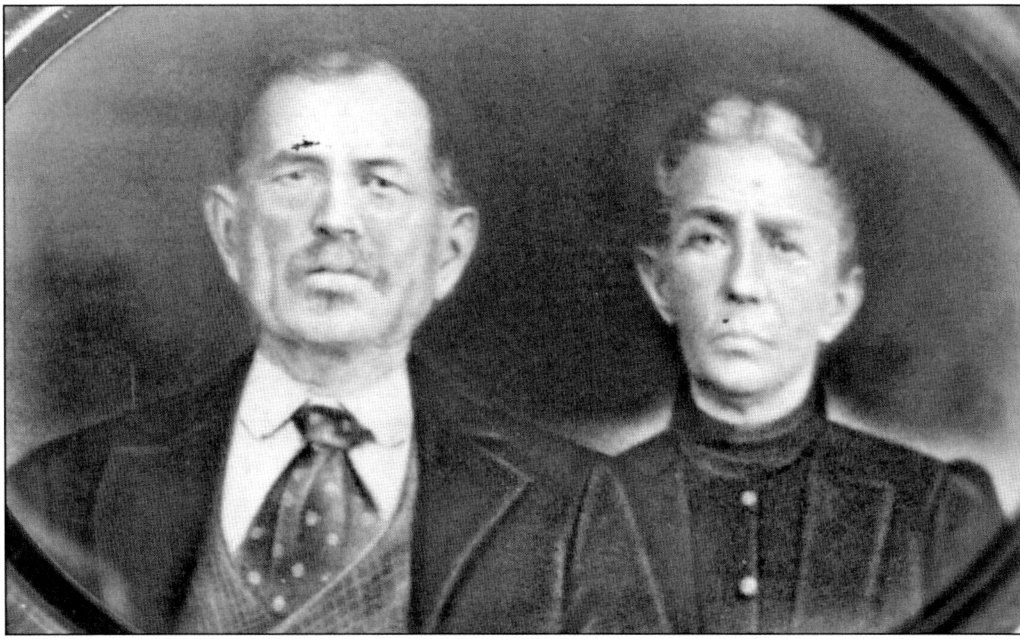

James Polk Burson (1845–1916) and wife Hannah Louisa Humphries (1859–1944) were early settlers in the Omaha community, where they ran a small store. The couple had six children. As each child married, she or he was given 40 acres of land and a mule. Only one child, James Cody, kept his land, raised his family of seven on it, and at his death willed it to his youngest sons, Paul and Kenneth. (Courtesy of Paula [Burson] Lambert.)

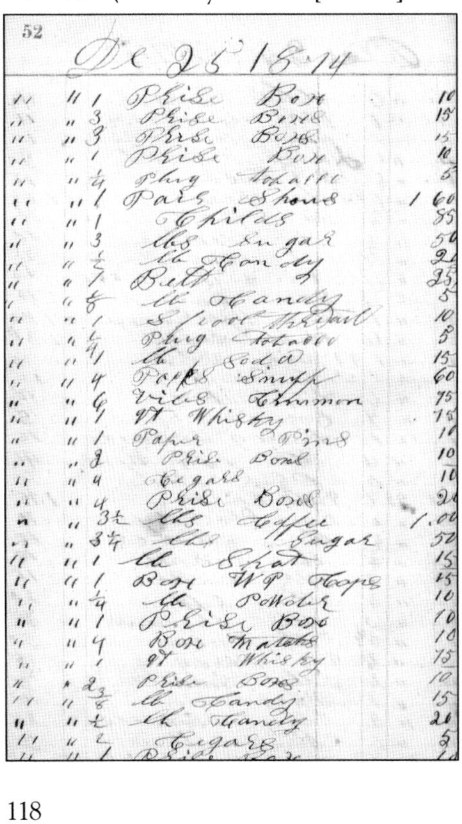

52

Dec 25 1874

"	" 1	Prize Box	10
"	" 3	Prize Boxs	15
"	" 3	Prize Boxs	15
"	" 1	Prize Box	10
"	" 1/4	Plug Tobacco	5
"	" 1	Pair Shoes	1 60
"	" 1	Childs	85
"	" 3	lbs Sugar	50
"	" 1/2	lb Candy	2[illegible]
"	" 1	Belt	25
"	" 1/8	lb Candy	5
"	" 1	Spool Thread	10
"	" 1/4	Plug Tobacco	5
"	" 1	lb Soda	15
"	" 4	Papers Snuff	60
"	" 6	Vials Cinnamon	75
"	" 1	Pt Whisky	75
"	" 1	Paper Pins	10
"	" 2	Prize Boxs	10
"	" 4	Cigars	10
"	" 4	Prize Boxs	20
"	" 3 1/2	lbs Coffee	1.00
"	" 3 1/4	lbs Sugar	50
"	" 1	lb Shot	15
"	" 1	Box WP Caps	15
"	" 1/4	lb Powder	10
"	" 1	Prize Box	10
"	" 4	Box Matches	10
"	" 1	Qt Whisky	75
"	" 2	Prize Boxs	10
"	" 1/8	lb Candy	15
"	" 1/2	lb Candy	20
"	" 2	Cigars	5
"	" 1	Prize Box	[illegible]

Shown here is a page from the Burson General Store ledger, dated December 25, 1874. The store was open for business on Christmas Day, and business was good. James Polk served in the Civil War, during which time he lost most of his eyesight, a handicap he is said to have borne cheerfully. (Courtesy of Kenneth Burson.)

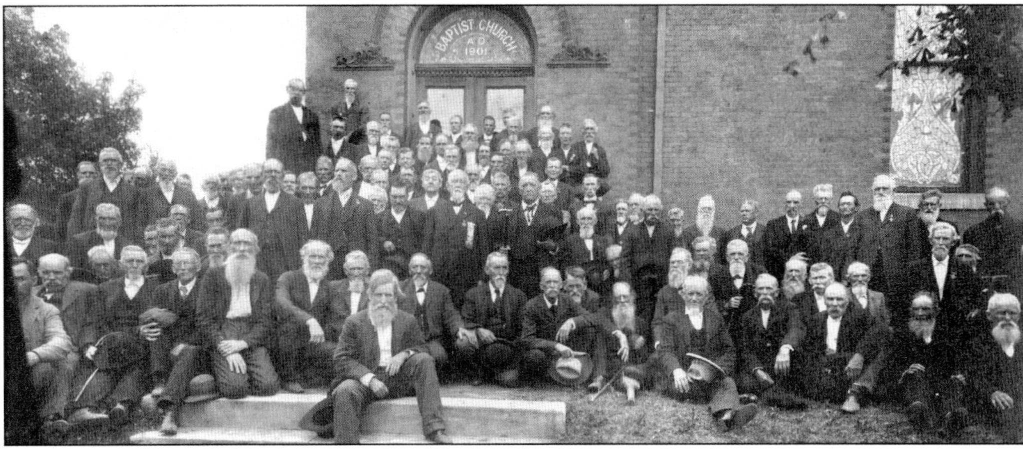

Gathered for the April 1906 Memorial Day at Roanoke First Baptist Church were more than 100 Confederate war veterans of the Aiken-Smith Camp, No. 293. The center figure on the top step is unidentified, and kneeling right behind him is Bill Radney. At his left is Jess Fausett. Directly behind Radney, with his eyes closed, is M. R. Taylor. In the first row, standing with a scrambled tie and clutching a bowler hat is Capt. W. A. Handley. Second behind him is clean-shaven Martin Pittman. To the right of Pittman is J. B. Carlisle. The man with the wooden leg seated in the front row is Major Coleman. Buck Weathers is kneeling with a full beard. Behind him against the brick wall, also with a full beard, is Gen. B. F. Weathers. The man with his head at the corner of the stained-glass window is John. H. Oldham. Mack Wood is seated third from the right. Behind Wood and to the left is Benjamin Walker. Holding a light-colored hat in his right hand and kneeling in the front row is G. O. Hill. F. D. Powers is seated fourth from the left. (Courtesy of W. T. [Bill] Belcher III.)

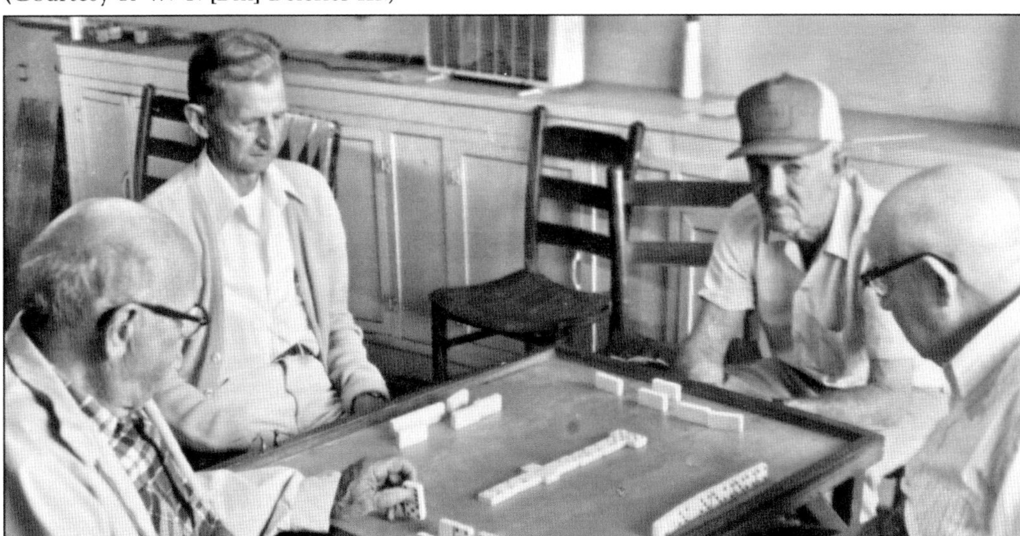

The Wadley Domino Club was a social outlet for many Wadley men for more than 40 years. The building in the heart of downtown was provided by Jim and Betty Sue Cleveland, and a dozen players could frequently be found playing on any week day. It was necessary to be a quick thinker, good mathematician, and a good conversationalist, all at the same time, to keep up with the flow of the game. The players at this table from left to right are Hoyt Welsh, Wyatt Lee Harris, Lester Jackson, and Oakley Evans. (Courtesy of Wyner Phillips.)

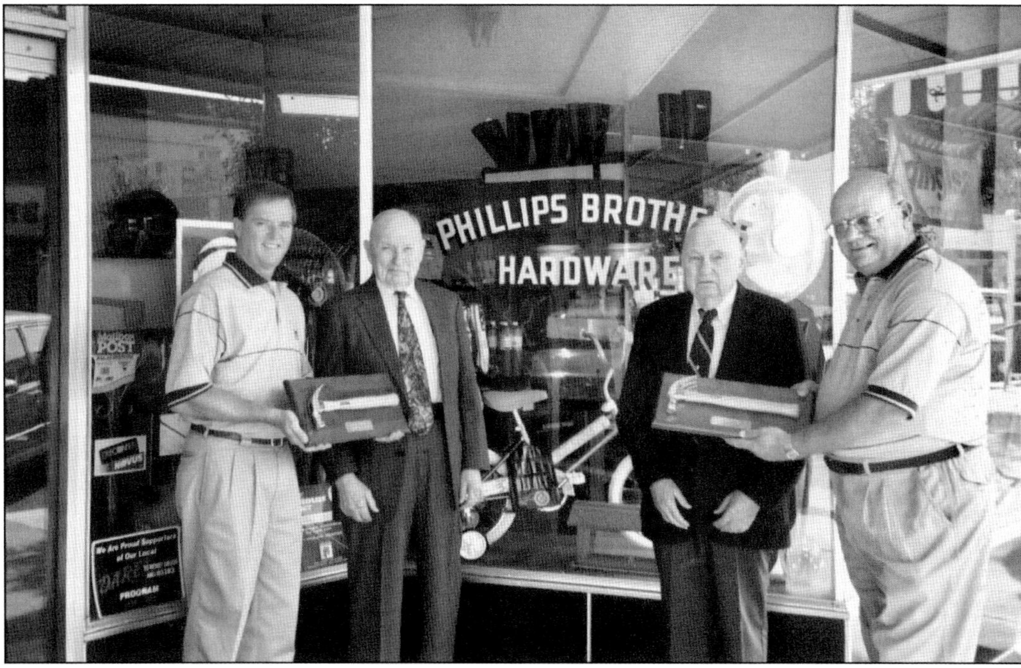

Phillips Brothers Hardware was a Roanoke store for 68 years. Standing in front of the store are: J. P. Phillips (left) and Leon Phillips with two representatives from Moore-Handley Hardware Company presenting them with gold hammers for 60 years of continuous business in 1997. (Courtesy of Wyner Phillips.)

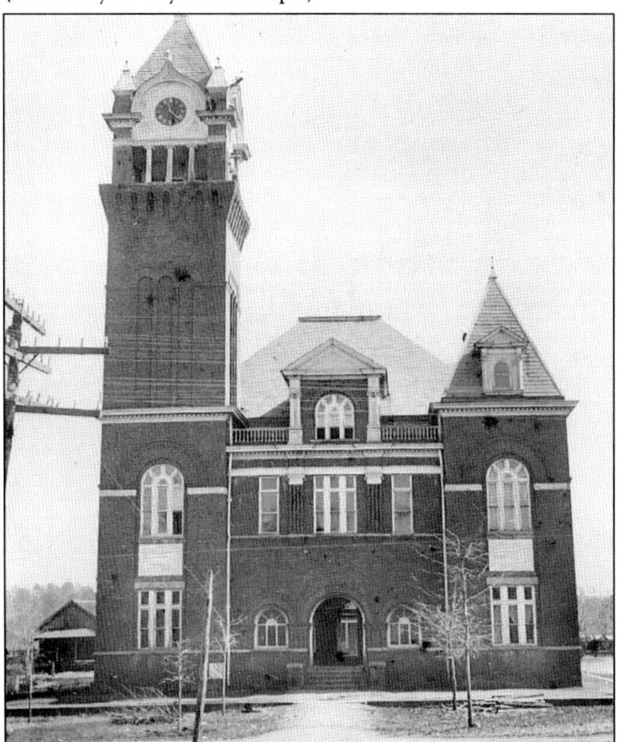

Randolph County was created by an act of the Alabama General Assembly on December 18, 1832, from former Creek territory. The county is named for the Virginia statesman John Randolph. Wedowee became the county seat in 1835 because it was located in almost the geographical center of the county. The first courthouse was built of logs in 1836. A new courthouse was built by Isaac Baker in 1840 at a cost of $2,000. In 1857, a new brick courthouse was constructed but was destroyed by fire in 1897, along with all courthouse records. The courthouse in the photograph was built in 1897 at a cost of $21,000 and was considered fireproof, but in spite of efforts to make it so, it also burned in 1940. (Courtesy of Shelby Green.)

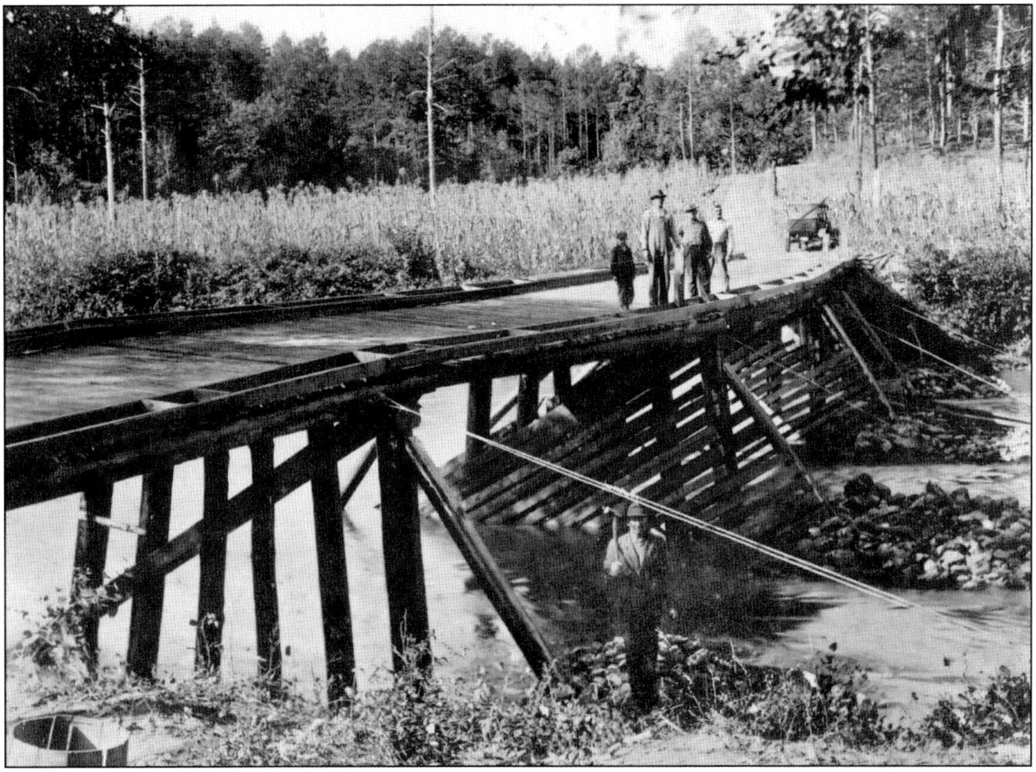

The first bridge in the county was built on the Little Tallapoosa at Bridge Forge by H. E. Meadows on August 25, 1920. The first logs were cut from virgin long-leaf pines on the G. H. Traylor place at a cost of $1 per tree. A keg of 60 D nails cost $6. Laborers on the bridge were paid $1 to $1.50 per day, and the overseer, H. A. Merrill, was paid $7 per day. The bridge was ready to cross in 30 days. To finance the bridge, Meadows sold 53 head of cattle for approximately $650. It was built for a toll bridge but proved to be an unsuccessful venture. He later sold the bridge to the county for $250. (Courtesy of Ellen Traylor.)

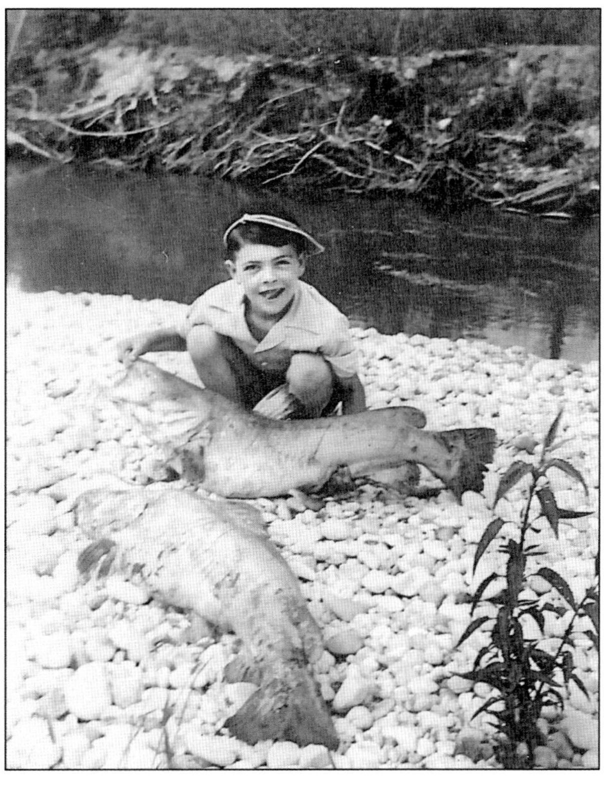

James Edward Beverly had a good day fishing in the creek c. 1941. (Courtesy of Dwayne Pate.)

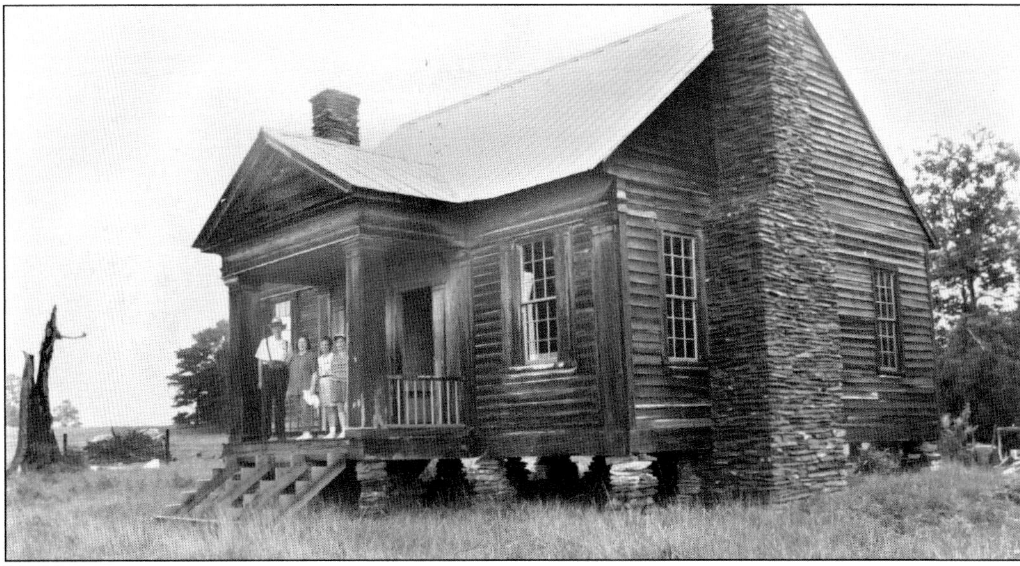

Louina, located on the east bank of the Tallapoosa River, became a settlement and trading post with the friendly Native Americans in 1834, and for half a century was the chief business center and largest town in Randolph County. There were about 30 residences, 8 stores, two schools (one for boys and one for girls), a hotel/tavern, saloons, a Masonic lodge, a Methodist and a Baptist church, a wheat mill and a corn mill, a wool factory, and a cotton gin. Second-generation citizens of Louina moved to other places, many of them to become prominent, and the last store closed in 1902. The only surviving, original structure is the Harrington Phillips residence. Here standing on the front porch are Phillips descendants. From left to right, they are Dr. Ellis West, Phyllis Phillips West, Jane Phillips Cato, and Mary Ann Phillips Vann. (Courtesy of Wyner Phillips.)

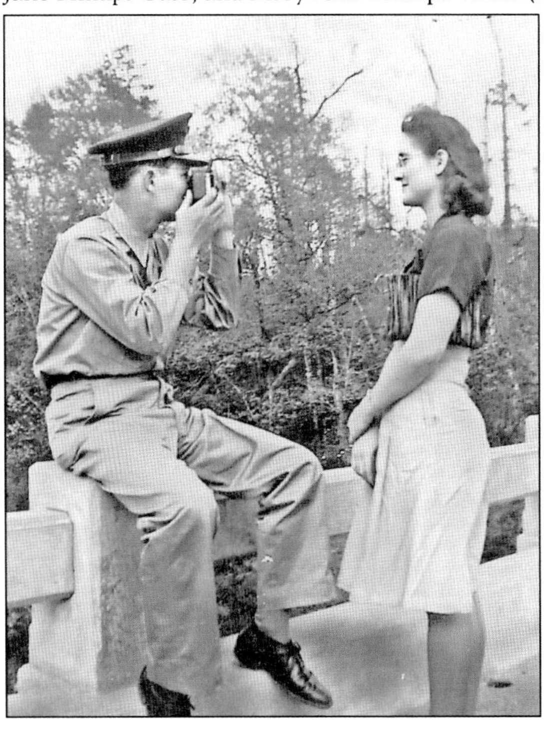

Pason Stephens, on military leave in the early 1940s, is enjoying the sights from the Wadley bridge with Ella Mae Beverly. (Courtesy of Dwayne Pate.)

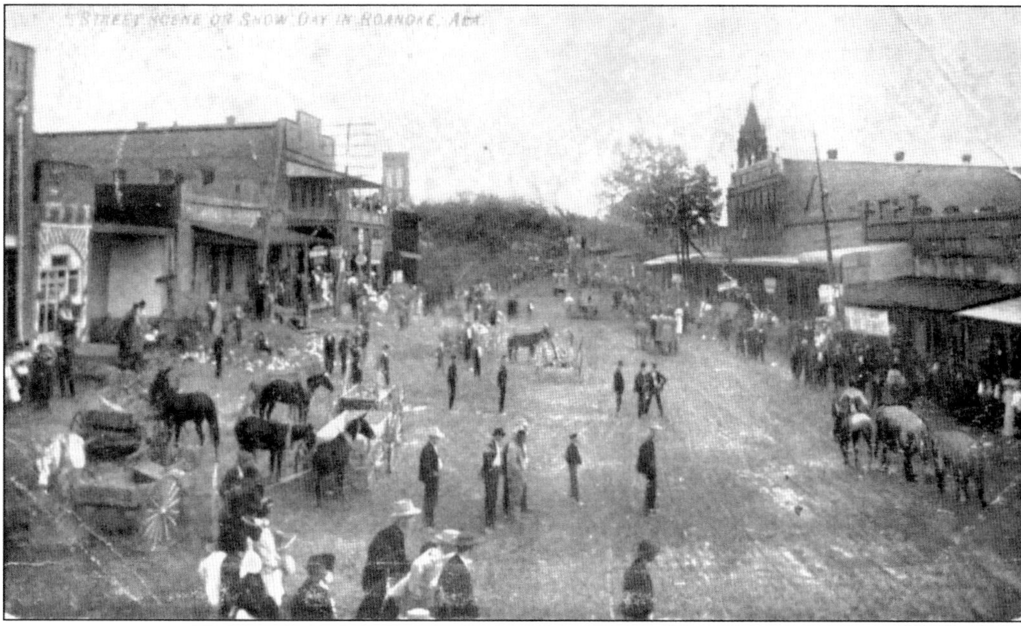

October 6, 1906, the Gentry Brothers Famous Shows circus came to Roanoke, and people lined the street to view the parade down Main Street. The street scene reveals that there were no litter laws in Roanoke at that time, and some store buildings were relatively unkempt. In the October 24, 1906, issue of the *Roanoke Leader*, O. H. Stevenson strongly suggested that citizens keep downtown clean, and if need be, the city pass an ordinance. Subsequent photographs reveal that the editor's suggestion was well taken without the passing of an ordinance. (Courtesy of the Randolph County Museum.)

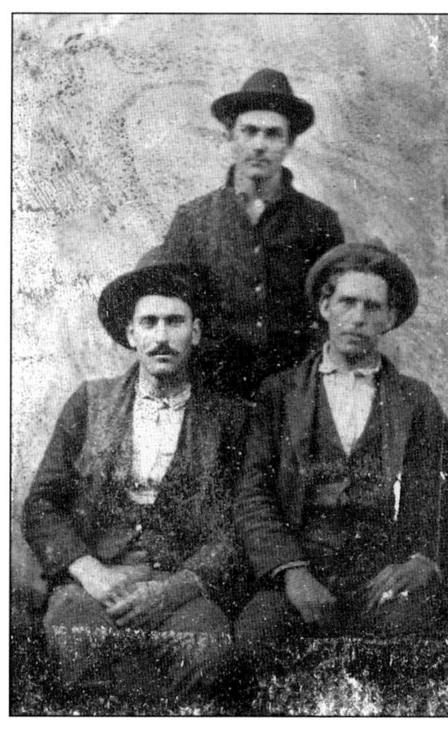

In this c. 1880 photograph are Tom May (seated left) and Charley May (seated right), whose grandson was Randolph County sheriff Fred May. The man standing is unknown. (Courtesy of Dwayne Pate.)

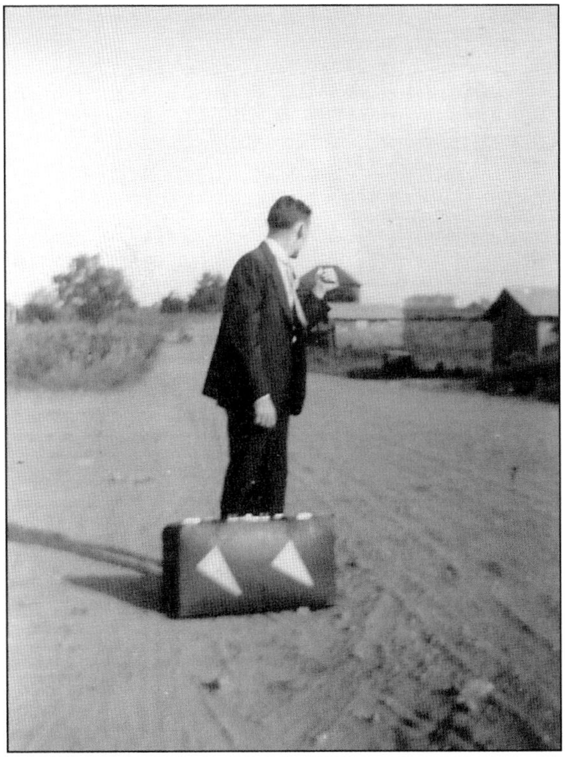

Wilson Beverly is standing in front of Beverly's Store in 1938 waiting for the bus to take him to Howard College. In the background is Rock Stand School. The two-story building behind his hand is the Woodmen of the World building, and the other buildings are Carlos Beverly's automobile and blacksmith shop and barn. (Courtesy of Dwayne Pate.)

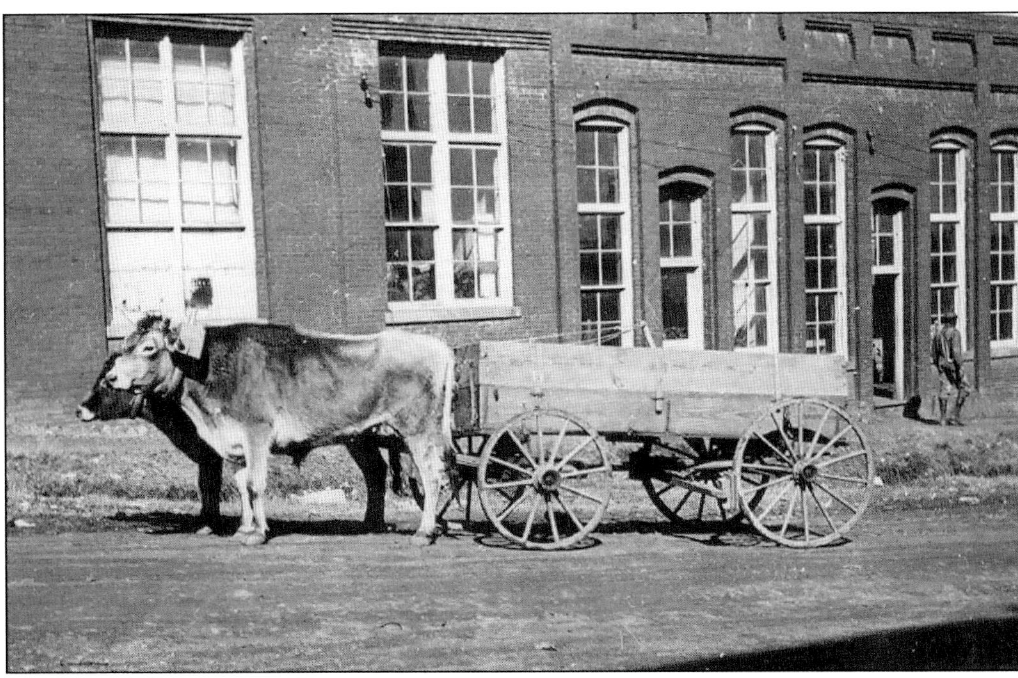

A farmer came to town with cows pulling his wagon. The cows are obviously well trained since they do not appear to be tied, and no one is supervising them, but the brake on the wagon is tied. They are parked beside the Bank of Wadley. (Courtesy of Southern Union State Community College.)

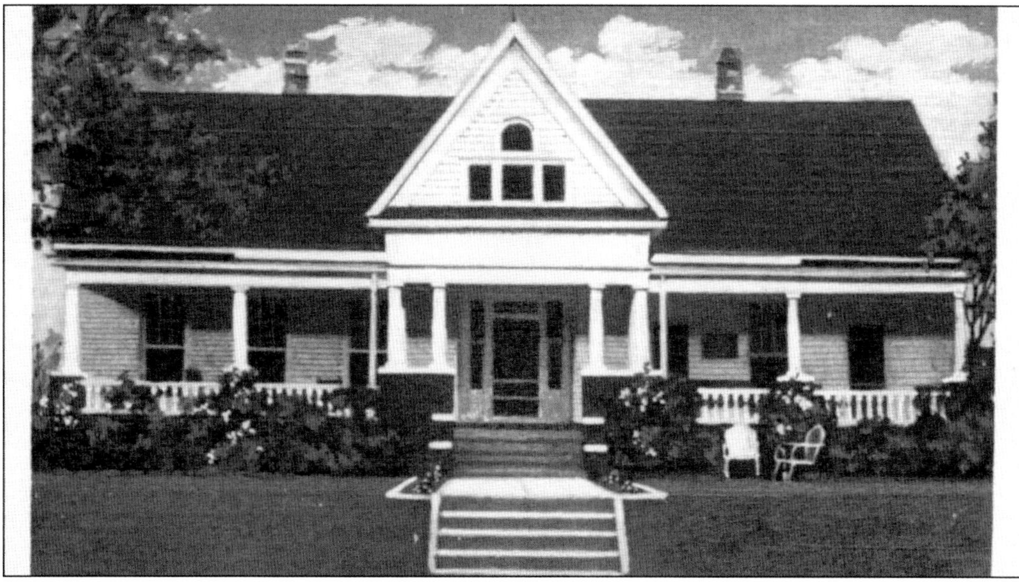

The first pastorium of First Baptist Church of Roanoke was next door to the Methodist parsonage, the second house from the Methodist church, and was built in 1906. Mr. and Mrs. Jessie Hearn purchased the house in 1941; they lived in part of it and used the other part as offices for the Hearn Insurance Agency. It was occupied by daughter Lou Ellen Huskey until it was demolished for the construction of First Methodist Christian Life Center on the site. (Courtesy of Lou Ellen Huskey.)

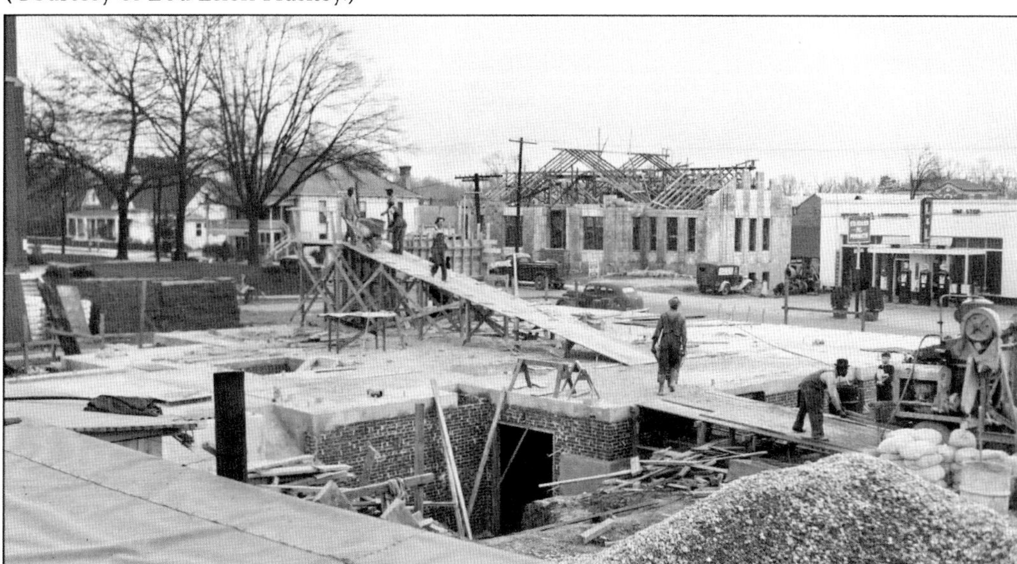

The building in the forefront of the photograph is the beginning of construction of the Roanoke Post Office in December 1940. The building under construction across Main Street is the Roanoke City Hall. The house to the left of city hall is Dr. D. M. Yates's home with his family living quarters on the lower floor. His dental office was the front left room of the second story. Other second-story rooms were rented to boarders. The extreme left house was the residence of Ella Smith, the inventor and manufacturer of the Alabama Indestructible Doll, also known as the Ella Smith Doll. (Courtesy of the Randolph County Museum.)

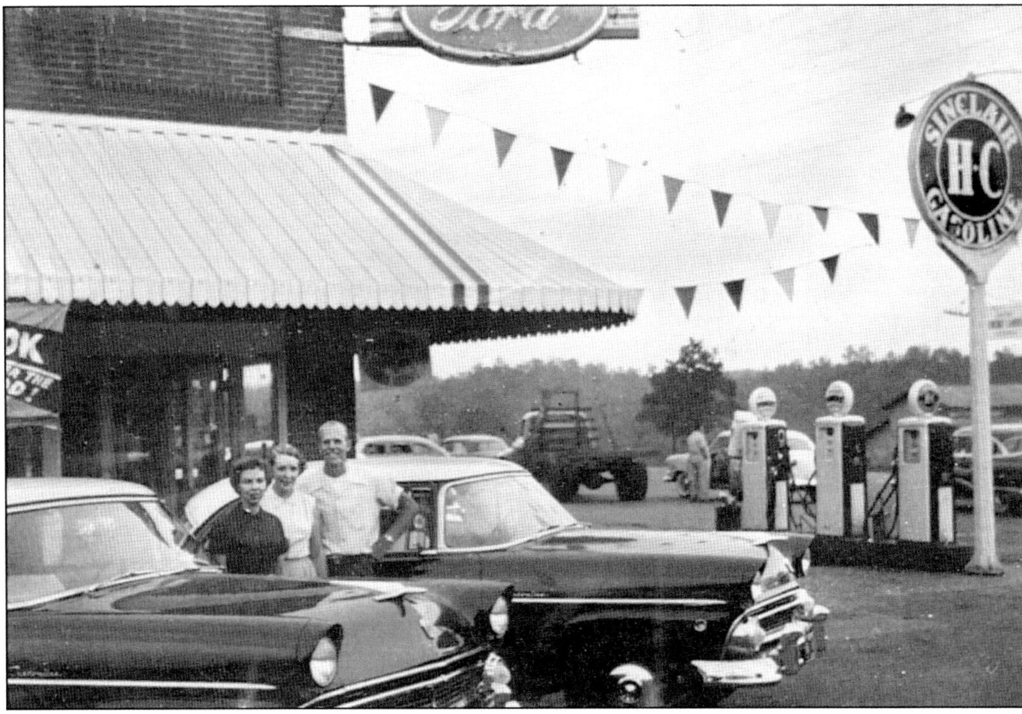

Considering the purchase of a new 1955 Ford car at J. V. Perry and Company in Wadley are, from left to right, Jen Bugg, Helen Bugg, and Bob Bugg. (Courtesy of Carol [Bugg] Knight.)

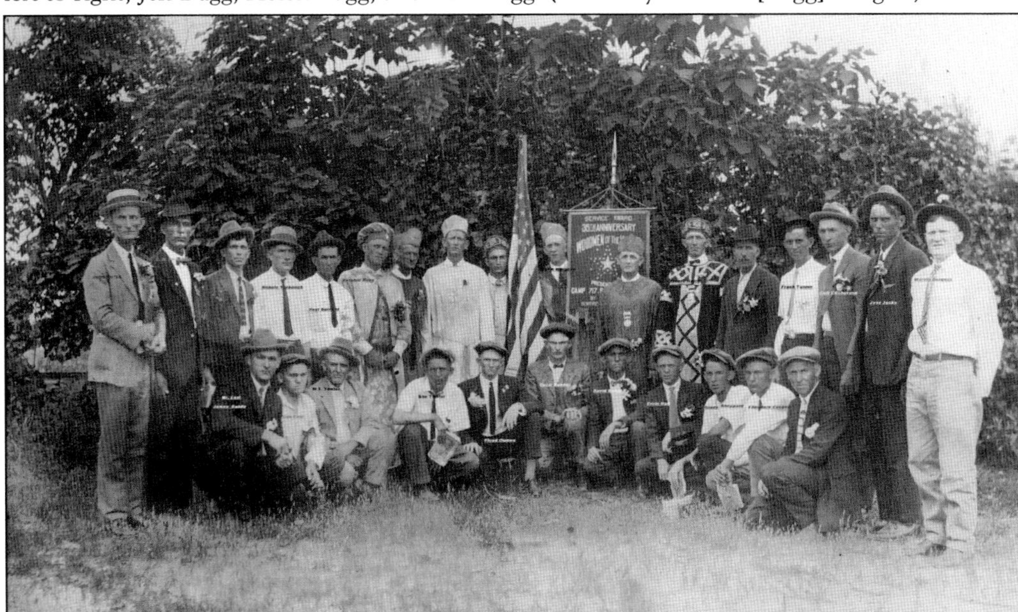

Some of the Woodmen of Rock Mills pictured here are Peter Ruston, Theodore Cooper, Grady Sheppard, Earvin Hall, David Breed, Cecil Bonner. Floyd Hall, Bon Towler, W. S. Towler, Ode East, James East, John Norred, C. B. Yarbough, Ronnie Yarbough, Hershall Huey, Worth Burgess, Ciscero Harry, Frank Turner, Cuff Eitcherson, Jessie Jacks, and Marvin Burgess. (Courtesy of Harold Breed and Jeff Towler.)

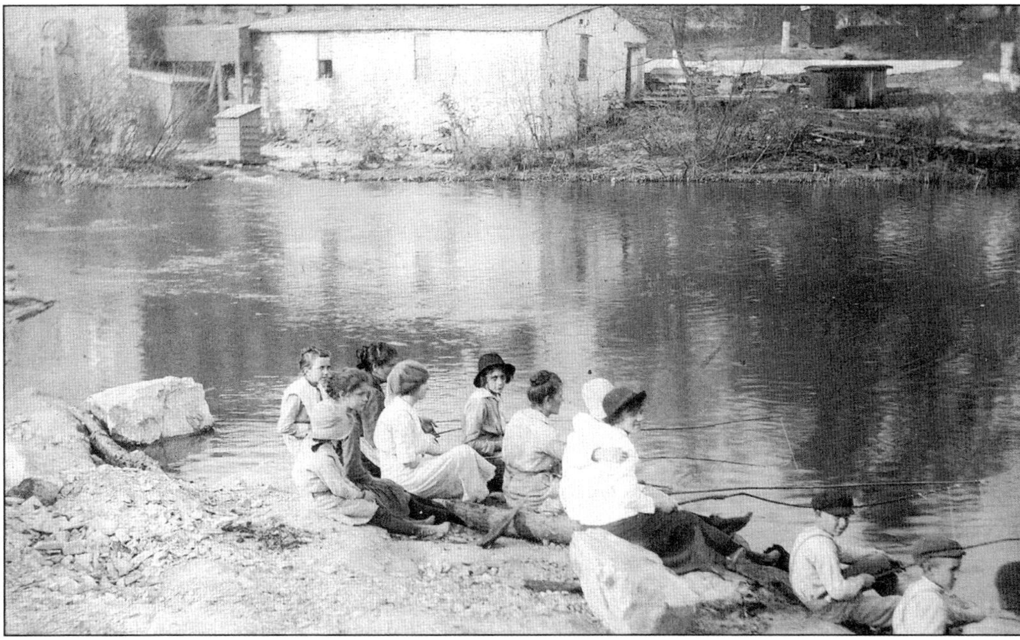

The current from the flow of Wehadkee Creek turned the wheel that generated electricity for Wehadkee Yarn Mills, and it also provided recreation for Rock Mills residents. (Courtesy of Harold Breed and Jeff Towler.)

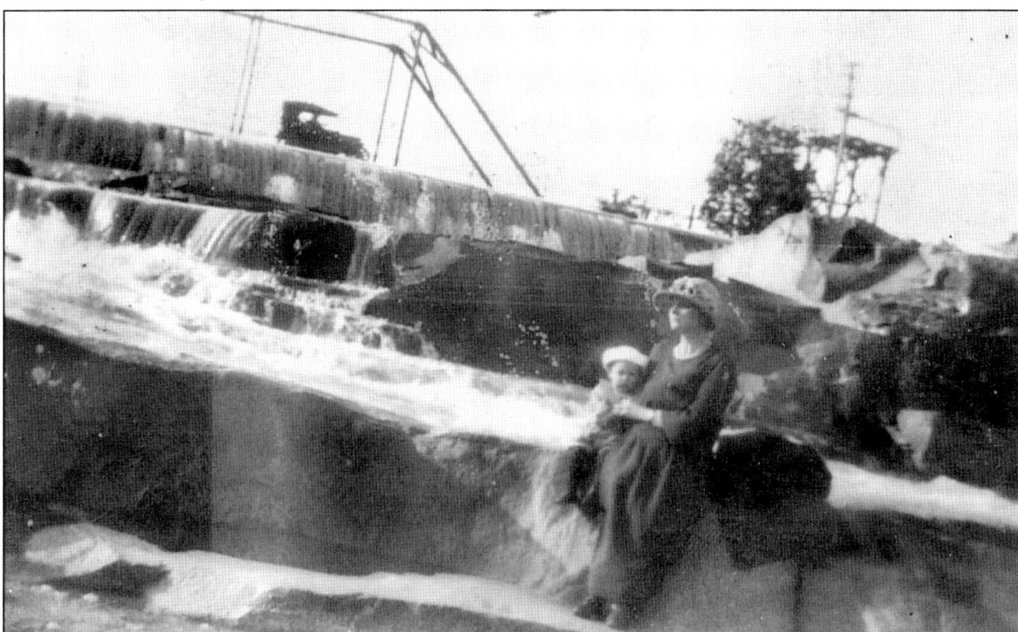

Sitting on a dry rock with water from the Wehadkee Creek streaming all around is Docia Mathews, third-grade teacher at Rock Mills School, with her nephew, Jesse L. Mathews. The photograph was made c. 1924, when the car crossing the bridge was a modern conveyance, and the tower in the background held the transformers that supplied electricity to the Wehadkee Yarn Mill, located just to the right of the creek. (Courtesy of Jesse Mathews.)